Whitehead and the Pittsburgh School

Contemporary Whitehead Studies

Edited by Roland Faber, Claremont School of Theology, and Brian G. Henning, Gonzaga University

Contemporary Whitehead Studies, co-sponsored by the Whitehead Research Project, is an interdisciplinary book series that publishes manuscripts from scholars with contemporary and innovative approaches to Whitehead studies by giving special focus to projects that: explore the connections between Whitehead and contemporary Continental philosophy, especially sources, like Heidegger, or contemporary streams like poststructuralism; reconnect Whitehead to pragmatism, analytical philosophy and philosophy of language; explore creative East/West dialogues facilitated by Whitehead's work; explore the interconnections of the mathematician with the philosopher and the contemporary importance of these parts of Whitehead's work for the dialogue between sciences and humanities; reconnect Whitehead to the wider field of philosophy, the humanities, the sciences and academic research with Whitehead's pluralistic impulses in the context of a pluralistic world; address Whitehead's philosophy in the midst of contemporary problems facing humanity, such as climate change, war & peace, race, and the future development of civilization.

Recent Titles in This Series

Whitehead and the Pittsburgh School: Preempting the Problem of Intentionality, by Lisa Landoe Hedrick

On Philosophy, Intelligibility, and the Ordinary: Going the Bloody Hard Way, by Randy Ramal

Untying the Gordian Knot: Process, Reality and Context, by Timothy E. Eastman

Mind, Value, and the Cosmos: On the Relational Nature of Ultimacy, by Andrew M. Davis

Whitehead's Radically Temporalist Metaphysics: Recovering the Seriousness of Time, by George Allan

Propositions in the Making: Experiments in a Whiteheadian Laboratory, edited by Roland Faber, Michael Halewood, and Andrew M. Davis

Whitehead and Continental Philosophy in the Twenty-First Century: Dislocations, edited by Jeremy D. Fackenthal

Beyond Whitehead: Recent Advances in Process Thought, edited by Jakub Dziadkowiec and Lukasz Lamza

Tragic Beauty in Whitehead and Japanese Aesthetics, by Steve Odin

Creaturely Cosmologies: Why Metaphysics Matters for Animal and Planetary Liberation, by Brianne Donaldson

Whitehead and the Pittsburgh School

Preempting the Problem of Intentionality

Lisa Landoe Hedrick

LEXINGTON BOOKS
Lanham • Boulder • New York • London

Chapter 2 reprint: Thanks to Editors John R. Shook and Maria Baghramian of *Contemporary Pragmatism* for permission to republish content here. Part of chapter 2 appeared in *Contemporary Pragmatism* 16.1 under the title "Analytic Philosophy and the Need for Pragmatist Metaphysics." Reprinted with permission from Brill.

Chapter 3 reprint: Thanks also to Editor John McCarthy of *The Review of Metaphysics* for permission to republish content here. Part of chapter 3 appeared in *The Review of Metaphysics* no. 288 (June 2019) under the title "McDowell, Whitehead, and the Metaphysics of Agency." Reprinted with permission.

Published by Lexington Books
An imprint of The Rowman & Littlefield Publishing Group, Inc.
4501 Forbes Boulevard, Suite 200, Lanham, Maryland 20706
www.rowman.com

Copyright © 2021 The Rowman & Littlefield Publishing Group, Inc.

All rights reserved. No part of this book may be reproduced in any form or by any electronic or mechanical means, including information storage and retrieval systems, without written permission from the publisher, except by a reviewer who may quote passages in a review.

British Library Cataloguing in Publication Information Available

Library of Congress Cataloging-in-Publication Data

Library of Congress Control Number: 2021933358

ISBN 978-1-7936-4657-6 (cloth)
ISBN 978-1-7936-4659-0 (pbk)
ISBN 978-1-7936-4658-3 (electronic)

Contents

Acknowledgments	vii
Introduction	1
1 Reading Plato, Aristotle, and Kant with Whitehead	5
2 Whiteheadian Anticipations of Pittsburgh Neo-Hegelianism	31
3 Pittsburgh's Problem with Intentionality	49
4 The Aesthetics of Experience	75
5 McDowell and the "Connivance of the World"	113
6 Symbolism and Language	139
Conclusion	175
Epilogue: Reclaiming Whitehead's Theology	179
Bibliography	195
Index	201
About the Author	213

Acknowledgments

I would first of all like to thank the faculty at the University of Chicago Divinity School for their sustaining presence during this book's development. Thanks especially to Dan Arnold, Ryan Coyne, and Kevin Hector for their helpful comments over the years.

Many thanks also to the members of the Metaphysical Society of America and the Institute for American Religious and Philosophical Thought for their graciousness in allowing me to workshop many earlier drafts of material included here—and even more so for their engagement with the material that did not prove so auspicious. Special thanks go to Nancy K. Frankenberry, who has been one of the most committed interlocutors of my work. She has been my teacher, my colleague, and my friend.

My final and deepest thanks go to my family. Thank you to my mother, whose confidence in me consistently preempts my own; to my father, who daily exemplifies the value of hard work and integrity; to my brothers, for their steadying companionship; and to my husband, Hunter, who regularly renews my spirit.

Introduction

This book is both an historical revision and a constructive proposal. With respect to the former aspect of the project, I investigate Whitehead's early critiques of analytic philosophy and examine the ways in which those critiques anticipate the problem of intentionality. Moreover, I locate surprising moments in scholarly accounts of the history of analytic philosophy that manifest a forgetting of Whitehead. With respect to the latter aspect, I propose Whitehead's aesthetics of experience and/qua symbolism as a constructive resource for contemporary analytic philosophers' attempts to reconcile mind and world. Combining the two elements of the project, I proceed to suggest how a better understanding of Whitehead's critique of early trends in analytic philosophy can help us to identify some of the habits of thought that impede it today. Here, my focus is specifically on the work of John McDowell and the ways in which Whitehead's own carries us further toward a reconciliation of nature and normativity.

HISTORICAL CONTEXT

The problem of intentionality originated when, in the latter half of the nineteenth century, the iconic anxiety of modern epistemology about one's ability to known "things in themselves" took on a new tone. The change occurred when thinkers such as Gottlob Frege and Bertrand Russell began to shift the focus of their philosophy from mind to language. When language (specifically sentences) instead of mind (specifically its ideas) came to be regarded as the bearer of meaning, the problem of how mind relates to world was no longer about how mental entities relate to non-mental ones, but of how linguistic signs can refer to or signify something else—specifically, something non-linguistic.

What was left standing in place of epistemological skepticism after the linguistic turn was the problem of how to make sense of the directedness of our sentences. And yet, it is the directability or intentionality of our speaking, writing, or thinking that facilitates claims about ourselves and the world—what may be referred to as the "objective purport" of our linguistic practices. If we cannot account for how this intentionality works, for how it achieves what it claims to achieve (e.g., in being about something), it isn't clear how we could identify the determinants or criteria by which to adjudicate between such claims. Moreover, it isn't clear how we could account for the reality of causality or the responsibility of moral agents if we cannot account for how it is that our thinking gains traction with the state of things.

My project attempts to address this problem in a number of ways. I begin with an historical analysis of the relationship between Whitehead and early analytic philosophers, primarily at Cambridge, in order to show how many of the problems he identified in the philosophy of, for instance, Bertrand Russell, could have preempted the contemporary manifestation of the problem of intentionality in analytic philosophy—a problem which thinkers of the so-called Pittsburgh School of Philosophy like Robert Brandom and John McDowell attempt to solve by returning to G. W. F. Hegel. Second, I explore recent efforts by Brandom and McDowell to account for the traction between nature and normativity. I substantiate McDowell's critiques of Brandom, and aim to show how McDowell's effort to reconceive of "experience" and "mind" in ways that obviate the epistemological need to bridge a gap between the thinking subject and the objective environment are on the right track, yet crucially limited by implicit metaphysical assumptions of which Whitehead can disabuse him. Second, I try to tease out of Pittsburgh-style analysis, with the help of Whitehead's own critique of classical substance metaphysics, the tacit metaphysical assumptions that have contributed to analytic tendencies to spatialize thought and language. The immediate effect of treating thought or language as if they exist in or create ontologically distinct realms of reason is to begin with the premise that mind is some sort of exception to nature.

Instead of beginning with an account of mind or the human subject as ontologically exceptional or distinct from the world, Whitehead begins with an event-based ontology whereby subjectivity becomes by means of the objectification of the past and eventuates its own objectification for the future. By taking the event as the final unit of analysis, he resists spatializing facthood such that objectivity is conceived as on the other side of an unbridgeable divide. Subjectivity and objectivity are modes of relation having to do with the full spatiotemporal continuum that makes up the passage of nature.

However we draw the line between mental and physical experience is a matter of convention, as Whitehead would be the first to acknowledge, and there can be no mistake that either is similarly a mode of relation, emerging from and acting back upon one another is ways that resist explanation by way of unidirectional models of causality. For Whitehead, then, mindedness qua mode of experience is emergent and therefore suited to the world it was designed to known in at least some of its perspectives. For Whitehead, in short, subjectivity is not epistemologically at a distance from the world precisely because it is not ontologically so.

Finally, my focus shifts toward exegesis of Whitehead's philosophy of symbolism in order to develop an alternative framework for understanding the relationship between nature and normativity after the problem of intentionality.

CHAPTER OUTLINE

Chapter 1 begins on a historical note. I examine some of Whitehead's earlier critiques of some of modern philosophy's bad habits. In particular, I investigate his critique of the neglect of temporality and the resultant spatialization of rationality in an intellectual lineage running circuitously from David Hume to Bertrand Russell. This neglect is a symptom of a misreading of Plato and a misuse of Aristotle that owe to the hermeneutical importations of the so-called Semitic theory of a wholly transcendent God. To adumbrate the nature of this misreading and misuse, I discuss A. E. Taylor's *A Commentary on Plato's Timaeus* (Oxford: Clarendon Press, 1928), whose work Whitehead regarded as the primary authority on the subject. Whitehead's alternative reading suggests that the bifurcation of nature so detrimental to modern epistemology—the very one, I argue, upon which the contemporary problem of intentionality is premised—need never have occurred.

Chapter 2 demonstrates how this bifurcation survives in the form of tacit metaphysical assumptions that have manifested in recent anti-metaphysical retrievals of Hegelian thought. It is here that I explore how Whitehead's early critiques of analytic philosophy anticipate the eventuation of Pittsburgh Neo-Hegelianism, while also foretelling its inadequacies.

Chapter 3 takes a closer look at the recent history of the problem of intentionality in analytic philosophy. Whereas in chapter 1, I focus on the intellectual environment surrounding the birth of analytic philosophy, and then fast-forward to John McDowell's appeal to Aristotelian naiveté as exemplary of a recurring impediment within this tradition to thinking about the relationship between mind and world, chapter 2 broadens the prehistory to McDowell's work by examining the post-Sellarsian intellectual environment he inherited. I discuss the writings of Wilfrid Sellars, Donald Davidson, Richard Rorty, Robert Brandom, in addition to John McDowell, insofar as they are in conversation with one another and have served to lay the groundwork of the contemporary exemplification of the problem. In the latter half of the chapter, I suggest ways in which this tradition is open to a metaphysics of the sort Whitehead exhibits.

Chapter 4 marks my shift from historical-diagnostic to constructive-therapeutic. Here, I exposit Whitehead's aesthetic ontology of perception and judgment. I situate his aesthetics in critical contrast to the tacit metaphysics of perception and judgment that funds McDowell's account of mind and world. It is Whitehead's aesthetic approach to perception and judgment, I argue, that provides the "real togetherness" without which we will continue to struggle to account for epistemological togetherness, that is, intentionality. This chapter transitions into the next by way of the continuity afforded by Whitehead's account of "symbolic reference." The real togetherness of mind and world depends upon the aesthetics of signification in general, and linguistic signification in particular.

Chapter 5 pivots back to McDowell's work on the epistemological significance of perception, exploring it in more detail in concert with some of his contemporary interlocutors. The purpose of this chapter is to show why the highly technical conceptual legwork presented in chapter 4 is just the sort that remains lacking in McDowell's reconception of experience and, as a result, his reconception remains inadequate to account for the very significance he wants to attribute to perception.

Chapter 6 offers my interpretation of Whitehead's theory of symbolism. I argue that his account of the concreteness of relations of symbolic reference provides a non-bifurcated view of symbols and meanings so as to demystify meaning. The effect is to finally avoid bifurcating nature in the ways even McDowell continues to do by reintegrating reason and experience. I conclude the project by distinguishing it from a call to conversion.

A NOTE ABOUT THE EPILOGUE

I make no mention of Whitehead's "God" in the book. The Epilogue is both a justification for and a correction of this omission.

Chapter 1

Reading Plato, Aristotle, and Kant with Whitehead

INTRODUCTION

The purpose of this chapter is to examine Alfred North Whitehead's early twentieth-century critiques of David Hume, Immanuel Kant, and Bertrand Russell as a pretext to showing how we might better understand the recent retrievals of Hegel's thought in analytic philosophy, vis-à-vis antimetaphysical or metaphysically minimalist readings (addressed in chapter 2). In order to understand these critiques, it will help to first gain some purchase on Whitehead's untraditional reading of Plato and Aristotle. This is because Whitehead attributes many of the problems of modern philosophy as stemming from a misunderstanding of Plato's realism and misappropriation of Aristotle's logic—two mistakes that resulted in modern philosophy's neglect of temporality and the resultant spatialization of rationality. The relevance of Whitehead to contemporary analytic efforts to make sense of the relationship between mind and world is directly related to how these efforts remain encumbered by spatialized accounts of "the conceptual," due to the very presuppositions Whitehead critiqued at the beginning of the twentieth century.

PLATO'S REALISM, ARISTOTLE'S IDEALISM, AND MODERN PHILOSOPHY'S BAD HABIT

In his Presidential Address for the 1922/23 Proceedings of the Aristotelian Society, Alfred North Whitehead stated the following: "I do not like this habit among philosophers, of having recourse to secret stores of information, which are not allowed for in their system of philosophy. They are the ghost of Berkeley's 'God,' and are about as communicative."[1] Although Whitehead had a knack for unearthing incoherent presuppositions, those of David Hume were what he had in mind on this occasion. Whitehead was speaking to the question of the uniformity of nature, which he defined as the problem as to whether "any isolated portion of our experience has any character which of itself implies a corresponding character, extending beyond the domain of the immediate example."[2] His point of departure was the implicit versus explicit status of space-time continuity in Hume's *Philosophical Essays Concerning Human Understanding*; more specifically, he was concerned with the incoherence of Hume's account of the idea of necessary connection between events, or the inference to causality.

In Essay 12 on "The Academic or Sceptical Philosophy," Hume claims that we acquire the idea of extension (spatiality) through perceptions of the "sensible qualities of objects," qualities which he takes to be "secondary" in the sense of existing only in the mind and not in the objects themselves. The rightful conclusion from this claim is the skeptical one, which asserts no ground for the future to conform to the past. But in the same essay, Whitehead observes, "Hume runs away from his own conclusion."[3] The "Pyrrhonian," he says in effect, must acknowledge that, if such skeptical principles were true, life would not be possible, because organisms can only survive in dependable environments. But Whitehead wants to know how Hume knows this, if in his own philosophy he has yet to account for the reality of space-time continuity as anything other than mere appearance. This discord, between the implicit and explicit status of space-time, was not specific to Hume for Whitehead, but was pervasive throughout modern philosophy. In fact, one of Whitehead's primary critiques of the early philosophy of Bertrand Russell—Whitehead's former student, *Principia* co-author, and close friend—was that he displayed just such "secret stores" of information. Archived correspondence between the two men, which will be treated later on, demonstrates as much.

Commenting on Russell's *Analysis of Mind*, published just a year earlier but drafts of which he had surely seen, Whitehead questions the distinction between theory and practice which Russell relies upon as if it were self-evident, even while his explicit system makes no room for its reality. In Lecture 5 on "Causal Laws," Russell writes,

> If, however, we know a very large number of cases in which A is followed by B and few or none in which the sequence fails, we shall in *practice* be justified in saying "A causes B," provided we do not attach to the notion of cause any of the metaphysical superstitious that have gathered about the word.[4]

Insofar as neither Hume nor Russell allow for any A to rationally justify the mind's expectation of B, each thinker tries to explain the origin of this expectation through appeal to justification "in practice" owing somehow to an observed "accumulation" of instances. But this very appeal to "accumulation" smuggles back in the notion we were denied at the beginning: the so-called external reality of extensionality and temporality.

The problem, according to Whitehead, is that each thinker operates on the suppressed premise that particular instances or events share no intrinsic character. Here we find the early indications of Whitehead's dismissal of vacuous entities, as evidenced in *Process and Reality* (1929). He insists that we can only escape Hume's difficulty if we admit what is implicitly assumed throughout his whole philosophy of nature: that instances are internally related and so "tell the tale" of the world with the patience for such events. Hume resists his own conclusion, and Russell speaks of being justified "in practice," because of the tacit assumption that particular instances are significant of something beyond it. This significance is spatio-temporal significance; a uniformity of nature is assumed by Hume's "accumulation" of events or Russell's "sequences."

Albert Einstein had only published his theory of general relativity seven years prior to these proceedings, and Whitehead published his *The Principle of Relativity with Applications to Physical Science*[5] in the same year of this address. In this work, Whitehead had critiqued the atomistic theory of space that regarded causal relations as action at a distance, albeit infinitely small distances. He dismissed the notion of infinitesimals. Whitehead's *Principle of Relativity* was not well received by physicists because he wrote the bulk of it using the same logical notion he had developed for the *Principia Mathematica*. It is for this same reason that I refer to his own analysis of the work that book performed, as recorded seven years later in *Process and Reality*. Here, Whitehead laments the treatment of time throughout modern philosophy as merely a fourth dimension of space. It is treated as such, moreover, when causality is accounted for by means of an infinite regress of "spaces." When causality is "spatialized" in this way, it relies on geometrical measurements (mainly Euclidean ones) that cannot wholly account for events. Whitehead suggests we stop identifying the units or instances of experience in terms of "distance," and instead understand such integrals in terms of "impetus." Such integrals, then, are no longer particulars in the classical sense, but internally related events. These are what Whitehead terms "actual entities," and it is because of this intrinsic character that he maintains the ontological principle: that the reason for one actual entity can only be other actual entities. Actual entities, in his words, "atomize the extensive continuum."[6] He writes further that if perception "merely concerns a private psychological field, science is the daydream of an individual without any public import."[7]

This is to say that the task of showing what the world must be like for inductive knowledge to be possible was at the forefront of Whitehead's mind in his 1922/23 address. Two years prior, his *The Concept of Nature* had criticized the "bifurcation of nature" implied by Hume's "secondary" qualities, Kant's "things in themselves," and the framework of Russell's "acquaintance."[8] In fact, Whitehead had read a paper only four months earlier for the 1921/1922 *Proceedings,* titled "The Philosophical Aspects of the Principle of Relativity."[9] In this book, Whitehead faulted the "standard form"[10] of Aristotelian logic for supplying the "two-termed relation of predication" he found largely responsible for this bifurcation.[11] The primary significance of the principle of relativity, he concludes, is that it displaces this Aristotelian logic, because it forces us to take account of time, and not just space, when thinking about the relationality of events.[12] As the title of the paper indicates, the "philosophical" aspects of the principle of relativity are its implications for our understanding of ultimate facts in terms of processes (events) instead of vacuous entities.

The misuse of Aristotle (and the misunderstanding of Plato) is one helpful way in which to understand what *Process and Reality* aimed to correct. Whitehead notes that Aristotle's philosophy was responsible both for the overemphasis on final causation in the Christian middle ages, and then on efficient causation in the modern scientific period. "One task of a sound metaphysics," he says in response, "is to exhibit final and efficient causes in their proper relation to each other."[13] Quite counter to the dominant contemporary caricatures of Plato and Aristotle, Whitehead argues, in effect, that the problems underlying the ignorance of time owes to the *idealist* treatments of Aristotle's logic and the misunderstanding of Plato's *realism.* The "Semitic theory" is mainly to blame on his account, insofar as its notion of a "wholly transcendent God creating out of nothing an accidental universe" made no room for a conception of the evolution of matter. And since "Newton held the Semitic theory," both the middle ages and the early scientific period could make no sense of Plato's cosmogony in the *Timaeus* by which "the origin of the present cosmic epoch is traced back to an aboriginal disorder, chaotic according to our ideals."[14] Distinctively, then, there is no bifurcation between a realm of ideas and a world of appearances in Whitehead's reading of Plato. What there *is* is an account of ultimate fact in terms of process, where the actual is always becoming and, therefore, "never really is."[15]

The interpretation of Plato (and Aristotle) with which Whitehead was working was A. E. Taylor's. Some consideration of Taylor's exegesis will help us understand Whitehead's argument—especially insofar as Taylor himself alludes to Whitehead's own terminology to explicate what he calls the "correct Platonic view."[16] Like Whitehead, Taylor read Plato's cosmology as more compatible with modern science than that of Aristotle:

> What Timaeus wants to insist on is that, to use a phrase of Dr. Whitehead's, "passage" is the fundamental fact about "Nature." This is why . . . natural

science is "progressive" in a sense in which pure mathematics[17] is not. . . . This correct perception that there is no finality in natural science is one of the things which most markedly distinguishes Plato from Aristotle for the better.[18]

Taylor's comment is significant because, when readers of Whitehead accuse his doctrine of "eternal objects" of being too "Platonic," they are both correct and incorrect, insofar as they do not intend what Taylor calls the "correct Platonic view" but rather an idealist reading, which will not help them as interpreters of Whitehead (or Plato, for that matter).

Commenting on varieties of the "bifurcation" of nature that Whitehead critiques in modern philosophy, Taylor argues that the more insidious variety—that leading to Kant's *noumena*—is nowhere to be found in Plato *or* Aristotle:

> The main point to be grasped is that the *Timaeus* is wholly free from any form of the doctrine which Professor Whitehead calls the "bifurcation" of nature. In Aristotle we find 'bifurcation' beginning in the distinction between "substances," which are imperceptible and the 'accidents' of the substances, which are what we perceive.
>
> But the very distinction between "substance" and "accident" plays no part in the *Naturphilosophie* of Timaeus. The other two more elaborate forms of "bifurcation" mentioned by Whitehead (*Concept of Nature*, lect. Ii)—the distinction between an unperceived "Nature as cause" and a perceived "Nature as effect," and the distinction between "Nature as she is" and "Nature as she appears to us"—are absent from both Plato and Aristotle.[19]

These passages lay a telling groundwork for an understanding of why Whitehead thinks modern philosophy mistreats the notion of time, and the heuristic role the "Semitic view" played in its appropriation of Greek philosophy. What we see in Taylor's commentary is a rejection of classical theological notions of eternity and absoluteness, which both he and Whitehead argue have been misread into Plato. Taylor writes, "It seems to me a sheer mistake to discover in the imagery by which Timaeus tries to lead up to the concept of 'timeless space' any novel 'later theory of (Platonic) Ideas'. We shall see on 51 b ff. that when the Forms are expressly spoken of, it is precisely in the spirit of *Phaedo*."[20] It is this notion of "timeless space" which has been misunderstood as a wholly transcendent realm of Ideas outside of the temporal process. If this is not what Plato endorsed, then it is not what Whitehead endorses when he writes of the handful of ways in which "the organic philosophy only repeats Plato."[21] Taylor continues,

> we must begin by forgetting all about the artificial "materialistic" interpretation of nature which assumes solid bits of "matter" as permanent things. This

interpretation of nature has, as it happens, coloured our language so deeply that it is hard for us at first to realize how very artificial an interpretation it is. But we must make the attempt to get back to a condition in which we can look at the "appearances" as they present themselves to an observer not yet biased unconsciously in favour of a "materialistic" theory. Then we shall see nature simply as a great complex of overlapping events of various kinds each with its own duration and volume. (For the point of view compare Whitehead *Concept of Nature* i–ii.)[22]

The doctrine of the non-evolution of matter that Whitehead identified in Newton treats as finally real a mathematical abstraction—"absolute space"—that depends on the artificial removal of time for the purposes of Euclidean geometrical measurements. Whitehead, a mathematician, but also passionate about the philosophy of education, had critiqued the teaching of Euclidean geometrical principles as if they were *the* axioms of geometry, and not merely *our* axioms of geometry.[23]

Whitehead was severely critical of the way primary school students were taught to accept the logical premises of subjects like geometry as self-evident propositions, implying that they are incapable of proof. This tendency is perpetuated by what he calls "fallacious views of logical method."[24] Whitehead regarded Bertrand Russell as exhibiting this fallacious view, which to a large degree contributed to Russell's "Platonism"—that is, his treatment of logic as containing the transcript of reality, as opposed to its being simply a tool developed to more efficiently communicate ideas. Whitehead did not see logic as adding anything to our knowledge of the world; Russell did. It was this tendency of the early Russell that would contribute not only to his account of sense-data, which Wilfrid Sellars would critique, but also to his insinuation of a logical Given, which Robert Brandom would critique. As Paul Redding writes, "For Russell, the immediate intuitive apprehension of sense-data was only *one* of the applications of the idea of 'acquaintance.' Our *a priori* knowledge of *logical and mathematical truths* were also accounted for by this means."[25] Whitehead avoided both notions of "givenness" because he rejected the concomitant philosophy of space that underwrites them.

For Whitehead, there is a given, but it is not the sort that is liable to postanalytic critiques. It is the sort of givenness he credits Plato with recognizing as the limit of "theory," insofar as any theory at all presupposes something given to be theorized. Again deferring to Taylor's interpretation, Whitehead quotes him on the following:

> In the real world there is always, over and above "law," a factor of the "simply given" or "brute fact," not accounted for and to be accepted simply as given. . . .
> It is the presence in nature of this element of the given, this surd or irrational as

it has sometimes been called, which Timaeus appears to be personifying in his language about Necessity.[26]

Whitehead follows the passage by stating, "a clear understanding of the 'given' elements in the world is essential for any form of Platonic realism."[27] Throughout *Process and Reality,* Whitehead speaks about this givenness in terms of "decision," not because it is a conscious activity, but because it is decisive—it is a "cutting off" or an "activity procuring limitation."[28] In his words, "'Actuality' is the decision amid 'potentiality'."[29] It is a regrettable irony that Whitehead's own metaphysics has been accused of the mistaken Platonism that he intended it to correct.

WHITEHEAD AND CONCEPTUAL SPACE

The benefit of getting Whitehead right on Plato is that it affords a clearer appreciation of his notion of conceptual space—a notion that has been spatialized in contemporary analytic accounts of intentionality. Whitehead was particularly moved by William James's image of the "blooming, buzzing confusion." He was insistent upon the fact that, in our direct observations, we encounter the whole passage of nature. It is only in analysis that we can construct for various purposes, like those of logic or pure mathematics, notions of "timeless space" or "absolute time."

In chapter 5, "Space and Motion," of his *Concept of Nature* Whitehead begins by naming the topic of his lecture as "the continuation of the task of explaining the construction of spaces as abstracts from the facts of nature."[30] Space and time are ultimately descriptors of relations that make up the structure of events. In chapter 3, "Time," he writes, "The germ of space is to be found in the mutual relations of events within the immediate general fact [of sense-awareness]."[31] Later, he writes, "There is time because there are happenings, and apart from happenings there is nothing."[32] Spatial and temporal extension are modes of relations constitutive of events, of the passage of nature; they are not qualities to be attached to bits of matter. What's more, they are not *additives* of one another, because they are nothing except events. We abstract them from one another for the purposes of measurement. It was the recognition of this abstractiveness that Einstein's theory of relativity demanded.

What relativity means is that time is a mode of relation peculiar to an event. For Whitehead, the distinction we are prone to make between mind and nature is ultimately one between two contemporaries in spatial relations pictured through the imagery of inner and outer. Only through such spatialized thinking are we tempted to equate the "immediacy" of sense-awareness ("mental" events) with the "instantaneousness" of nature ("non-mental" events).[33] Whitehead refers to such thinking as "materialist," and includes the idealism of the eighteenth and nineteenth centuries under the same banner insofar as it also shared the belief "that nature is an aggregate of material and that this material exists in some sense *at* each successive member of a one-dimensional series of extensionless instants of time."[34] He amplifies his critique of materialism in the following passage:

> Furthermore the mutual relations of the material entities at each instant formed these entities into a spatial configuration in an unbounded space. It would seem that space—on this theory—would be as instantaneous as the instants, and that some explanation is required of the relations between the successive instantaneous spaces. The materialistic theory is however silent on this point; and the succession of instantaneous spaces is tacitly combined into one persistent space. This theory is a purely intellectual rendering of experience which has had the luck to get itself formulated at the dawn of scientific thought. It has dominated the language and the imagination of science since science flourished in Alexandria, with the result that it is now hardly possible to speak without appearing to assume its immediate obviousness.[35]

In an exceptionally clear passage, Whitehead describes the speciousness of what those beholden to a materialist picture call the present:

> On the materialistic theory the instantaneous present is the only field for the creative activity of nature. The past is gone and the future is not yet. Thus (on this theory) the immediacy of perception is of an instantaneous present, and this unique present is the outcome of the past and the promise of the future. But we deny this immediately given instantaneous present. There is no such thing to be found in nature. As an ultimate fact it is a nonentity. What is immediate for sense-awareness is a duration. Now a duration has within itself a past and a future; and the temporal breadths of the immediate durations of sense-awareness are very indeterminate and dependent on the individual percipient. Accordingly there is no unique factor in nature which for every percipient is preeminently and necessarily the present. The passage of nature leaves nothing between the past and the future.[36]

The immediacy of perception is not equivalent to the instantaneousness of events in nature, precisely because the conflation of the two is premised on a false notion of the present. The present is not one part of the triad of time, but a particular interrelation between the passage of mind with the passage of non-mental events in nature. *Our* present, on a Whiteheadian description, is best described as "the vivid fringe of memory tinged with anticipation."[37]

It is *ours* and no one else's. If we want to speak of simultaneity in terms of "instantaneous spaces," we can only speak of parallel moments in one time-system (which he defines as different families of durations). To do this is to develop the notion of "absolute space," which is the domain of the physical sciences.[38]

Taylor relies on Whitehead's notion of time-systems to explain what he reads Timaeus as having in mind; that is, a notion of "absolute space" which is always derivative of "perceptual space." Both he and Whitehead credit Leibniz's ingenuity in this regard for having defined space in terms of the order of co-existences.[39] It is also, he notes, "what ought to be meant by the modern philosophers when they speak of 'conceptual' space." This last point is Whitehead's, and Taylor credits him for it. Whitehead himself was mystified by what modern philosophers *actually* meant by "conceptual space," writing, "I suppose that it is meant that the space is the conception of something in nature."[40] But when asking about what this "something" may be, Whitehead humorously demands "a definite Habeas Corpus Act for the production of the relevant entities" less we meander into the realm of "pure fantasy."[41] Whitehead's theory of space, in contrast to those like Russell's, ceases to present space as a collection of brute facts. The nature of explanation is the discovery of interconnection, which is at root the interdependence of the character of space and the character of time.[42] When Timaeus speaks of what is "eternal" in terms of what does not "pass," according to Taylor, he "asserts that it is not 'in' anything except in the sense that it is 'in' itself, it 'fills' itself."[43] Interestingly, both Taylor and Whitehead commend John Milton on this point. According to Taylor, "Milton is affirming the eternity of [*nous*] when he says that the mind is its 'own place'."[44] Whitehead, however, sees Milton's *Paradise Lost* as wavering "between the *Timaeus* and the Semitic doctrine" of the order of nature.[45] Yet both Taylor and Whitehead are in full agreement when attributing to Aristotle the classical isolation of space from time "with all the paradoxes it involves."[46] It was Aristotle's "preoccupation with the notion of volume" that led to this separation, Taylor claims, which is why "the latest philosophical work on the concepts of physics, work like Professor Whitehead's, strikes a reader familiar with Greek philosophy at once as an attempt to get back from Aristotelian positions to the general standpoint of Plato's Pythagorean cosmologist."[47]

This is true to an extent. Whitehead himself only explicitly notes two ways in which his philosophy of organism "repeats Plato."[48] That is to say that he also means to modify Plato "so as to avoid the pitfalls which the philosophical investigations of the seventeenth and eighteenth centuries have disclosed."[49] In his 1919 *An Enquiry Concerning the Principles of Natural Knowledge*—the manuscript which he refused to share with Russell for fear he would run away with his ideas[50]—Whitehead makes a distinction in his preface between natural philosophy and metaphysics which suggests such pitfalls. He writes,

> The discussion of the deduction of scientific concepts from the simplest elements of our perceptual knowledge at once brings us to philosophical theory. Berkeley, Hume, Kant, Mill, Huxley, Bertrand Russell and Bergson, among others, have initiated and sustained relevant discussions. But this enquiry is touched by only one side of the philosophical debate. We are concerned only with Nature, that is, with the object of perceptual knowledge, and not with the synthesis of the knower with the known. This distinction is exactly that which separates natural philosophy from metaphysics.

The difference between metaphysics and the natural philosophy of Hume, Kant, and Russell is that natural philosophy asks only about the object of perceptual knowledge and believes this to be the only place to begin. And yet, because of tacit metaphysical presumptions, the epistemologies of modern philosophy lead either to solipsism or contradiction. Whitehead shows the only way to refute the solipsist is to refuse to play his game. He continues, "Accordingly none of our perplexities as to Nature will be solved by having recourse to the consideration that there is a mind knowing it. Our theme is the coherence of the known, and the perplexity which we are unraveling is as to what it is that is known."[51] We could read Whitehead here as saying that we set ourselves up for inadequate and inaccurate theorizing if we operate according to the same tacit presumptions that lead one to think they can speak of a conceptual realm with any sense without being able to account for how it coheres with what is "given" in the non-problematic sense of what is the prerequisite material prompting theorization. In one sense, it was the neglect of temporal extension in consideration of spatial extension that led to the bifurcation of nature into "primary" and "secondary" qualities. This bifurcation, on Whitehead's account, precipitated an incorrect view of the nature of physical science. The Kantian notion of *mere* appearance illustrates this neglect of temporality.

H. A. PRICHARD AND THE REAL PROBLEM OF KANT'S FIRST *CRITIQUE*

Whitehead the mathematician cannot be extricated from Whitehead the philosopher. To study his regard for the nature of geometrical and arithmetical rules, and the relation of logical notation to them, is arguably one of the most elegant routes to appreciating the ways in which Whitehead anticipates post-analytic critiques before analytic philosophy had come of age. As with Plato, however, Whitehead never gives us an extended exegesis of Kant. We must first gain some purchase on the interpretation of Kant with which Whitehead was working in order to appreciate the "Kant" who was the subject of contention not only for Whitehead, but also for Russell. Later in this section, after considering H. A. Prichard's *Kant's Theory of Knowledge*[52]—which was the scholarship on Kant most familiar to Whitehead—I will examine Whitehead's correspondence with Russell, in which he critiques Russell's putative refutation of Kant in his early drafts of *The Problems of Philosophy* for not being "within a hundred miles of Kant's position." This will ultimately be in service of showing how radically Whitehead disagreed with the premises of the analytic tradition.

Prichard begins with an investigation of the problems of Kant's first *Critique*—not the problem as Kant himself understands it, but the problem of Kant's misunderstanding of what his problem actually was and should have been explicitly. Paraphrasing Kant's own set up of the problem of the first *Critique*, Prichard writes:

> There, in fact, lies the importance to metaphysics of the existence of such judgments in mathematics and physics. For it shows that the difficulty is not peculiar to metaphysics, but is a general one shared by other subjects; and the existence of such judgments in mathematics is especially important because there the validity or certainty has never been questioned. The success of mathematics shows that at any rate under certain conditions *a priori* synthetic judgments are valid, and if we can determine these conditions, we shall be able to decide whether such judgments are possible in metaphysics. In this way we shall be able to settle a disputed case of their validity by examination of an undisputed case.[53]

Insofar as Kant took metaphysics to be making *a priori* synthetic judgments, and insofar as metaphysics is not unique in doing so, but keeps company with mathematics and physics, he thought that we could investigate the nature of such judgments in the latter cases in order to determine the extent to which we can make them in the former.

Prichard claims that Kant's so-called Copernican revolution only appears as such due to a rhetorical sleight of hand, unnoticed even by Kant. When he claims to reverse the ordinary view of the relationship between mind and objects, Kant is using "objects" to mean things in the world, or noumena. His alternative is to conceive objects as having to conform to the mind. But in this second use, "objects" now refers to things as they appear to us, or phenomena. As "object" refers to something different in each instance, Prichard argues, Kant's position is only verbally a reversal of the traditional one.

We can notice Kant's mistake if we make explicit the spatial motifs on which he implicitly relies. If the ordinary view is that objects are things outside the mind and ideas within the mind, the former being independent and the latter dependent upon the mind, then traditional conformity holds between something within the mind to something without the mind. "Hence," writes Prichard, "the real contrary of this view is that ideas, within the mind, exist first and that objects outside the mind, coming into existence afterwards, must adapt themselves to the ideas."[54] But Kant does not claim this; he claims only, in effect, that our knowledge of mind must conform to mind. Contrary to Kant's own construal of his position as reversing the ordinary relation of conformity between mind and object, his actual position is "we ought not to speak of conformity at all."[55]

It is interesting to note the resemblance Prichard's claim bears to Robert Brandom's own that what Kant was really doing in the first *Critique* was not asking how representations can be successful, but challenging the semantics of representationalism itself. In his 2006 article "Kantian Lessons about Mind, Meaning, and Rationality,"[56] Brandom claims that Kant is not asking the epistemological question of the Cartesian skeptic, but a semantic question about the nature of representation. Further, he claims that an adequate answer to the semantic question would dissolve the epistemological one; that is, we cannot talk about ideas being true if we are not clear on what it means to believe something to be true in the first place. Brandom thinks Kant nearly succeeds in answering the semantic question, too. "Kant tells us nearly everything we need to know about minds, concepts, and their use and contents," according to Brandom.[57] Of course, he does not explicitly tell us, but shows us, Brandom thinks. Like Prichard, he is arguing for what Kant was actually doing in the *Critiques*, despite what Kant thought he was doing. This is why Brandom titles the piece "Kantian Lessons"—they are Kantian, not Kant's.

To be sure, Prichard does not claim that Kant is asking the "prior" semantic question, like Brandom does; he claims that Kant thinks he has made an epistemological move when he has really made an ontological one—one impermissible by his own lights. Kant can both make and miss this move because of a prior oversight regarding the nature of synthetic *a posteriori* judgments or presumed empirical givens. The "problem" he intends the first *Critique* to address is, after all, that of synthetic *a priori* judgments, because these strike Kant as problematic in a way that analytic *a priori* or synthetic *a posteriori* judgments are not. Prichard, however, thinks that Kant has failed to notice that the difficulty that extends to synthetic *a priori* judgments extends equally to synthetic *a posteriori* judgments. He writes, "It can only be supposed that the conformity of empirical judgments to their objects is guaranteed by the experience upon which they rest, if it be assumed that in experience we apprehend objects as they are. But our experience or perception of individual objects is just as much mental as the thinking which originates *a priori* judgments."[58] In other words, the only reason Kant is able to make a distinction between synthetic *a priori* and synthetic *a posteriori* judgments is because he takes ideas to involve an *activity* of mind in the way perceptions do not. According to Prichard, Kant forgets that perceptions are equally dependent upon the mind, and so equally set up the problem of something within the mind conforming to something outside of it—at least, we can argue as much using Kant's own presuppositions. Prichard is simply pointing out an inconsistency in Kant's thinking, not endorsing any of the language—particularly the ascriptions of "mental" and "non-mental," "inside" and "outside." These distinctions perpetuate the very bifurcation of nature he would abandon.

The inconsistency owes to a tacit ontological assumption about particulars and universals. Kant assumes that the mind acts as intermediary when the subject relates to universals, but does not act as intermediary when the subject relates to particulars. It is assumed that, with respect to universals, because we have to *think* them, "what is related to the subject as the object of its thought must be subjective or mental."[59] That creates a question about the conformity of this object-qua-idea to the reality it "represents." Such is not the case for Kant in perception, because he assumes some sort of givenness. It is because Kant misconceives the nature of things like geometrical thinking that he takes it to be different in kind from perception and not just in degree.

But Prichard thinks that, if Kant is to be consistent with himself, it must be that his concern is not specifically with *a priori* judgments, but with the conformity of all ideas-qua-activities of the mind—including perception—to things outside of it. Therefore, in claiming that particulars must conform to universals, as he does with respect to geometrical and mathematical rules, he is not actually claiming that we can only really ever know phenomena—he only thinks he is claiming this because of his equivocation on the use of "object" in each rendition of the direction of mind/world conformity. To the contrary, what is shown, on Prichard's analysis, is that the problem of the first *Critique* "reduces itself to the question, 'What is the presupposition of the existence of definite laws of connexion in the world?' And the only answer possible is that reality is a system of a whole of connected parts, in other words, that nature is uniform."[60] If Kant were to deny the law of connection, then he would be unable to claim that particulars conform to universals. He does claim this, however, and is thereby committed to the uniformity of nature.

To sum up, thus far, Prichard has accused Kant of getting away with the distinction between problematic synthetic *a priori* judgment and unproblematic synthetic *a posteriori* judgments only because he acknowledges the relation of subject (mind) to object (world) in the former but not in the latter. Kant therefore operates with an ontological distinction between particulars-qua-things-independent-of-the-mind and universals-qua-things-dependent-upon-the-mind. His interpretation of this distinction, however, is informed by an Aristotelian tendency to regard individuals as the only realities, such that universals and the relations between universals are somehow "mere" fictions of the mind. Prichard calls this tendency the "conceptualist attitude."[61] Only because this view underwrites Kant's recognition of the activity of *thinking* in *a priori* but not *a posteriori* synthetic judgments, can he find the logical momentum to assume that thinking, qua activity, originates something in the former and not in the latter. In other words, thinking originates the object of the judgment in the case of universals but does not originate the object of the judgment in the case of particulars.

Had Kant not committed the first oversight, he would have noticed that there must be fallacious reasoning involved in the association of reality only with particulars; that is, he would have noticed that, since ideas and perceptions are equally mind-involving objects, his problem was not only with the nature of *a priori* but also *a posteriori* synthetic judgments. In fact, he would have been able to make sense of his difficulty in defining the nature of synthetic *a priori* judgments, instead of resting content to describe some as self-evident (those of mathematics) and some as requiring demonstration (those of physics). He would have been able to make sense of this difficulty because he would not have his mistaken epistemological claim authorized by a mistaken *ontological* one—one concealed by its very operation, and so, upon scrutiny, liable to the critique of performative self-contradiction. Indeed, he would have seen that the real problem of the first *Critique* was, according to the terms of his own discussion, the relationship between things in the mind with things outside the mind. And insofar as he believed the revolution of standpoint to be necessary in order to make sense of the direction of conformity in this relation, he would also need to admit that, entailed in the assumption of conformity, is the assumption of the uniformity of nature.

But then, the warranted conclusion is *not* that we can only know things as our mind constructs them, because we have rid ourselves of the ontological assumption that only individuals have reality *and* the concomitant epistemological one that mind is only involved when the object is a universal. Kant would not have claimed that what makes the universal judgments in mathematics (e.g., about the straight line being the shortest distance between two points) and the singular judgments in physics (e.g., the phenomenal world as demonstrative of the validity of this mathematical judgment) true is self-evident in the first but demonstrative in the second. Short of designating a unique category of judgments, such would be to say that the "truth of the law of causality is *not* apprehended in the same way that we see that 'two and two are four'."[62] Rather, if he were to be consistent with what counts as an *a priori* synthetic judgment, it "could then be defined as one in which the mind, on the presentation of an individual in perception or imagination, and in virtue of its capacity in thinking, apprehends the necessity of a specific relation," according to Prichard.[63] It turns out that, according to this more coherent definition of *a priori* synthetic judgments, they succeed *not* insofar as their objects are possible items of experience (some version of Kant's *phenomena*), but rather, they succeed insofar as their objects are the necessary relations constitutive of the individuals they apprehend. If *a priori* synthetic judgments are not true insofar as their objects are possible objects of experience, then the possibility of mathematics and physics no longer entails the impossibility of metaphysics.

KANT'S SPATIALIZATION OF THOUGHT

The foregoing discussion of Prichard's work on Kant illustrates a problematic tendency at the root of his first *Critique*, a tendency that owes to the very legacy of Aristotle that Taylor delegitimized and Whitehead sought to correct. This is the tendency in Western philosophy to spatialize thought—even to spatialize *time* by conceiving of it as an "inner" sense. Prichard argues as much in his chapter 5 "Time and Inner Sense," where he questions "whether Kant is, on his own principles, entitled to speak of an inner sense at all."[64] I might paraphrase his argument by saying that Kant is not so entitled because he takes sensations to be produced by the activity of things-in-themselves, and so internal sensation must likewise be produced by the activity of something within the mind. But if we cannot know the thing-in-itself, including what *we* are in ourselves, then how are we able to determine if a given sensation is due to *ourselves* and, therefore, an *inner* sense? If we take Kant at his word, we shouldn't be able to recognize an inner sense at all.[65] But then why does Kant maintain that time is merely the *form* of our internal sense, the form of our self-perception? Kant writes, "Time is nothing other than the form of inner sense, i.e., of the intuition of our self and our inner state. For time cannot be a determination of outer appearances; it belongs neither to a shape or a position, etc., but on the contrary determines the relation of representations in our inner state."[66] Notice that Kant says "outer" appearances, which are distinguished from "inner" sense by reason of the fact that they have shape or position. But if, as Prichard has already argued, we have no grounds to determine whether the cause of our affections is dependent or independent upon the mind, what sense does it make to speak of "outer" appearances—particularly insofar as "appearances" already implies something *dependent* upon the mind?

Kant has once again failed to consistently apply his own distinction, allowing some low-grade affirmation of "facts as they are outside of us" to creep in. As a consequence, he slips back and forth between two meanings of "external": the one, to mean phenomena of which the parts are external to one another, that is, spatial; the other, to mean phenomena independent of the mind. Time cannot be a determinant of external phenomena in the first sense, insofar as it has nothing to do with space or position, but regarding the second sense, it would seem to be an oxymoron, since "phenomena" are distinguished from "things-in-themselves" precisely on the grounds that they *are* dependent upon mind. He goes on to argue the unreality of time on the grounds that we can exhaustively describe the nature of its form by spatial analogy:

> And just because this inner intuition yields no shape we also attempt to remedy this lack through analogies, and represent the temporal sequence through a line progressing to infinity, in which the manifold constitutes a series that is of only one dimension, and infer from the properties of this line to all the properties of time, with the sole difference that the parts of the former are simultaneous but those of the latter always exist successively. From this it is also apparent that the representation of time is itself an intuition, since all its relations can be expressed in an outer intuition.[67]

Kant has seamlessly transitioned from the claim that time is the form of internal states, to the assertion that time is a way in which we *perceive* our internal states. In the first, our states *really are* temporally related; in the second, we *perceive* our *perceptions* to be temporally related.[68] (In the previous chapter, Prichard argues that Kant makes a similar transition with respect to space, beginning with the assertion that space is the form of things, and moving to the assertion the space is a form of our perception of things.[69]) The point, Prichard concludes, is that Kant cannot have it both ways:

> [he] is only justified in denying that we know things in themselves if he concedes that we really know our own states, and not merely the appearances which they produce. . . . Hence, since these states are really our states and not appearances produced by our states, these being themselves unknown, time, as a relation of these states, must itself be real, and not a way in which we apprehend what is real.[70]

Prichard concludes, in effect, that Kant cannot performatively sustain his own explicit commitment to the spatialization of time. This is the reading of Kant to which Whitehead notes his indebtedness in *Process and Reality*. For over a decade before writing his magnum opus, Whitehead had been advocating for the philosophical implications of the theory of relativity, and had been correcting Bertrand Russell's neglect of applied mathematics for some idealized version of pure mathematics. It would seem, then, that by the time of *Process and Reality*, Whitehead was already at the helm of what would later become post-analytic philosophy, before *analytic* philosophy even had its sea legs.

WHITEHEADIAN ANTICIPATIONS OF POST-ANALYTIC CRITIQUE

It is noteworthy that Prichard's efforts to correct the tacit ontological assumptions in Kant that rendered Kant's reasoning convoluted, in order to show how Kant's thought might differently resolve epistemological skepticism with a metaphysics of intentionality, resembles McDowell's rereading of Kant in *Mind and World* (1994). Ironically, McDowell takes his rereading of Kant on intuition to demand a sort of "Aristotelian innocence," by which he means what Whitehead means by the elimination of the bifurcation of nature. McDowell critiques *both* what he calls the "bald" naturalism of scientific materialism *and* post-Kantian idealist critiques of the supersensible for presuming a sort of "rampant" *Platonism*, insofar as each operates with an idea of "nature" as an unbounded "objective" realm that is structured by a "subjective" or "conceptual" realm.[71]

It should be noticed that the "Aristotle" that McDowell commends for this innocence is more akin to the "Plato" that Whitehead commends for the same, and that the "Platonism" McDowell seeks to exorcise from Kant is more akin to the "false Platonism" that Whitehead-via-Taylor identifies than the Plato whose *realism* Whitehead prescribes. This is important, because McDowell thereby exhibits the very misunderstandings of Plato and misappropriations of Aristotle that Whitehead sought to correct, and which unskilled readers of Whitehead continue to uphold. When he expressed mystification about what traditional philosophy had dubbed "conceptual space," Whitehead was talking about something very much like the problematic dichotomy that McDowell seeks to correct with his notion of "second nature." In fact, McDowell calls his corrective account of conceptual capacities a "naturalized" Platonism—a phrase that would strike Taylor and Whitehead as strange, if not redundant.

The retrieval by post-analytic philosophers of Hegel has been rather telling in its urgency to undo the damage caused by assumptions that make intentionality seem problematic. McDowell argues that we need that reading of Hegel that emphasizes his *Aristotelianism* in order to make sense of normativity coming from nature. When Brandom reads Hegel in an anti-Aristotelian way, he ends up unable to account for *perceptual* judgments. What such attempts suggest to me is that philosophers of the analytic tradition would do well to stop debating about whether Hegel was doing metaphysics—such debates are non-starters, because "metaphysics" has no static sense—and to pay attention to the thinker who anticipated the inadequacy of Anglo-American philosophy's dominant account of experience from the outset. Whitehead identifies, and more completely, the same inhibiting factors in this tradition as does McDowell a century later. When McDowell claims that we need a new conception of "nature" and "objectivity," along with "experience," he would do well to examine Whitehead.

It is one of the great ironies of intellectual history that the general impression among analytic philosophers is that Whitehead's ideas are too Platonist, too metaphysical, and too abstract. In fact, it was all these things that Whitehead resisted in analytic thinkers of his day, and the modern philosophical tradition to which they responded. Russell's logical atomism was not, in Whitehead's view, a departure from classical metaphysical ideas, but a particular type of extension of them.

Russell and Whitehead collaborated for a decade on the *Principia Mathematica*. But the collaboration did not extend beyond the project—the relationship of logic to mathematics exhausted the extent of their intellectual agreement. Once the subject became the relationship of logic to ontology, or the philosophy of mathematics, the two thinkers diverged. We see these differences expressed in Whitehead's 1911 critiques of *The Problems,* which was Russell's attempt to work out the philosophical problems that arose in their *Principia* project.

Keeping in mind the Prichard-inspired reading of Kant explored above, we can better understand Whitehead's critique of Russell's draft of *The Problems*, which we have in the form of fourteen handwritten pages dated August 28, 1911. It is difficult to decipher Whitehead's handwriting exactly, but on my best reading, after offering a Prichard-like paraphrase of Kant, he writes:

> Now if this is anything like Kant, you do not touch him. First, you muddle the physical objects (=scientific molecule) in "public space" with his thing-in-itself. Second, you have smuggled away and ignored the phenomenal object with which he starts. Thus the whole point of the "phenomenon" mentioned by you on p. 28 is lost. Third, your "main objection" on p. 29 is that our nature is a fact of the "existing world." What do you mean by "existing world"! Apparently something in time, for "tomorrow" applies to it. Kant would certainly have [end page 8] denied this. This would be the "phenomenal ego." The "transcendental ego" is not in time—rather conversely.[72]

The Kant that Whitehead says Russell misses entirely is the Kant that Prichard accuses of maintaining in *practice* the very reality of time that he denies in *principle*. Russell misses this Kant because he makes recourse to those "secret stores of information" that Whitehead accused so many modern philosophers of having in his address to the Aristotle Society in 1922. What these "secret stores" often hold are tacit assumptions about space and time that are either treated as needing no defense, or as explicitly contradicted by their purported principles.

As there is little indication[73] that Russell made any substantial changes to the text as a result of Whitehead's comments, we may use the text as we have it today to examine the parts Whitehead had in mind in the above statement. The first is quite straightforward. Russell writes,

> The physical object, which he calls the "thing in itself," (1) he regards as essentially unknowable; what can be known is the object as we have it in experience, which he calls the "phenomenon." . . . Kant's thing in itself is identical in *definition* with the physical object, namely, it is the cause of sensations. In the properties deduced from the definition it is not identical, since Kant held (in spite of some inconsistency as regards cause) that we can know that none of the categories are applicable to the "thing in itself."[74]

Whitehead has taken issue with what Russell refers to as "the physical object" here. Earlier in the letter, while commenting on Russell's chapter 2, Whitehead argued that Russell had entirely failed to refute the solipsist because of his loose application of terms. For instance, Russell writes, "The real table, if it exists, we will call a 'physical object.' Thus we have to consider the relation of sense-data to physical objects. The collection of all physical objects is called 'matter'."[75] Physical objects are what Russell understands as the objects causing our sensations. As the causes of our sensations, these physical objects exist outside us in spatial extension, which is the "physical space" that Russell understands as the "space of science."[76] We can already see why Whitehead-qua-Taylorian might have objected to this terminology, on several levels. First, with respect to his treatment of space, Russell is working with the very bifurcated picture of nature that he thinks he is critiquing in Kant. When Russell talks about "the real space" that is "public" versus "the apparent space" that is "private to the percipient,"[77] Whitehead sees that Russell is already playing the game he thinks he is challenging. When Russell says that it is this "physical space" with which geometry deals, Whitehead does not disagree; what he disagrees with is the ontological claim that this space is somehow the "real" one. Again, this explains why Whitehead and Russell ceased to collaborate after the *Principia Mathematica*—while their mathematics were not contentious, their philosophies of mathematics were. For Whitehead, if you are contrasting reality with appearance, you've already played right into the traditional doctrines of space to the neglect of time. Russell is employing the "nature as it really is" versus the "nature as it appears to us" picture, and in doing so, associates Kant's "thing in itself" with the former. Whitehead, however, thinks that Russell has failed to anticipate Kant's rightful reply to this association. Thus, though "you might say, 'At least Reality-in-itself is something.' [Kant] replies 'Yes, but now I am conceiving Reality-in-itself as a phenomenal object, [this] names the counterpart of my phenomenal self'."[78] Russell is wrong, he thinks, in making the association he does because, in speaking about "physical objects" as the causes in physical space of our sensations, Russell is applying the notions associated with the categories of the Transcendental Aesthetic: time, space, number, and causation. These notions cannot both apply to the "physical object" as Russell defines it and to Kant's "things-in-themselves."[79]

By equating the two, Russell is not objecting to Kant as much as he is creating a straw man argument for his hypostatization of logic and pure mathematics: "Apart from minor grounds on which Kant's philosophy may be criticized, there is one main objection which seems fatal to any attempt to deal with the problem of *a priori* knowledge by his method. The thing to be accounted for is our certainty that the facts must always conform to logic and arithmetic. To say that logic and arithmetic are contributed by us does not account for this."[80] On Whitehead-qua-Prichardian's reading, neither is it true to speak of the self-evidence of logic and pure mathematics (this was the critique he gave of mathematics education and the disuse of Euclid's *Elements* for historical context), nor is it true that Kant would have equated "things-in-themselves" with what Russell calls "the facts."

Neither, and for the same reason, would Kant have equated them with "the existing world" as Russell does when he writes, "Our nature is as much a fact of the existing world as anything, and there can be no certainty that it will remain constant. It might happen, if Kant is right, that to-morrow our nature would so change as to make two and two become five. This possibility seems never to have occurred to [Kant], yet it is one which utterly destroys the certainty and universality which he is anxious to vindicate for arithmetical propositions."[81] When Whitehead critiques Russell for thinking that "our nature" and the "existing world" correspond to Kant's "transcendental ego" and "things-in-themselves," he does so not because he is defending Kant, but because he thinks that Russell's efforts to refute him miss the mark because the position he is defending against Kant is also, on Whitehead's estimation, fallacious. Russell is trying to show why, if we go along with Kant's view, we cannot make sense of the *apodicity* of propositions like "2 + 2 = 4" or probability that "the sun will rise tomorrow," but the reason Russell thinks Kant cannot make sense of our certainty in such cases is because Russell wrongly attributes to Kant the view that science deals with things-in-themselves. Russell thinks that Kant must admit "the time-order of phenomena is determined by the character of what is behind phenomena," because even if the possibility of "2 + 2" equaling "5" is *formally* incompatible with Kant's view that "time itself is a form imposed by the subject upon phenomena," this is the logical implication, Russell thinks, that undermines Kant's hope of vindicating synthetic *a priori* judgments. In order to vindicate such judgments, Russell thinks that Kant must allow the "things-in-themselves" to at least cause the apparent time-order of our sensations. Whitehead holds that Kant need do no such thing, because he will simply point out that Russell's "existing world" and "physical space" are not merely Reality-in-itself-qua-phenomenal-object.

For Whitehead, Kant ought to be refuted precisely because he disseminates the very idea that Russell himself employs to critique him. In the same letter mentioned above, from August 26, 1911, Whitehead writes: "My general view of your philosophy is that it is in the same state of transition as that in which Kant unfortunately wrote his *Critique*. . . . You seem to lack the self-confidence (or rather, time) to systematize philosophy afresh, in accordance with your own views."[82] The "same state" to which Whitehead here refers is, on my reading, induced by, as he writes in *Process in Reality* eighteen years later, the "inconsistent presuppositions underlying [the] inherited modes of expression"[83] from Descartes to Hume. Exposing these presuppositions ought to be, he thinks, our means of refuting Kant: "At the end," Whitehead continues, "there should be no problem of space-time, or of epistemology, or of causality, left over for discussion."[84] It is precisely this endeavor to correct that line of thinking that bequeathed to philosophy a group of "problems" that is common to Whitehead and post-analytic philosophy.

In light of the foregoing, it is perplexing to learn that Russell reported to Victor Lowe in a letter on July 24, 1960, that he could say "definitely and with certainty" that "before 1918, [Whitehead] had no definite opinions in philosophy and did not actively combat mine."[85] Lowe wonders if it is a case of protective memory. I go a step further; in the next chapter, I argue that this protective memory has become institutionalized and has, as a result, inhibited analytic philosophers like Brandom and McDowell from assaying the conceptual impediments to their theories of intentionality.

NOTES

1. Alfred North Whitehead, "Uniformity and Contingency: The Presidential Address," *Proceedings of the Aristotelian Society.* New Series. Vol. 23 (1922–1923), 13. Read to the Society on November 6th, 1922.
2. Ibid., 1.
3. Ibid., 13.
4. Bertrand Russell, chapter 5 "Causal Laws" in *The Analysis of Mind* (New York: Macmillan Company, 1921), 96.

26　　　　　　　　　　*Chapter 1*

5. Alfred North Whitehead, *The Principle of Relativity with Applications to Physical Science* (Cambridge: University Press, 1922).
6. Alfred North Whitehead, *Process and Reality*. Eds. David Ray Griffin and Donald W. Sherburne (New York: The Free Press, 1929), 332.
7. Ibid., 333.
8. Russell had read his "Knowledge by Acquaintance and Knowledge by Description" for the 1910/11 *Proceedings* of the Society. He published *The Problems of Philosophy* in 1912.
9. Alfred North Whitehead, "The Philosophical Aspects of the Principle of Relativity." *Proceedings of the Aristotelian Society.* New Series, Vol. 22 (1921–1922). July 16th, 1922.
10. Whitehead is referring to how Aristotelian logic has been received and used in modern philosophy. Toward the end of the paper, he allows for some aspects of general relativity in Aristotle's *own* account of time (223).
11. Ibid., 218–219.
12. Ibid., 223.
13. Whitehead, *Process and Reality*, 84.
14. Ibid., 95.
15. Ibid., 82. Quoting the *Timaeus*.
16. A. E. Taylor, *A Commentary on Plato's Timaeus* (Oxford: Clarendon Press, 1928), 60.
17. Whitehead himself resisted the use of the term "pure mathematics" because it was liable to misunderstanding. In their collaboration on the *Principia*, Russell was the one who went through Whitehead's drafts and inserted "pure" before Whitehead's use of "mathematics." To paraphrase Victor Lowe in his biography of Whitehead, Russell was more prone than Whitehead to idealize logic, forgetting the distinction between a symbol and its object. Whereas Whitehead and Russell collaborated on the logical notation of the principles of mathematics, they could not have done so on the *philosophy* of mathematics. For Russell, mathematics was simply an outgrowth of logic, from which all its principles could be deduced. For Whitehead, logic was simply a critical element to any introduction to mathematics. As Lowe explains it, "Russell the logician was preoccupied with the truth of 'p implies q', but Whitehead the mathematician retained an interest in the truth of 'q' which went beyond the use of q as a premise in the chain of deductions constituting pure mathematics. If q is true, it may also be a premise in a branch of applied mathematics." [Victor Lowe, *Alfred North Whitehead: The Man and His Work*, Volume 1: 1861–1910 (Baltimore and London: The Johns Hopkins University Press, 1985), 284–285].
18. Taylor, *A Commentary on Plato's Timaeus*, 60.
19. Ibid., 62.
20. Ibid., 313.
21. Whitehead, *Process and Reality*, 95. See also: 82.
22. Taylor, *A Commentary on Plato's Timaeus*, 313.
23. Whitehead, "Mathematics and Liberal Education: An Address" (1912), *Essays in Science and Philosophy* (New York: Philosophical Library, 1947), 186. Whitehead made these comments in his inaugural address to the *Association of Teachers in*

Mathematics for the Southeastern Part of England, his audience being very much interested in practical pedagogy. See Victor Lowe, *Alfred North Whitehead: The Man and His Work,* Vol. 2, ed. J. B. Schneewind (Baltimore and London: The Johns Hopkins University Press, 1990), 43.

24. Whitehead, "Mathematics and Liberal Education," 185.

25. Paul Redding, *Analytic Philosophy and the Return of Hegelian Thought* (Cambridge University Press, 2007), 58.

26. Whitehead, *Process and Reality,* 42. The work to which he here refers is Taylor's *Plato: The Man and His Work* (New York: Lincoln MacVeagh, 1927).

27. Ibid.

28. Ibid., 43.

29. Ibid.

30. Alfred North Whitehead, *Concept of Nature* (Cambridge, UK: Cambridge University Press, 1920/1930), 99.

31. Ibid., 52–53.

32. Ibid., 66.

33. Ibid., 70.

34. Ibid., 71.

35. Ibid.

36. Ibid., 72.

37. Ibid., 73. It is the capacity for memory and anticipation that defines mentality in Whitehead's 1947 essay "Immortality." There he examines the mutual implications of four notions: life, consciousness, memory, and anticipation. Life without consciousness is not capable of a sufficient degree of novelty to be counted as having the capacity of mind. Life with consciousness that is restricted to the immediacy of the present is unable to pursue possibilities. But conscious life with the capacity for memory and anticipation alone is able to escape the dominate determination of the immediate past that is defining of mental capacity. To speak of life as emerging from a lifeless matter is to speak of the emergence of memory and anticipation as forms of relation. There are not two types of entities in Whitehead's world; there is only one type, with a "variety of recessiveness and dominance among the basic factors of experience, namely, consciousness, memory, and anticipation." If the present is nothing but duration, then when we perceive the present we perceive not something "in between" past and future, but the creative interplay between actuality and potentiality, between efficient and final causation in varying degrees according to varying combinations of factors of experience-qua-creativeness. See Whitehead, "Immortality" in *Essays in Science and Philosophy,* 1941 (New York: Philosophical Library, 1947), 91.

38. Whitehead, *Concept of Nature,* 106.

39. Taylor, *A Commentary on Plato's Timaeus,* 350.

40. Whitehead, *Concept of Nature,* 96.

41. Ibid.

42. Ibid., 98.

43. Taylor, *A Commentary on Plato's Timaeus,* 351.

44. Ibid.

45. Whitehead, *Process and Reality*, 95.
46. Taylor, *A Commentary on Plato's Timaeus*, 677.
47. Ibid.
48. Whitehead, *Process and Reality*, 42 and 95.
49. Ibid., 50.
50. The handwritten correspondence between Russell and Whitehead that is archived at McMaster University is quite revealing. In particular, see the letter from Whitehead to Russell from September 11, 1918.
51. Whitehead, *An Enquiry Concerning the Principles of Natural Knowledge* (Cambridge: The University Press, 1919), vii.
52. H. A. Prichard, *Kant's Theory of Knowledge* (Oxford: Clarendon Press, 1909). Prichard notes his indebtedness to Edward Caird's two-volume *The Critical Philosophy of Immanuel Kant* (London: Macmillan Publishing, 1889) as expositor, and to J. M. D. Meikeljohn, Max Müller, and John P. Mahaffy as translators.
53. Ibid., 8–9.
54. Ibid., 16.
55. Ibid.
56. Robert Brandom, "Kantian Lessons about Mind, Meaning, and Rationality," pp. 1–20, *Philosophical Topics*, Vol. 34, No. 1/2, 2.
57. Ibid., 20.
58. Prichard, *Kant's Theory of Knowledge*, 17.
59. Ibid., 19.
60. Ibid.
61. Ibid., 21–22.
62. Ibid., 26.
63. Ibid.
64. Ibid., 108.
65. Ibid., 109.
66. Immanuel Kant, *The Critique of Pure Reason*, trans. and eds. Paul Guyer and Allen W. Wood (Cambridge, UK: Cambridge University Press, 1998), A33/B49–B50.
67. Ibid.
68. Prichard, *Kant's Theory of Knowledge*, 114.
69. Ibid., 38–40.
70. Ibid., 113–114.
71. Redding, *Analytic Philosophy*, 26.
72. Whitehead's page 8.
73. See Lowe, *Alfred North Whitehead*, 20.
74. Bertrand Russell, *The Problems of Philosophy* (Oxford University Press, 1912/2001), 48.
75. Ibid., 4.
76. Ibid., 15.
77. Ibid.
78. Whitehead's, p. 11.
79. Whitehead's, pp. 5–6.

80. Ibid., 49.
81. Ibid., 49.
82. Whitehead's, pp. 1–2.
83. Whitehead, *Process and Reality*, xi–xii.
84. Ibid.
85. Victor Lowe, "Whitehead's 1911 Criticism of Russell's *The Problems of Philosophy*," *The Journal of Bertrand Russell Studies* [McMaster University Press, No. 13 (Spring 1974)], 3.

Chapter 2

Whiteheadian Anticipations of Pittsburgh Neo-Hegelianism

INTRODUCTION

In the previous chapter, I introduced Whitehead's early critiques of analytic philosophy. I did so on the promise that these critiques would help us understand the intellectual heritage that bequeathed to contemporary analytic philosophers the problem of intentionality—a problem which the Pittsburgh School (largely represented by Brandom and McDowell) has recently appealed to Hegel to solve. The purpose of this chapter is to demonstrate why these appeals are insufficient to their attempts to make sense of how mind and world relate non-problematically. Insofar as I take it to be the most promising, McDowell's work is my primary focus. I argue here and throughout the book that his notion of second nature and appeal to Aristotelian naïveté to deal with the problem of intentionality and establishing the normative constraints the world must have upon thought remain insufficient.

I will argue in later chapters that McDowell perpetuates a version of the bifurcation of nature insofar as his account of experience and reason remains complicated by the presuppositions that (1) both rely upon consciousness and (2) meaning is ingredient only in the latter. On his account, second nature, as that which is constitutive of rational, self-conscious human subjects, is acquired by language initiation. Linguistically initiated individuals are capable of new kinds of experience—experiences which are capacities for knowledge. For example, I argue in chapter 5 that McDowell fails to explain how human beings cross ontological threshold between non-rational and rational kinds of experience.

For the purposes of this chapter, it is sufficient to identify some early warning signs of his inability to do so, including (1) his continued conceptual isolation of reason from a notion of "first" nature due to (2) his taking natural human language to be the ontological catalyst of rationality, such that (3) first nature consists only of causal relations, not rational ones, with the implication that (4) meanings are entirely dependent upon actualized linguistic capabilities for their efficacy in the world. Whitehead's early critiques of analytic philosophy can help us to identify intellectual precursors to these problematic assumptions, in turn helping us to understand the eventuation of Pittsburgh Neo-Hegelianism.

WHAT WHITEHEAD CAN TELL US ABOUT ANALYTIC PHILOSOPHY'S RETURN TO HEGEL

In a statement that anticipates the very sort of move for which McDowell and Brandom are credited, Whitehead writes: "Indeed, if this cosmology be deemed successful, it becomes natural at this point to ask whether the type of thought involved be not a transformation of some main doctrines of Absolute Idealism onto a realistic basis."[1] Whitehead was very much in conversation with his contemporaries, so we should note that the idealism he had in mind was that of F. H. Bradley, and the realism he had in mind was likely that of T. Percy Nunn, who was President of the Aristotelian Society from 1923–1924, the year after Whitehead, and who had been, at least indirectly through years of the *Proceedings,* a conversation partner of Whitehead's.

Nunn was influential for Russell during Russell's early attempts to formulate a theory of perception, but, unlike Russell, Nunn was a defender of the reality of secondary qualities apart from perception. In his 1915/1916 paper on "Sense-data and Physical Objects," Nunn argues against Russell, G. E. Moore, and G. F. Stout that "the hypothesis of the existence of unperceived sense-data is not only tenable but, on the whole, the most satisfactory theory of perception hitherto advanced."[2] He continues, "Mr. Russell, in his paper on 'The Relation of Sense-data to Physics', seems to indicate that my views had some influence in leading him to adopt his theory of 'perspectives'. But although Mr. Russell prefers not to assume the hypothesis of unperceived sense-data, neither he nor, so far as I know, any other writer has directly criticized my arguments in its favour."[3] Nunn's "realism" refers to his affirmation of world as it appears to us, free of the bifurcation of nature that Whitehead critiqued. In his Presidential Address to the *AS* in 1923, Nunn contrasts his realism to "an unhealthy romanticism" about the nature of scientific objects, which he likely attributed to Russell. Nunn was talking about the nascent theory of general and special relativity when he wrote:

> I own that, as a layman following at a long distance the present heroic adventures and discoveries of physics, I put out of my mind all that I have said in

this paper and accept the wonderful tale as it is told. But when the book is set down the obstinate question returns: A wonderful tale it certainly is, but what does it really mean? And the only answer I can find is the one which I have once more tried to formulate and defend. I may summarize it by saying that the real achievement of science is not to have disclosed any reality behind the veil of sensible things, but to have greatly extended and deepened and rationalized the scheme of the world revealed in perception. It is perhaps only a sign of an unhealthy romanticism to be disappointed because it can do nothing more.[4]

Here, just as Whitehead did in *The Concept of Nature* three years earlier, Nunn refuses to treat perception as a "veil" behind which science seeks to peer, while critiquing the view that would beget logical positivism and other forms of scientism—whose heirs McDowell would critique for being beholden to a Platonist picture of "Reality as it appears" and "Reality as it is."

In accounts of the early years of analytic philosophy, there is usually a discussion of the intellectual exchanges between thinkers like Russell and G. E. Moore. The relationships between Russell and his other important contemporaries like T. Percy Nunn and G. F. Stout—not to mention Whitehead—are not as well known. In 2014, the Aristotelian Society published a virtual issue aimed at providing more insight into the debates surrounding the emergence of analytic philosophy in Britain at the turn of the twentieth century. The issue, titled "The Emergence of Analytic philosophy and a Controversy at the Aristotelian Society: 1900–1916," collected papers from the archives of the *Proceedings of the Aristotelian Society* and the *Proceedings of the Aristotelian Society Supplementary Volume* that were relevant to the titular controversy. More specifically, this controversy concerned the nature of sense-data (psychical or physical), their reality beyond perception, and how they relate to knowledge of the external world. Special guest editor Omar W. Nasim compiled essays that he thought relevant to a better understanding of the formation of Russell's early thought. Noticeably absent from his list, however, is Whitehead. In fact, in all 487 pages of the issue, Whitehead's name is never mentioned. This is a curious editorial decision, considering that other *AS* Presidents are incorporated in the collection, including Friedrich Schiller and Nunn, whose presidencies, respectively, bookended Whitehead's own. The protective memory appears institutionalized.

Whitehead's part in this controversy was sympathetic with Nunn's own, as his later statement about putting Absolute Idealism on a "realistic basis" suggests. What Nunn called "unhealthy romanticism," Whitehead repeatedly identified as a misguided appropriation of Plato—the very one *his* work has been accused of displaying and *Russell's* work was, at least to a larger extent and until recently, regarded as rejecting. As Victor Lowe puts it, "If Whitehead when younger was ever attracted to extreme Platonism [a descriptor I, anachronistically for Lowe, equate to the sort Whitehead deemed illegitimate], the doctrine of evolution and the discovery of alternative geometries—both of which suggest that Nature is patient of many patterns of order—had taken him away from it."[5] It was Whitehead's attention to the process of our thinking, rather than just the product, that allowed him to identify cases in which other thinkers presumed the self-evidence of a product by forgetting the process.

A discussion between Whitehead and Quine is telling in this regard. In his "Whitehead and the Rise of Modern Logic" (1941),[6] Quine criticized Whitehead's account of the fundamental idea expressed by "=" in an algebraic calculus, which Whitehead had treated in his *A Treatise on Universal Algebra: With Applications* (1898). There, Whitehead claimed "Equivalence . . . implies non-identity as its general case."[7] He goes on:

> Identity may be conceived as a special limiting case of equivalence. For instance in arithmetic we write, $2 + 3 = 3 + 2$. This means that, in so far as the total number of objects mentioned, $2 + 3$ and $3 + 2$ come to the same number, namely 5. But $2 + 3$ and $3 + 2$ are not identical; the order of the symbols is different in the two combinations, and this difference or order directs different processes of thought. The importance of the equation arises from its assertion that these different processes of thought are identical as far as the total number of things thought of is concerned. [8]

His emphasis on the processes of thought, for which arithmetical notation stands as a *substitute*, indicates that Whitehead never lost sight of the material conditions in which and for which mathematics is carried out. In calculus, the mathematician is freed from having to think explicitly through concrete inferences in order to focus simply on the rules of interchanging the signs.[9] Whitehead attributes to calculus, then, the task of facilitating our reasoning, not providing a window into "Reason's" own language. Whitehead rejected the logicism of the early Russell's efforts to reduce all mathematical notions to logical ones, and, therefore, also the Leibnizian enterprise of reducing *all* notions to logical ones.

In 1900, Russell published *The Critical Exposition of the Philosophy of Leibniz*, in which he attempts to systematize Leibniz's philosophy by way of geometrical deduction. This is two years after Whitehead's *Universal Algebra*, three years before *The Principles of Mathematics* (1903), and ten years before the *Principia Mathematica* (1910). Russell credits Leibniz for teaching him the importance of relations, while also critiquing him for not fully committing to this importance, leading to his failure to produce a body of systematized thought—something Russell endeavored to correct. Indeed, Russell writes in his *Critical Exposition* that, even while Leibniz insisted that all propositions are reducible to a subject and a predicate, which would amount to a monadology, it was Leibniz's "assumption of a plurality of substances [that] made the denial of relations peculiarly difficult, and involved him in all the paradoxes of the pre-established harmony."[10]

It is in the latter work, from 1903, that Russell discovers the paradox of set theory that would unsettle Frege and motivate Russell's theory of Types. Inchoate expressions of this paradox existed before 1903 in Russell's work, however, particularly in what he called the "contradiction of infinity" with which "[m]athematical ideas are almost all infected."[11] As discussed at the outset of this chapter, Whitehead did not share the same sort of concern for infinity, precisely because, as I have tried to show, he did not commit the same error of spatializing logic and reasoning that Russell did.

We may regard Whitehead's rejection of Russell's logicism, then, as another instance of his insistence on the process-qua-temporal-extension of logic in addition to its product-qua-spatial-extension visualized by notation, which we find in his disagreement with Quine. Whitehead anticipated his critiques of logicism in *Universal Algebra* when he writes how, from arithmetical perspective of equivalence as a *limited* case of identity, "it is tempting to define equivalent things as being merely different ways of thinking of the same thing as it exists in the external world." This is the temptation to think, "there is a certain aggregate, say of 5 things, which is thought of in different ways, as 2 + 3 and as 3 + 2."[12] But Whitehead argues that if we mistake 2 + 3 and 3 + 2 as interchangeable symbols for 5, we treat mathematical notation not as shorthand for our rational *processes*, but rather as corresponding to ultimate realities that exist independent of the processes. The problem with treating 2 + 3 and 3 + 2 as identical, insofar as they each represent an aggregate of 5, is that this distinction once again introduces an ontological bifurcation between Reality-as-it-appears to us (2 + 3 or 3 +2) and Reality-as-it-is (5). Only someone with this bifurcated picture could maintain the absolute identity of 2 + 3 and 3 + 2. This is why Whitehead thinks that a "sufficient objection" to those who maintain this identity, like Quine, is to suggest how this claim of mathematical identity is akin to the philosophical claim to have solved the problem of the distinction between self and world, by which I take him to mean that to claim the mathematical identity of 2 + 3 and 3 + 2 (which assumes a represented reality, i.e., the aggregate of 5) is to claim that sensory objects are identical with the objects of perception (which assumes a Reality-in-itself like Russell's "Physical Objects"). "As there is no universally accepted solution of this problem," he writes, "it is obviously undesirable to assume this distinction as the basis of mathematical reasoning."[13] Mathematical figures, for Whitehead, symbolize the process of forming a synthesis between two things and then of considering a third thing that is not equivalent to but internally related to the others. He generalizes this emphasis on process in mathematical reasoning into his Ontological Principle in *Process and Reality*.

Each of these encounters—with Quine and with Russell—demonstrate Whitehead's embeddedness vis-à-vis the "controversy" ensuing throughout the *Proceedings* of the Aristotelian Society between 1900 and 1916. He was very clearly engaged in debates regarding the nature of sense-data and what sorts of ontological and epistemological commitments questions about their reality entail, specifically with respect to the language of "externality." Even more broadly, these encounters indicate how Whitehead understood the need to recast certain doctrines of Absolute Idealism onto a realistic basis. He understood it, in short, as a need to reject both Bradley's doctrine of the absolute-qua-a-single-experience *and* Leibniz's doctrine of many windowless monads, the two alternatives resulting from a view of experience as in some way illusory.[14] Once we have found ourselves engrossed in this illusoriness, our only recourse is to something like Leibniz's "pious dependence upon God," as we see in Descartes. Such a recourse is "repugnant to a consistent rationality," insists Whitehead; "the very possibility of knowledge should not be an accident of God's goodness; it should depend on the interwoven nature of things. After all, God's knowledge has equally to be explained."[15]

Whitehead insists in *Process and Reality* that any metaphysical theory that starts from a commitment to the disjunction between "the component elements of individual experience" and "the component elements of the external world" will encounter two problems: (1) an ontological problem about the nature of the truth and falsehood of propositions, and (2) an epistemological problem about the grounds for judging truth and falsehood.[16] So long as we subscribe to Hume's doctrine of "impressions of sensation," which assumes that experience is analyzable without remainder in terms of universals *and* that experience is composed of "mere" sensations received by a passive subject, we will fail to take account of the necessary ontological togetherness needed to provide the epistemological togetherness that alone can rejoin propositions and judgments by way of the actual entity. We must completely reject the Absolute Idealist's (i.e., Bradley's) trust in the subject-predicate mode of expression and transferal of this format onto an account of experience, rendering the datum of experience fully analyzable in terms of universals. Whitehead's philosophy of organism is "in sharp disagreement with Bradley" on these points, even if "the final outcome is after all not so greatly different," insofar as their shared goal is to dispute the "doctrine of 'vacuous actuality'."[17] By taking relatedness to be dominant over quality, rather than vice versa, Whitehead brings actual occasions to the center of his event-based cosmology: "All relatedness has its foundations in the relatedness of actualities; and such relatedness is wholly concerned with the appropriation of the dead by the living."[18] It is relatedness that has quality, not substances. These qualities or modes of relatedness, when spoken of in abstraction from their realization, he calls "pure potentials" or "eternal objects," insofar as they indicate the various modes by which a subject becomes by objectifying its immediate past. Only when we start with the "experiential togetherness" of actual occasions will temporality seem inextricable from spatiality. To be able to do this, however, requires a new understanding of experience in which the classical distinction between primary and secondary qualities is entirely eliminated.

It is also the case that we can only make sense of false propositions by recasting our account of them upon the notion of actual occasions (also called actual entities in all cases but one, but the exception need not concern us here). Whitehead first considers propositions in their role in the "actual world" and not primarily in their "connection with logic" and some "moralistic preferences for true propositions."[19] He regards propositions, like pure potentials, as "definite potentialities *for* actuality with undetermined realization *in* actuality," but unlike pure potentials, they are not absolutely general but involve one or more actual occasions or entities as "logical subject(s)."[20] In short, "The proposition is the possibility of *that* predicate applying in that assigned way to *those* logical subjects."[21] Propositions play a role in Whitehead's cosmology beyond the role they play in conscious forms of judgment about their truth or falsehood, which enables him to account for the importance of false propositions, which have "fared badly" at the hands of logicians.[22]

Another way to understand Whitehead's emphasis on relation over quality is to say that Whitehead achieves his recasting of idealist doctrines upon a "realist basis" by allowing Aristotle's notion of "generation" to dominate on subjects where previously his classificatory logic had. I have already noted the ways in which Whitehead regarded the philosophy of organism as simply a "restatement" of Plato—as well as the senses in which it was decidedly *not*—but it is also the case that Whitehead recognized Aristotle's *Metaphysics* as offering unparalleled resources for accounting for the very sense of internal relations among individuals that the long history of European overemphasis on his logic had obscured. The subject-predicate "habit of thought" dominated European thought on the nature of mentality so extensively, Whitehead believed, that by current standards "probably Aristotle was not an Aristotelian."[23] The Aristotle with whose thought Whitehead found analogies for his own was the one who developed the notion of appetition, rather than that of substance.[24]

RETHINKING THE RETURN TO HEGEL WITH WHITEHEAD

It is relevant for the purposes of this chapter to note that, according to Paul Redding, McDowell's reclaiming of Hegel differs from that of Brandom insofar as he emphasizes Hegel's Aristotelianism and Brandom ignores it.[25] McDowell argues that we must pay attention to Hegel's Aristotelianism in order to find the resources analytic philosophy needs to make sense of the way normativity stems from nature, properly understood.[26] To be sure, this distinction is seldom explicit; it is Redding who suggests that, while both Brandom and McDowell want to recover idealist thought after Russell's dismissal of it as anachronistic,[27] the differences in their readings of Hegel can be accounted for by looking at what they do with Aristotle.

If analytic philosophy's return to Hegel is, indeed, motivated by dissatisfaction with how, throughout its history, modern philosophy has rejected some motivating concerns of Absolute Idealism, and the tacit dogmas that led its proponents to do so,[28] then attention ought to be paid to Whitehead's indictment of those habits of thought in modern philosophy that he foresaw leading to just the sorts of problems with which analytic philosophy now finds itself.

According to Redding, Brandom and McDowell can "link" their projects back to the idealist tradition insofar as it concerns the world as *exhibited* not *represented.*[29] That is, because Hegel was talking about "the world" as that which is "exhibited rather than represented in thought," he was not, like Kant, looking for "the structure of 'being' from the logical structure of one's assertions about knowable objects or states of affairs."[30] The reason Hegel is so attractive to McDowell, Redding seems to imply, is because he avoids the mistakes that led to the problem of reconciling normativity and nature: (1) Aristotle's mistake in his *Categories* of trying to derive logical categories from assumptions about "being"; (2) Kant's mistake in his "Transcendental Analytic" in the *Critique of Pure Reason* of trying to derive the structure of "being" from the logical structures of one's assertions about knowable objects. Hegel, in contrast, is attractive to Brandom and McDowell because he does not start with an ontological gap between mind or "logical structures" and world or "structures of being."

In this way, Redding identifies Hegel's approach as more akin to that of the "Frege-Wittgenstein" than the "Russell-Moore" tradition within analytic philosophy, which is precisely what Brandom and McDowell are eager to point out. By redefining "the world" in expressivist rather than representationalist terms, the point goes, Hegel refuses to treat "the world" as an object generalized from empirical experience; instead, Hegel means by "the world" the whole semantic content of thought accrued by "horizontal" inferential relations, not "vertical" representational relations to things "in" the world.[31] Hegel thereby avoids what McDowell calls the "remnant Platonism" of traditional philosophy by refusing to understand "objectivity" in terms of some "God's-eye" point of view. It was precisely this traditional ontological opposition, between human-qua-finite and divine-qua-infinite, that Hegel wanted to avoid through his neo-Aristotelian theology.[32] The activity of philosophy, by which mind takes itself as its object, was how Hegel sought to resolve "the lack of self-consciousness of Aristotle's immanent deity."[33] According to this reading of Hegel as a reformed analytic philosopher *avant la lettre,* Hegel's most "metaphysical" claim was actually a response to what he took to be "the most problematic metaphysical feature of ancient and modern thought"—that is, a Platonic positivism, which may be regarded as "the metaphysical concomitant of the epistemologically conceived 'Myth of the Given'."[34] For "Sellarsian neo-Hegelians" like Brandom and McDowell, the problem with metaphysics is equivalent merely to the limits of Aristotelian substance metaphysics, but this Platonic positivism is embedded within its appropriation.[35] This is why, the argument goes, Hegel does not "advocate a *negation of* metaphysics," but, rather, "refashions metaphysics around the primacy of the notion of *negativity*."[36] Hegel's dialectical method exhibits this primacy, most prominently, perhaps, in his notion of "determinate negation" that has become so central to Brandom's inferentialism.

The "Hegel" of Sellarsian neo-Hegelians stands as a corrective to what Richard Watson calls Russell's "shadow Hegel." This shadow Hegel, argues Watson, "is the rock that logical atomism could take as a jumping-off place ... The shadow Hegel's system authenticates the philosophy that casts off from and corrects it."[37] It was this shadow idealism that analytic philosophy denied any philosophical viability to at its very inception. And, yet, the acceptance of Russell's "shadow Hegel"—and, therefore, of his rejection of post-Kantian idealism—was so complete that it took three-quarters of a century for the tradition to gain critical distance from it.

One argument for why Kantian idealism maintained its influence on the analytic tradition, while post-Kantian idealism did not, is because of the impact of Wittgenstein's *Tractatus Logico-Philosophicus*. In the *Tractatus*, Wittgenstein employed a version of the "context principle" that Frege had first developed in *The Foundations of Arithmetic*: "Only the proposition has sense; only in the nexus of a proposition has a name meaning."[38] The idea of a word's meaning depending on the context provided by the proposition in which it appears stood in tension with the assumptions of logical atomism, such that Redding argues that this principle "marked a deep distinction separating the approaches of Frege and Wittgenstein on the one hand and those of Russell and Moore on the other, the former pair's approach to metaphysics being more 'judgment-based' and, because of that, 'Kantian', the latter pair's, more ontological or 'object-based'."[39]

Turning to Michael Friedman's analysis of the relationship of analytic philosophy to nineteenth-century idealism, Redding suggests that it was Russell and Moore's ontologism that separated them from the neo-Kantian logical positivists who, working in a post-Newtonian scientific milieu, "were doing essentially what Kant *would have* done" had he appreciated the historicity of models of knowledge. But Kant, having taken Aristotle to have "definitively established the basic forms of right inference, and Euclid the basic structures of geometric knowledge," also "thought Newton had definitively established the science of the phenomenal world."[40] According to Friedman, "the logical positivists' main philosophical concern did not arise within the context of the empiricist philosophical tradition at all. Rather, the initial impetus for their philosophizing came from late nineteenth-century work on the foundations of geometry by Riemann, Helmholtz, Lie, Klein, and Hilbert—work that, for the early positivists, achieved its culmination in Einstein's theory of relativity."[41] It was the popularization of non-Euclidean geometries, and thereby the loosening of the apparent ahistorical and apodictic nature of mathematical principles, Friedman argues, that was the primary catalyst for neo-Kantian ("judgment-" versus "object-based") philosophical semantics. In effect, the logical positivists transformed the nature of Kant's *a priori* into the language of the new science, turning away from talk of apriority, but maintaining a claim to some non-empirical structure of knowledge.[42]

Friedman's analysis is worth discussing at length at this point, because his framing of the impetus for logical positivism (and the nature of its distinction from Russell and Moore's alleged ontologism) reveals the centrality of debates about space and time to the formation of logical positivism (with a notable absence of Whitehead's contribution to these debates). There are two main things Friedman wants his readers to understand about the original logical positivists, and, therefore, about the origin of the Frege-Wittgenstein line of thought that would eventually lend itself to a reconsideration of Hegel. First, the early nineteenth-century "axiomatization" of the foundations of geometry problematized Kant's claim that our knowledge of geometrical principles are synthetic. In particular, the deductions of Euclidean geometry were no longer taken to depend on "spatial intuitions," and the popularization of non-Euclidean geometries (practically evidenced by Einstein's theory of relativity) made it impossible to say that there was any straightforward empirical way to determine if space was Euclidean or non-Euclidean. Friedman's second point, then, is that the early logical positivists did not replace Kant's synthetic *a priori* with a bald empiricism of physical geometry; rather, they "followed the example of [Henri] Poincaré in maintaining that there is no direct route from sense experience to physical geometry: essentially nonempirical factors, variously termed 'conventions' or 'coordinating definitions', must necessarily intervene between sensible experience and geometrical theory."[43] It was precisely the appreciation for the "plasticity of epistemic structures" that Redding argues rendered its trajectory open to a Hegelian, rather than a Kantian, rectification.[44]

While I am not here fully endorsing Friedman's rewriting of analytic philosophy's birth narrative—partially because I find the claim that logical positivism originated with an appreciation of the "plasticity of epistemic structures" incompatible with my understanding of the logicism of Russell and Frege alike—I think it is necessary context for understanding Redding's explanation of Brandom and McDowell's return to Hegel. What seems obvious, in any case, is that however we characterize the intellectual lineage within which Brandom and McDowell are working, it does indeed remain "judgment based" in the sense of taking judgments to be the basic unit of awareness. It is this Kantian ontological commitment that continues to undermine their neo-Hegelianism, and I propose that it is a product of an original failure by the logical positivists. This was the failure of the Frege-Wittgenstein tradition of thought to properly integrate the new notions of spatial and temporal extension of the new geometrical thinking. That failure enabled the Frege-Wittgenstein to remain beholden to the Kantian "judgment-based" approach to metaphysics—the approach which today characterizes the Sellarsian neo-Hegelians. This failure may, at least in part, be explained by Whitehead's account of the misunderstanding of Plato and the misappropriation of Aristotle through seventeenth- and eighteenth-century European philosophy.

Indeed, notably absent from Friedman's and Redding's treatments of the intellectual catalysts for analytic philosophy is any alternative picture of how the original members of the Vienna Circle might otherwise have understood the irreconcilability of Kantian and post-Kantian idealist treatments of mind and world in light of the mathematical and physical discoveries of the early twentieth century. It is not unimportant, after all, that Whitehead and Russell's *Principia* is considered to have provided part of the intellectual foundation of logical positivism's "unique, innovative scientific culture."[45] Neither, then, should the strikingly distinct philosophies of mathematics of its co-authors be ignored. Insofar as Russell later repudiated his own then-philosophy of mathematics for its naïve Platonism, after Wittgenstein, his student, convinced him that all mathematics was composed of tautologies, it seems prudent to take seriously the thought of Russell's own teacher, who was not so prone to such extreme positions.[46]

The failure to recollect Whitehead's contributions to the debates surrounding the origins of analytic philosophy has hindered conversations about intentionality. This erasure of Whitehead is what enables McDowell to repeat many of the same Whiteheadian critiques of analytic modes of thought to the present day, but to do so without a genuine reconsideration of the unskillful readings of Plato and Aristotle, and, therefore, also without a radical enough reconception of experience.

A WHITEHEADIAN ASSESSMENT OF MCDOWELL'S REVISED KANTIANISM

The fifth lecture of McDowell's *Mind and World* (1994), entitled "Action, Meaning, and Self," presents a reading of Kant according to which he had to resort to a transcendental framework in order to preserve some connection between concepts and intuition, a relation which he could not find in "nature."[47] According to McDowell, Kant knew very well that this connection ought to be maintained if we were to make any sense of the objective purport of our observations. In refusing both the Myth of the Given and a radical coherentism, Kant was unable to see any other option other than the transcendental one, McDowell argues.[48] But the transcendental solution doesn't really solve the purpose for which it was created, he thinks, because by placing the connection between spontaneity and intuitions *outside* of nature, the connection ends up being one that is between the conceptual, on the one hand, and the world of appearances as distorted by the conceptual, on the other. Rather, what we need is a connection between the conceptual and the ordinary empirical world.

Besides failing to achieved any real connection between concepts and intuitions, McDowell thinks this transcendental framework also prohibits any real connection between consciousness and self-consciousness: "The result of Kant's move is that the subjective continuity he appeals to [the Transcendental Unity of Apperception], as part of what it is for experience to bear on objective reality, cannot be equated with the continuing life of a perceiving animal. It shrinks, as I said, to the continuity of a mere point of view: something that need not have anything to do with a body, so far as the claim of interdependence is concerned."[49] He continues,

> This is quite unsatisfying. If we begin with a free-standing notion of an experiential route through objective reality, a temporally extended point of view that might be bodiless so far as the connection between subjectivity and objectivity goes, there seems to be no prospect of building up from there the notion of a substantial presence in the world. If something starts out conceiving itself as a merely formal referent for "I" (which is already a peculiar notion), how could it come to appropriate a body, so that it might identify itself with a particular living thing?[50]

McDowell's dissatisfaction with Kant's appeal to a Transcendental Ego is reminiscent of Whitehead's comment to Russell in his letter from August 26th, 1911. Paraphrasing his understanding of Kant, Whitehead wrote: "I, by a self-activity which can be analyzed into an application of the pure forms of time and space and a synthetic unity of apperception [to me mysterious (ANW)], weld these relations (experienced in sensation) into perceptions of objects, the phenomenal objects. All my ordinary ideas apply to these phenomenal objects necessarily, because they are merely expressive of an analysis of the process of formation by me."[51] The synthetic unity of apperception *would* be mystifying to Whitehead, because he was never tempted to first begin with a notion of experience as separate from "objective" reality (the bifurcation) and *then* try to reconcile it with the "continuing life of a perceiving animal." For Whitehead, it is precisely the *continuing life* which we encounter in experience—the becoming, the process, and the fluency of the world is what is immediate to us, and any notion of experience as composed of bits of sense-data is abstracted after the fact, according to a spatialized picture not only of "objective reality" but also of the "conceptual realm" by which we are said to categorize it. For Whitehead, then, we need never find ourselves in a position from which "there seems to be no prospect of building up . . . the notion of a substantial presence in the world." If we never begin with Aristotle's substances, we can never wind up with a picture of the world as bifurcated into subject and object.[52]

For McDowell, Kant *tries* to avoid Descartes's solipsism, and "he gets to the very brink of success." "But," he continues, "[Kant] thinks the only alternative is a transcendental self-awareness, something that has no object substantially present in the world. . . . Kant's insight would be able to take satisfactory shape only if he could accommodate the fact that a thinking and intending subject is a living animal."[53] Significantly, Whitehead's philosophy takes as a guiding insight that "the key to the history of mankind lies in this fact—as we think, we live."[54]

Whitehead resisted in Russell just those habits of thought that led to and created a version of the Myth of the Given which Sellars and his followers would oppose. Russell regarded Kant as having compromised the objectivity of both mathematics and logic by psychologizing, albeit "transcendentally," those two types of knowledge.[55] But, as Redding notes, "having eliminated Kant's way of holding onto the normativity of logic, Russell reverted to the type of Platonic intuitionism that had been espoused by Moore."[56] Russell thereby resorted to the view that "the objectivity of logical laws was a consequence of the way that logical relations were ultimately grounded in ontology."[57] By resorting to the Myth, McDowell would argue, Russell actually embedded himself deeper into the remnant Platonism that sees mind and nature from "sideways on," as presenting a gulf to be bridged. "Bald naturalists," who represent the position that Russell moved closer to in his critique of Kant, also share this "sideways on" view, says McDowell. As Redding explains, Russell

> reverted to a position closer to Aristotle's representationalist interpretation of the logical categories than to Kant's. For Aristotle, it would seem, the categories

reflected in the logical behavior of our worlds reflect structures properly belonging to *being*, while for Kant the worldly structures—in the sense of the way they are *for us*—reflect the logical structures of our judgments. So for Russell, the *laws* of logic are normative for us in so far as there can be questions of thought's form correctly or incorrectly representing the *world's* form. The laws of thought are made true by an ontology which we must be able to somehow directly grasp *if* we are to apply those laws in our thinking. In fact, the universal principles of logic, and following them, the laws of pure mathematics, must be grounded in a form of acquaintance in which relations between universals are given in a way *analogous* to that in which *sense-data* are given to us in sensation.[58]

In contrast to Russell's recoil back into a bifurcated picture of nature, McDowell takes himself as going a different way with Aristotle. By employing the notion of habituation developed in Aristotle's philosophy of ethics, McDowell seeks to create a new form of naturalism that can connect concepts to intuition without resort to a transcendental framework. "Second nature" is modeled after the process by which an individual acquires Aristotle's *phronēsis* or (by some translations) "practical wisdom."[59] Although he is somewhat cryptic about it, McDowell relates Aristotle's *phronēsis* to Hegel's forms or *Sittlichkeit*—for instance, when he writes, "The way to correct what is unsatisfactory in Kant's thinking about the supersensible is rather to embrace the Hegelian image in which the conceptual is unbounded on the outside."[60] By seeking to introduce a new conception of nature into Kant's system, McDowell takes himself to have erased the gap between our rationality and our animality, where rationality remains "appropriately conceived in Kantian terms."[61] Rationality, in Kantian terms, means for McDowell responsiveness to meaning or rational relationships that is autonomous or *sui generis*, even if it remains (in a way Kant did not allow) grounded in nature.

McDowell is very aware that any attempt to connect our responsiveness to meaning with our natural sentient capacities will not succeed using "naturalistic" terms that presuppose a "realm of law" where causal relations obtain and a "space of reasons" where rational relations obtain. And yet, he is concerned just as much with maintaining the distinctiveness of conceptual capacities as he is with showing the continuity of sapience with sentience. Conceptual capacities are, by definition, a distinctive type of freedom. To account for the connection between the space of reasons and the realm of law, to review, McDowell argues that we must cease to equate the realm of law with what counts as "nature."

By coming to see our responsiveness to meaning as "our way of actualizing ourselves as animals," McDowell takes himself to have removed, like Whitehead, "any need to try to see ourselves as peculiarly bifurcated."[62] Like Whitehead, he even laments the difficulty he faces in trying to offer a re-reading of Aristotle's picture of ethical understanding, given the prevalence of baldly naturalistic readings of him. This is a frustration he shares with Whitehead, who himself insisted (as discussed earlier) that Aristotle (*and* Plato!) knew nothing of a bifurcation of nature. Reading Aristotle as presuming "nature" in the scientific sense is what McDowell calls "a historical monstrosity."[63] But insofar as McDowell believes rationality is "appropriately conceived in Kantian terms," he inherits Kant's mistreatment of time in accounting for conceptual capacities, and, therefore, remains complicit within a framework built upon those aspects of Aristotle that Whitehead identified as involving an overemphasis on the static, spatialized view of his categories. Here is the true taproot of the modern bifurcation of nature.

TOO LITTLE, TOO LATE

It is an injustice to Whitehead and his intellectual interlocutors that such critiques of anachronistic "naturalist" readings of these ancient Greek sources have, as far as I can tell, only recently influenced analytic philosophy's attempts to solve the problem of intentionality. And it is an injustice to these attempts that they continue to be such poor readers (if readers at all) of Whitehead. This is particularly the case with respect to McDowell, because unlike Whitehead, McDowell does not appreciate the true extent to which this anachronistic reading of Aristotle—this "historical monstrosity"—has compromised the very conception of rationality he tries to revive. His corrective reading of Aristotle's "nature"—and its relations to Hegel's *Bildung*—is insufficient to root out the spatializing account such readings (owing, on Whitehead's account, to the "Semitic view") have effected in modern philosophy's conceptions of experience—conceptions that continue to suppose the "two-term" relation of predication that Whitehead sees as responsible for the bifurcation of nature.

As I will continue to show throughout the book, McDowell does not sufficiently rehabilitate his notion of experience to address the problem of mind and world. In this chapter, I have argued that this insufficiency owes, at least in part, to a failure to appreciate the underlying presuppositions that motivated the "baldly naturalist" readings of Aristotle, and how those presuppositions persist in Kant's conception of rationality. Even after McDowell introduces "second nature," he continues to speak of the realm of law and the space of reasons as separate "logical spaces." Rationality "appropriately" conceived in Kantian terms continues to think of events—mental or physical—in spatial terms, as if they occur within rational relations or causal relations, *even if* rational relations are seen as potentiated out of merely causal ones.

In so doing, McDowell fails to take account of what Whitehead, in his paper for the 1921/1922 *Proceedings* of the *Aristotelian Society*, calls the "philosophical aspects of the principle of relativity" for the "standard form" of Aristotelian logic. It is this standard form of Aristotelian logic, Whitehead warns, that eventuated into Hume's skepticism and forced Kant's hand when it came to rescuing spontaneity by means of a transcendentalist framework—a rescue that could, by that point, only be achieved by self-contradicting and idealist means (as earlier evidenced by Prichard).

The very terms of discussion, which defined the problem of normativity after Kant, established the framework within which Hegel's solution could count as such. But these terms are precisely what are at issue in Whitehead's work, such that to work with them is already to be compromised by the fallacies upon which they are premised. What this means is, in effect, that despite the many ways in which McDowell succeeds, his efforts to solve the problem of mind and world will always—so long as he retains a Kantian conception of rationality—be too little, too late.

NOTES

1. Whitehead, *Process and Reality*, xiii. The absolute idealist he had in mind was not Hegel, however, but F. H. Bradley, though British idealism was strongly influenced by German idealism.
2. T. Percy Nunn, "Sense-data and Physical Objects," *Proceedings of the Aristotelian Society*, New Series, Vol. 16 (1915–1916), pp. 156–178, esp. 157.
3. Ibid.
4. T. Percy Nunn, "Scientific Objects and Common-Sense Things: The Presidential Address," *Proceedings of the Aristotelian Society*, New Series, Vol. 24 (1923–1924), pp. 1–18, esp. 18.
5. Lowe, *Alfred North Whitehead*, Vol. 1, 198.
6. W. V. Quine, "Whitehead and the Rise of Modern Logic," *The Philosophy of Alfred North Whitehead*, ed. Paul Arthur Schilpp (Evanston and Chicago: Northwestern University Press, 1941), 127–163.
7. Alfred North Whitehead, *A Treatise on Universal Algebra: With Applications* (Cambridge: Cambridge University Press, 1898), 6.
8. Ibid.
9. Ibid., 10.
10. Bertrand Russell, *A Critical Exposition of the Philosophy of Leibniz* (London and New York: Routledge, 1900/1992), 18.
11. Ohad Nachtomy, "Leibniz and Russell: The Number of all Numbers and the Set of all Sets," in *Leibniz and the English-Speaking World*, eds. Pauline Phemister and Stuart Brown (The Netherlands: Springer, 2007), 207–218, esp. 209.
12. Whitehead, *A Treatise on Universal Algebra*, 6.
13. Ibid.

14. Whitehead, *Process and Reality*, 190.
15. Ibid.
16. Ibid., 189.
17. Ibid., xiii.
18. Ibid.
19. Ibid., 259.
20. Ibid., 258.
21. Ibid.
22. Ibid., 259. The early Russell worried about the "existence" of propositions. After reading a draft of his work on the subject, Whitehead wrote in a letter to Russell on May 5, 1906: "I have read over your ms on propositions three or four times with the greatest care.... False propositions are a great difficulty to me. You say—and this seems sense—there is only the fact that Caesar is dead, and there is not in addition ... the true proposition, 'Caesar is dead'. But then what the devil is there in respect to 'Caesar is not dead'?" [Lowe, *Alfred North Whitehead*, Vol. 1, 280–281.]
23. Whitehead, *Process and Reality*, 51.
24. Whitehead indicates reliance upon W. D. Ross's 1923 translation of Aristotle's *Metaphysics*. See Whitehead, *Process and Reality*, 50 and 344.
25. Redding, *Analytic Philosophy*.
26. I would venture to say, albeit prematurely, that McDowell's critiques of Brandom's "transcendental sociologism" gains credence to the extent that Brandom fails to appreciate that one must have positive ontological commitments in order to be an epistemological quietist.
27. Redding, *Analytic Philosophy*, 15.
28. See W. V. Quine's "Two Dogmas of Empiricism" (1951) and Donald Davidson's "On the Very Idea of a Conceptual Scheme" (1974).
29. Redding, *Analytic Philosophy*, 234.
30. Ibid., 232. Redding explains, "'The absolute', Hegel's way of referring to the Neoplatonic 'one', is not something talked *about* like a finite substance—an idea that even Kant seems to remain committed to with his conception of the type of knowledge that we, finite knowers, are *denied*. Rather, the absolute is to be thought of as something the structure of which is expressed or shown in the logic of our self-correcting attempts to talk about the world."
31. Ibid., 234.
32. Ibid.
33. Ibid., fn. 46.
34. Ibid., 20.
35. Ibid.
36. Ibid.
37. Richard A. Watson, "Shadow History in Philosophy," *Journal of the History of Philosophy* 31 (1993), 95–109, esp. 99; Redding, *Analytic Philosophy*, 7–8.
38. Ludwig Wittgenstein, *Tractatus Logico-Philosophicus,* trans. C. K. Ogden (London: Routledge and Kegan Paul, 1922), 3.3; quoted by Redding, *Analytic Philosophy*, 9.

39. Redding, *Analytic Philosophy*, 9. Redding attributes this distinction to Peter Hylton's *Russell, Idealism and the Emergence of Analytic Philosophy* (Oxford: Oxford University Press, 1993), 223.

40. Ibid., 10.

41. Michael Friedman, *Reconsidering Logical Positivism* (Cambridge: Cambridge University Press, 1999), 6. According to Friedman, "Most of the early writings of the positivists focused on these revolutionary mathematical-physical developments." (Fn. 10)

42. Friedman, *Reconsidering Logical Positivism*, 7–8; Redding, *Analytic Philosophy*, 9–10.

43. Friedman, *Reconsidering Logical Positivism*, 6. He notes, further, "This radically new conception of physical geometry—neither strictly Kantian nor strictly empiricist—was formulated by Reichenbach (1920) in a especially striking fashion in his first book, *The Theory of Relativity and A Priori Knowledge*."

44. Redding, *Analytic Philosophy*, 11.

45. Friedrich Stadler, *The Vienna Circle and Logical Empiricism* (New York, Boston, Dordrecht, London, Moscow: Kluwer Academic Publishers, 2003), xiv.

46. Lowe, *Alfred North Whitehead*, Vol. 1, 285.

47. McDowell, *Mind and World* (Cambridge, MA: Harvard University Press, 1994), 98.

48. Ibid.

49. Ibid., 102.

50. Ibid., 102–103.

51. Whitehead's pp. 6–7.

52. Whitehead, *Process and Reality*, 50.

53. McDowell, *Mind and World*, 104.

54. Alfred North Whitehead, "The Study of the Past—Its Uses and Its Dangers" in *Essays in Science and Philosophy*, 1933 (New York: Philosophical Library, 1947), 200.

55. Redding, *Analytic Philosophy*, 59.

56. Ibid., 61.

57. Ibid.

58. Ibid.

59. McDowell, *Mind and World*, 79.

60. Ibid., 83.

61. Ibid., 85.

62. Ibid., 78.

63. Ibid., 79.

Chapter 3

Pittsburgh's Problem with Intentionality

INTRODUCTION

This chapter details the more recent history of how intentionality became a "problem" for analytic philosophy. My first goal is to map the contemporary conversational terrain of the so-called problem of intentionality (specifically, the intentionality of *belief*) among those scholars for whom it has been, in various ways, a central concern: Wilfrid Sellars, Donald Davidson, Richard Rorty, Robert Brandom, and John McDowell. My second goal is to pursue an immanent critique of the discourse about intentionality-qua-problem, which these thinkers have generated and within which some of them have sought to solve or dissolve this problem. My hope is that, if I can achieve this second goal, I will have demonstrated how contemporary analytic philosophy is well disposed for a Whiteheadian interlocutor.

THE "PROBLEM" OF INTENTIONALITY

In the sense used throughout this project, questions about intentionality concern the directedness or aboutness of our thoughts. These questions already assume a certain picture of "thought" that will itself require reworking in later chapters, but in the interest of gaining some clarity about the analytic debates, I will be relying upon their common parlance. Intentionality becomes problematic when we cannot make sense of the nature of "aboutness" in the sense of knowing when our thoughts are, in reality, somehow related, in a perspicuous way, to what we take them to be about.

As I understand it, the problem of intentionality is a linguistic inflection on the older forms of Cartesian skepticism. Descartes and Locke, for instance, worried about how our ideas functioned as interfaces with the world. They spoke of ideas as essentially private entities, belonging to internal discourse, which literally re-presented the objects of the world to us. This is not a problem of intentionality, because it takes for granted that our ideas match up with things in the world through a one-to-one correspondence. Intentionality became a problem when the internal discourse of ideas was no longer seen as a private affair—that is, when analytic philosophy took the so-called linguistic turn. When ideas became something contingent upon language, rather than something simply expressed by language, this meant that there were no longer such things as "true signs." Ideas were now derivative, conventional, and incapable of retaining a static meaning.

In what follows, I rely upon Rorty's account of the manifestation and implications of the linguistic turn for philosophy. I then introduce McDowell's contestation of this account. This confrontation, between Rorty and McDowell, will lead us to two different interpretations of the major conceptual resources funding *both* Rorty's neopragmatist assault on objectivity and McDowell's attempt to rehabilitate the notion of objectivity: the attacks on classical empiricism by Sellars and Davidson. Sellars challenged the premises of the so-called framework of givenness, and Davidson challenged the premises of scheme/content dualism. I then move to the work of Brandom who, in many ways, is heir to the Sellarsian theory of mind.

In preview, McDowell reproaches Brandom for his "transcendental sociologism," while Rorty accuses Brandom of abandoning his commitment to the priority of social practices by claiming that facts would still have existed had there never been any claimers. Rorty suspects that Brandom has reinstated, late in his career, the metaphysical picture of a world that places demands on us independent of our practices. I discuss how Jeffrey Stout attempts to split the difference between these two interpretations of Brandom, arguing that inferentialism is neither guilty of idealism, nor of abandoning its pragmatism.

THE LINGUISTIC TURN

In 1975, Ian Hacking wrote "the discovery that all names are conventional thunders us into modern philosophy."[1] As Richard Rorty understands this statement, it was the turn away from epistemological questions about the truth of statements, and toward pragmatic questions about the rules of language games that constituted the linguistic turn in philosophy.

Once this turn is made, one can no longer speak of "meaning" as something over and above what is said. Semantics becomes answerable to pragmatics, such that conceptual content is composed of conventional uses of a word. When the problems of philosophy are reduced to the problems of language, the analytic argument went, then there is no longer any sense to the question of how we can know that our ideas "line up" with reality. This question no longer makes sense, because words are no longer seen to represent timeless ideas; rather, ideas are the negotiated content of linguistic practices that constantly evolve in public discourse. Epistemological skepticism was only possible when ideas were understood as veils between the subject and the object. But with the linguistic turn, the meaning of ideas was no longer seen in an atomistic way. Conceptual content was seen to reside in the uses of words in sentences. Words, or the "ideas" they purportedly stood for, no longer lined up with items in reality; sentences as a whole, understood in terms of determinate uses in discourse, became the focus of analytic philosophy.

What was left standing in place of epistemological skepticism after the linguistic turn was the problem of how to make sense of the directedness of our sentences, because with the Scylla of classical correspondentism out of the picture, the danger was the Charybdis of idealism. Some philosophers of language, most notably Davidson, wanted to say that to worry about idealism was not to have taken the linguistic turn. Holding on to the idea of a web of ideas that, to speak metaphorically, spins in a frictionless void, Davidson argued, was to cling to a final dogma of classical empiricism: the idea of scheme/content dualism. Such dualism is implicit in the notion that ideas are interfaces with reality.

In contest of this last dogma of empiricism, Davidson argued that meaning could never operate in a self-subsisting system unmoored from the objects of the world. This is because meaning is always indexed to the more basic concept of truth, such that we cannot analyze truth in terms of meaning, but only meaning in terms of truth. We cannot, that is, determine which sentences are true and which are false simply by analyzing their meaning. We cannot do this, Davidson argued, because the practice of truth-taking is more basic than semantic interpretation. We cannot even begin to interpret what another person means until we have established a pattern of practices of truth-takings that significantly overlaps with another person—such overlap is the condition of our being able to recognize an activity as a *linguistic* one. So the very idea of interpretation presupposes a shared world and a substantial agreement on what two people take to be true. We can begin to talk about meanings only after we realize that they obtain amongst the patterned truth-takings of different individuals.

Davidson thereby shows that linguistic practices become instituted only through a three-way relationship between two speakers and a shared world in continual exchange. Properly understood, on this account, the linguistic turn does not mean a loss of objectivity: "Of course the truth of sentences remains relative to language," he writes, "but that is as objective as it can be.

In giving up the dualism of scheme and world, we do not give up the world, but re-establish unmediated touch with the familiar objects whose antics make our sentences and opinions true or false."[2] This sentiment echoes his 1973 essay "Radical Interpretation," in which he argued that what ultimately ties our language to the world is that the truth conditions (and, therefore, meanings) of our sentences are actually *constituted* by the conditions, or ostensive presentations of an object, that typically cause us to hold sentences true.

Moreover, the concept of belief requires a grasp of the notion of objective truth, Davidson argues, since belief is basically the concept of a sentence held true that might not actually be so. Truth is not agreement or shared belief, then, because the very concept of belief itself entails the implicit distinction in interpersonal communication between what a speaker takes to be true in contrast to other standards of truth directed toward the same objects. So, whereas truth is not an epistemic notion (as idealized rational acceptability or justification), it is also not entirely divorced from belief. Truth is tied to meaning and belief just because language is a tool used by human beings to talk about a shared world. Truth is unified by the role it plays in enabling us to interpret speakers of any language and is, therefore, pre-analytically grasped. Truth, though relative to language, is not conceptually relative—it is relatively expressed, but universally grasped.

My reading of Davidson as defending objectivity in light of the linguistic turn, and thereby as dismissing the problem of intentionality, is not a standard reading by all accounts. In fact, Davidson has been appropriated by some neopragmatists like Rorty who think that objectivity as such is an obsolete notion once we have made the linguistic turn. According to Rorty, once we come to see meaning in terms of the practical employments by linguistically initiated human beings, then the idea of sentences being "true" in an objective sense—a sense not reducible to what a particular linguistic community currently agrees upon (and agreement instantiated by the rules of a language game)—becomes nonsensical. To argue that there is a "truth" that somehow floats free of linguistic practices is, he would say, a confusion between the relationships of justification, which hold between sentences, and the causal relationships, which obtain between events. Rorty concludes that we must limit our projects to mere description, because there can be no connection between the idea of truth as merely descriptive of certain linguistic practices, and the prescriptive sense of truth as a norm for inquiry.

One implication of Rorty's position is that there is nothing outside of discourse that could put a check on our thinking; there is no wider context or causal matrix that could provide a norm for inquiry. With the loss of such a "world"—a world that was never even threatened in Davidson's estimate—we can no longer appeal to the likes of "experience" or "nature" as extra-linguistic bearings on our beliefs.

If language is no longer seen as a medium of representation, it is because there is no longer anything to represent beyond the brute happenings of aural, oral, visual, and tactile interaction. Rorty writes, "one cannot be Davidsonian about language and still think of language as an interface, nor as itself having an interface with what it 'represents'. For the behaviorism that Davidson shares with Quine . . . makes language into something people do, rather than something standing between them and something else." He continues, "It can, to be sure, be viewed as a system of representations—but then so can anything—the rings in trees or the grooves on phonograph records. We cannot see representation and knowledge as posing philosophical problems unless we can reinvent something like the seventeenth-century gap between two kinds of reality, and thus reinvent an interface."[3] The skepticism of the seventeenth century was formulated in terms of the relationship between ideas and the world. This skepticism cannot, Rorty thinks, be reformulated in terms of the relationship between language and the world because "asking how languages manage to represent reality seems a bit like asking how it is possible for wrenches to wrench. That is what we *made* them to do."[4] Fifteen years later, Rorty would regret having said that we "make" language to represent reality. Correcting this formulation of his point, he writes that he should not have said that the idea of language representing reality was unproblematic, but that it was unnecessary.

According to Rorty, Davidson encourages us to give up the idea that certain aspects of the world "make" sentences true or false. This idea of "truthmakers" is central to the realism/antirealism debate in analytic philosophy. Davidson and Quine both, in a rejection of logical positivism, challenged the distinction between analytic and synthetic judgments. The dismantling of this dualism achieved, in Rorty's estimate, the simultaneous undoing of the dualism between language and facts. Once this dualism is given up, so is the debate between realists and antirealists, because language is no longer understood in representationalist terms (such that it could *fail* to accurately represent reality). Rather, according to Rorty, once we cease to see sentences "as expressions of experience" or as "representations of extra-experiential reality" and rather as "strings of marks and noises used by human beings" to "achieve their ends" (ends which "do not include 'representing reality as it is in itself'"), we will realize that there *is* no such thing as "'a language' as a structured medium of representation."[5] If language is something we *do* instead of something that can stand in determinate relation between us and some distinct entity we call "the world," then there can no longer be any "problems of language."[6]

THE STATUS OF OBJECTIVITY: DAVIDSON, RORTY, AND MCDOWELL

The issue with Rorty's assessment of the implications of Davidson's thought for philosophy after the linguistic turn is that, in denying that there is any problematic interface between "us" and "the world," he fails to maintain the distinction between the two. McDowell argues as much when he criticizes Rorty's reading of Davidson for ignoring that part of Davidson that says that the reason there are no problems of language is not just because truth is relative to language and, therefore, there is no "world" to get wrong, but because, we recall from the earlier passage from Davidson, truth and meaning are not separable from "the familiar objects whose antics make our sentences and opinions true or false." In other words, Rorty loses the sense in which states of affairs exert a normative force on our beliefs.

Thus, while denying that there is such a thing as the problem of intentionality, Rorty is all the while perpetuating it by saying that there is nothing outside of discourse that makes our sentences true or false. McDowell recognizes the insidiousness of saying that objectivity can be reduced to solidarity when he points out, "The only authority that meets [Rorty's] requirement is that of human consensus. If we conceive inquiry and judgment in terms of making ourselves answerable to the world, as opposed to being answerable to our fellows, we are merely postponing the completion of the humanism whose achievement begins with discarding authoritarian religion."[7] There is a distinction to be made between the perfectly functional idea of objectivity, and the idea that this objectivity is on the other side of an unbridgeable divide. These are not the same ideas, and yet Rorty thinks that the former must go along with the latter—or, rather, he interprets the former such that the latter exhausts its relevance to discourse. McDowell continues his critique:

Attacking the vocabulary of objectivity as such, as Rorty does, rather than the conception of the world as withdrawn, distracts attention from a necessary task. If we are to achieve a satisfactory exorcism of the problematic mainstream modern epistemology, we need to uncover and understand the specific historical influences—which, as I have been insisting, are much more recent than the vocabulary of objectivity itself—that led to a seeming withdrawal on the part of what we wanted to see as the empirically knowable world, and thus to philosophy's coming to center on epistemology in the sense of the attempt to bridge the supposed gulf.[8]

The notion of objectivity, in and of itself, need not be problematic. In "Solidarity or Objectivity?"[9] Rorty makes a helpful distinction between relativity and ethnocentrism that McDowell is invoking here. Rorty argues that the pragmatist is not a relativist, committed to the positive theory that everything is relative and nothing can be better or worse. Rather, he argues, the pragmatist is making only a negative claim: that we should do away with the traditional epistemological distinction between "knowledge" and "opinion," because this distinction reinforces a metaphysical picture of truth as one-to-one correspondence with reality, where "knowledge" is such correspondence and "opinion" is a degree of justified belief. "The reason the realist calls this negative claim 'relativist' is that he cannot believe that anybody would seriously deny that truth has an intrinsic nature," writes Rorty.[10] I agree with McDowell, however, that Rorty very quickly collapses this helpful distinction.

On my assessment, the problem has to do with Rorty's blindness to certain assumptions he makes about how evidence works. Consider the following statement: "From a pragmatist point of view, to say that what is rational for us now to believe may not be *true*, is simply to say that somebody may come up with a better idea. It is to say that there is always room for improved belief, since new evidence, or new hypotheses, or a whole new vocabulary, may come along."[11] Of course, what counts as evidence is relative to the terms of the question and the purposes for which it is asked. But the testing of such evidence must always be, at some level, practical—that is, must have to do with causal interactions illustrative of certain orders of nature beyond what we can debate. This is to reinstate the distinction between knowledge and opinion, but it is *not* to commit us to a "wishful denial of contingency," as Rorty would label it. Another way of saying this is that the idea of being answerable to the world is not the same as a denial of contingency.[12] Speaking "from the midst of the practices of our ethos" is combinable with making ourselves "answerable to the world." To deny this is to deny the distinction between relativism and ethnocentrism. As McDowell argues, "The thesis that 'justification is relative to an audience' is, as explicitly stated, relativistic, not just ethnocentric."[13]

To use standard alethiological terminology, Rorty is trying to make a distinction between normative and disquotational uses of "true." Descriptive uses of "true" in the form of Tarskian T-sentences exhaust, according to Rorty, the disquotational use of "true" and must remain purely descriptive. To be clear, a Tarkian T-sentence is a formal sentential structure serving as the basic guide to his semantic account of truth. It follows the form:

"*P*" is true if and only if *p*

Such that,

"Schnee ist weiß" if and only if snow is white.

In this example, German is the object language of the theory and English is the metalanguage. The formal structure indicated above embodies Tarski's material adequacy condition for the truth of a sentence, also known as Convention T. Tarski admitted that T-sentences only work for formal languages, not natural ones, because a natural language is, so to speak, semantically self-enclosed, such that there is no way to determine, from without, whether a sentence is properly constituted. Davidson famously inverted Tarski's semantic theory of truth into a truth theory of meaning. Instead of taking meaning as basic, Davidson took practices of taking-true as elemental, thereby developing a theory of interpretation that would work between natural languages.

Rorty reads Davidson as indefinitely maintaining the distinction between the descriptive and normative uses of "true," and this is why he can claim Davidson as substituting solidarity for objectivity. But, my ongoing argument has been, this is to misunderstand Davidson's understanding of semantics as instituted by relationships of triangulation, as well as his account of the irreducibility of normativity by way of the constitutive ideal of rationality. McDowell agrees: "For a given sentence ["*p*"] to be true—to be disquotable—is for it to be correctly usable to make a claim just because [*p*]." He goes on, "Truth in the sense of disquotability is unproblematically normative for sentences uttered in order to make claims."[14] Far from avoiding philosophical dualism, Rorty reinstates a dualism between reason and nature by insisting on the separation between normativity and disquotability in speaking about truth. It is this picture of the separation of reason and nature with which Rorty is covertly operating—all the while taking himself to have deflated the latter into the former—that leads him to miss the radicality of Davidson account of *radical* interpretation.

For Davidson, the radical interpreter begins from outside of the putatively linguistic behavior and seeks to gain some purchase on the norms that constitute the language; that is, she aims to translate what begins as a disquotational use of language into her own normative use. As McDowell points out in *Mind and World*, "When Rorty suggests that the results of the field linguist's endeavours to employ a notion of truth unconnected with norms, and hence separate—by the supposed gulf between two standpoints—from, for instance, a conception in which the truth is seen as what ought to be believed [. . .], he obliterates the significance of the transition from starting predicament to achieved interpretation."[15] It is fairly clear that Rorty inherits this dualism from Sellars's strict separation of the realm of reasons and the realm of nature. The semantical, for Sellars, strictly operates in the realm of reasons, such that there can be no relations between elements in the real order and elements in the linguistic order. He argues that this non-relational character of meaning is "key" to understanding "the correct place of mind in nature."[16] But to think of mind in this way is not to clarify intentionality, but to problematize it once more. This time, however, it is not the classical metaphysics of correspondence that introduces the gap, but rather a deflationary pragmatism that runs into confusion at critical points.

Language, for Sellars (and for Rorty), can be exhaustively described by reference to "rule-governed uniformities" without any appeal to semantics.[17] Meaning-involving relations only obtain from within the conceptual realm. The problem with this sort of isolationist philosophy of language is that it leads, almost without exception, to an inability to account for the constraints reality has on our normative practices. McDowell calls this sort of philosophy of language, in which there can be no meaning-involving relations with anything outside the linguistic realm, "transcendental sociologism," and he ascribed this label to Brandom's inferentialism.

SOCIAL PRACTICES AND THE LEVEL OF THE SEMANTIC

McDowell too quickly accuses Brandom's inferentialism of metaphysical idealism. Brandom knows that he ought to make more of the material constraints on our linguistic practices (what he calls "discursive entries" and "discursive exits"). He writes,

> What must not be lost is an appreciation of the way in which our discursive practice is empirically and practically *constrained*. It is not up to us which claims are true (that is, what the facts are). It is in a sense up to us which noises and marks express which claims, and hence, in a more attenuated sense, which express true claims. But empirical and practical constraint on our arbitrary whim is a pervasive feature of our discursive practices . . . [D]iscursive practices as here conceived do not stand apart from the rest of the world.[18]

It is clear that Brandom is aware of the need to account for observation and action in relation to our linguistic practices. He is fully aware that one of the greatest challenges to inferentialism is the need to account for how something like the notion of objectivity or truth beyond mere justified belief could have arisen in the first place—indeed, notions which he himself employs in order to explicate his own theory of normativity:

> For those practices are not things, like words conceived as marks and noises, that are specifiable independently of the objects they deal with and the facts they make it possible to express. Discursive practices essentially involve to-ing and fro-ing with environing objects in perception and action. The conceptual

proprieties implicit in those practices incorporate both empirical and practical dimensions. All our concepts are what they are in part because of their inferential links to others that have noninferential circumstances or consequences of application—concepts, that is, whose proper use is not specifiable apart from consideration of the *facts* and *objects* that responsively bring about or are brought about by their application.[19] (emphasis added)

Rorty sees statements such as this as evidence of Brandom conceding, late in his career, to the idea of the world making demands of our practices. One upshot of Brandom's above emphasis on perception and action (discursive entries and discursive exits) is the idea that "facts" exist independently of someone asserting them. It is interesting that Rorty and McDowell seem to be accusing Brandom of opposite things—Rorty, of a degree of realism, and McDowell, a degree of idealism. Whereas I think Rorty is simply wrong in failing to make the distinction between justification and truth, I think McDowell fails to appreciate the grasp Brandom has on this distinction.

Inferentialism, at least in Brandom's use, means that we must look to practices of inference to understand justification. This means that only a belief that can serve as either the premise or the conclusion of inference can serve to justify other beliefs. There are causal relations between beliefs and the world, but only beliefs can justify other beliefs. The "world," that means, cannot make beliefs correct or incorrect, because correctness is strictly a matter of playing by the rules of the inferential game. Such rules are negotiated through practices of giving and asking for reasons. The crucial point that I think McDowell misses in his aforementioned ascription to Brandom's theory is that Brandom is not thereby claiming that states of affairs in the world cannot make beliefs *true*.[20] We need the distinction between truth claims and true claimables.[21]

However, I do not think Brandom makes enough of this last point, and because of this, McDowell's concern doubles as mine. We need more than mere causal relations between the world and our beliefs—we need rational relations. But how do we achieve such relations without falling prey to the Myth of the Given; that is, to the idea that bits of the world line up with bits of language in a relationship of justification? The question, as Brandom puts it, asks "why we shouldn't think of our claims as standing in normative relations to facts, which make them correct or incorrect in the sense of true or false."[22] To Rorty's point, conceptual norms exist only because vocabularies exist. So to speak about facts in the sense of true claimables *is* to talk of something that is conceptually structured and, therefore, already presupposing linguistic practices. Facts, for Rorty, *are* conceptually structured—they are not the sort of thing that can *make* claims true, because they always already are claims. He thinks that we will always worry about intentionality—about the success of our thinking and speaking gaining traction with objects in the world, or with *the* world—as long as a merely causal relation is not enough to satisfy us. McDowell is dissatisfied with merely causal relations between the world and our thinking, and for this, Rorty faults him for "keeping alive the pathos of possible distance from the world."[23] All the while, it is this distance that McDowell fears Rorty is perpetuating. McDowell hopes that we can escape Cartesianism once and for all if we read Kant on intuition differently than has been done. He points to the Transcendental Deduction as a key to understanding Kantian intuition in a way that does not lead to the classical divide between appearances and things-in-themselves. Rather than being immediacies that figure into the "framework of givenness," McDowell argues, intuitions have logical structures.

The issue McDowell takes with Brandom's theory is that he gets Kant wrong on judgment and intuition. Brandom takes a judgment, as Kant understood it, as the basic unit of awareness. Such judgment is always already conceptually structured, and is, therefore, always already caught up in normativity. If awareness *begins* in the normative realm thus conceived, then it is caught up from the beginning in the rules of the linguistic game. As Sellars and Brandom understand it, the rules of this game can be formulated in pre-semantic terms, such that they form the structure upon which semantic relations supervene. If we conceive the directedness of thought (meaning, aboutness, or intentionality) as supervening upon rule-governed proprieties, then we will never conceive of spontaneity as having rational relations to receptivity. For Brandom and Sellars, the level of social practices is pre-semantical and so meaning-involving relations can never obtain between words and things in the so-called real order. But McDowell thinks that this way of viewing meaning-relations is confused. There are no grounds to think, he argues, that the directedness of thought must be constituted by norms that are social but not yet semantical.[24] He writes, "once we see that the relevant 'oughts' can be as it were on the semantic surface, we can take in stride that meaningful speech, and thought directed at the world, are unproblematically part of our lives—as Wittgenstein says, 'as much a part of our natural history as walking, eating, drinking, playing'."[25] I expand in my next chapter upon McDowell's reading of Kant, at the same time that I consider the limitations of McDowell's attempt to reestablish the world's rational constraints on our thinking. For now, we are concerned with getting clear on Rorty's side of the argument in order to provide an outline of the problem of intentionality is contemporary Analytic philosophy.

To be sure, Rorty and McDowell are united against the empiricist worldview and its attendant framework of givenness. But Rorty would say he resists the temptation to establish something beyond causal relations between our beliefs and the things they purport to be about. By his lights, giving in to this temptation "keeps alive the pathetic Kantian question about the 'transcendental status' of the world."[26] This "transcendental status" attributed to the world strikes Rorty as merely a sugar coating of the "bitter Platonic pill," just another form of the "Platonic disease."[27] He simply cannot see what is to be gained by making a distinction between trying to express truth claims about the world and aiming to be justified in one's claiming among one's peers: "What, I still want to ask, is so 'mere' about getting together with your fellow inquirers and agreeing on what to say and believe?"[28]

Reducing objectivity to solidarity is just that, a reduction. And it is a reduction from what the idea of objective purport means on the face of it: not *mere* intersubjective agreement. So regardless of what Rorty thinks objectivity "really is" all about, what it claims to be about is not that. One of the greatest challenges to theories of language that want, like Brandom's, to focus on discursive practices alone to account for normative authority (the power to determine what counts as a correct inferential move, as evidence, as meaningful, and so forth) is how to account for this very idea of objectivity as something *beyond* discourse in the first place—a notion that has been around much longer than empiricist epistemology and Cartesian skepticism.

Brandom's move is to take a step back from Rorty's way of speaking and to make an observation: that what Rorty is doing, by saying that facts only exists when vocabularies exist, is employing a *vocabulary* of vocabularies. That is, he is developing a way of speaking about implicitly normative discursive practices. But applying vocabularies—even to be able to talk *about* our vocabularies—is, nevertheless, something that we *do*. It is the *social articulation* of our linguistic practices of giving and asking for reasons that is the key to understanding how our claims "answer normatively to the facts."[29] To be sure, a pragmatist about norms will hold that nothing can confer normative status other than discursive practices. This means that something can justify a belief only insofar as it serves a role in some actual vocabulary.

This is what Sellars meant when, critiquing the idea that certain nonconceptual "givens" in perception could make a belief true, he said that only beliefs can justify other beliefs. This amounts to a critique of sense-datum theorists, or those who want to say that, once we have made all the available moves in the space of reasons to justify a belief, we can make one more move: we can *point* to something that is simply received in experience, as some brute impact from the exterior that can serve as a reason. McDowell writes that sense-datum theorists thereby give us "exculpations" where we want "justifications."[30] But whereas Sellars thinks that we must renounce empiricism altogether in order to avoid the temptation to appeal to empirical descriptions as justifiers, McDowell aims to retain an account of normative authority that has room for both spontaneity *and* receptivity (see my chapters 4 and 5).

The important point, at least for getting clear on the contemporary texture of the problem of intentionality in analytic philosophy, is that we must never treat vocabularies as things that exist out of relation from our actual use of them, such that something like a dichotomy between reason and nature could ever creep back into our thinking. When we speak about vocabularies, we must never lose sight of the fact that we are using a vocabulary of vocabularies to do so, and so are caught up in the very practices we seek to elucidate. But because we can make this observation, we can also point out that we create vocabularies in order to make explicit practices that were implicit in our use of other vocabularies. Through this process of explicitation, we are creating new ways of speaking for new purposes, purposes that were not determined for us by previous vocabularies. And in so creating, we are demonstrating the ways in which constraint by linguistic norms makes possible new forms of freedom. We can use our metavocabulary to critique other vocabularies, such as the vocabulary of representation, gaining a historicist perspective on our own normative practices. All the while, however, we are receiving and acting in determinate relations with other discursive partners in a material matrix.

It is *within* these determinate relations that practices capable of normative constraints can arise—practices uninterpretable apart from the material matrix. "Norms," Stout writes, "are initially proprieties implicit in practices." These implicit proprieties are made explicit in the form of "rules and ideals."[31] For instance, if someone makes an observation such as "This violin is made from old-growth cedar from the Italian Alps" after examining the instrument, we recognize her as making a non-inferential report about the object in hand. If she is an expert in wood identification, we will draw an inference from this fact to the one that she has made an informed claim, thereby *endorsing* her claim. Thus, as Brandom writes, "The causal relation [between, for instance, an observation and a claim about it] can underwrite a justification just because and insofar as those assessing knowledge claims *take* it as making good a kind of *inference*." He continues, "Non-normative causal relations between worldly facts and someone's claims do not exclude normative epistemic justificatory relations between them, since others can *take* the causal relations *as* reasons for belief, by endorsing reliability inferences."[32] I think that this is a very strong aspect of Brandom's theory, and one that complicates McDowell's ascription of "transcendental sociologism" to it.

RELATIONS OF JUSTIFICATION AND RELATIONS OF CAUSATION

Whether or not we think we need to worry about the possibility of "getting things right" in any robust sense turns out to have a lot to do with whether or not we think that an endorsement of reliability inferences is the same as taking the facts (or causal relations) as the reasons. Rorty, for one, doesn't think so.[33] In so rejecting this move by Brandom, I suspect, Rorty is doing just what McDowell has said: he is perpetuating the very dichotomy between mind and world which his entire philosophical career has been dedicated to showing doesn't exist.

The act of endorsing a reliability inference about an expert reporter will only come to look like taking causal relations as reasons if we can see how pragmatism ought to resist reduction of the social-practical to either pole of the Cartesian dualism; that is, to either mere appearance or absolute reality. In order to see this, I argue, we need to make explicit the metaphysics of pragmatism. As Brandom writes, "Once the metaphysician renounces the adoption of an exclusionary or dismissive attitude toward non-conforming vocabularies, the project of metaphysics modestly understood represents one potentially useful discursive tool among others for getting a grip on our multifarious culture. This is not an enterprise that the enlightened pragmatist ought to resist."[34] The committed pragmatist can also be (indeed, might have to become) a metaphysician.

What the pragmatist cannot coherently claim is that any particular vocabulary has greater cognitive value owing solely to its ontological status, to some ability to mirror the final real things better than another vocabulary.[35] Such a claim would be complicit in classical ontotheology—that pejorative form of metaphysics that is parasitic upon an absolute correspondentist epistemology. Such ontotheology was delegitimized in large measure through modern philosophical critique, culminating in Friedrich Nietzsche's declaration (if not lamentation) of the death of God, with Martin Heidegger delivering a proper eulogy. It is this type of metaphysics that is indicted by Sellars's critique of the framework of givenness. Rorty argues that the framework of givenness is a monotheistic hangover from a time when the ontotheological synthesis was still intact. The pragmatist could never pursue metaphysics in this vein.

And yet, per Brandom's description, metaphysics in the sense of a discursive tool useful for making sense of the multifariousness of the world is entirely consistent with the pragmatic enterprise. Such a stance with respect to metaphysics speaks to Brandom's desire to navigate between the two, self-defeating extremes of postmodernism: on the one side, a deflationary pragmatism that leads to the death of the subject and the annihilation of truth-talk, eventually leading nihilism in through the front door and, on the other side, a metaphysical realism that slips representationalism in through the back door.[36] The former is self-defeating because it ends up denying the very presuppositions that make it possible: the ideas of truth, objectivity, and subjectivity in any robust sense. It ends up conceding these notions to philosophy in a Cartesian vein, rendering any rehabilitation efforts trivial. As

Stout notes, "What gives impetus to the more extreme forms of postmodernism is the view that ordinary talk of truth and of subjects is wholly vitiated by a form of metaphysical philosophy that runs through the entire culture."[37] Rorty shares this view, and it informs his entire understanding of the ontological status of our dominant vocabularies. He writes, "If one wishes to wed historicism and scientism, then one will marry Hegel and Darwin not by finding a holistic, panpsychist way of describing the relations between experience and nature, but rather by finding a historicist and relativist way of describing Darwin's claim upon our attention."[38] The reference to panpsychism is, I can only presume, a dismissal of systems like Whitehead's. This presumption is supported by the continuance of Rorty's statement: "[A] historicist way of avoiding this conflict cannot invoke an appearance-reality distinction. Nor can it resort to notions of misleading abstractions and misplaced concreteness, for 'concrete' implies a special relation of closeness to reality for which historicism has no room."[39] The direct target of this statement is undoubtedly William James and (in some moods) John Dewey, but Whitehead is conceivably a secondary target.

It is no secret that Rorty often accused Dewey of not remaining Wittgensteinian (in Rorty's Rortyan reading of Wittgenstein) enough, restraining himself to description without redescription. The Dewey at which he takes aim is primarily the Dewey of *Experience and Nature*. Here, Rorty claims, Dewey falls into the representationalist trap of claiming that some descriptions of nature and experience are more or less accurate than others. The only sense that "more accurate" or "more concrete" could have for the consistent pragmatist, Rorty thinks, is "more useful" for purposes of our own design.[40] This is to substitute "expediency" for "accuracy" as a term of epistemological "approbation," such that we can avoid arguing that scientific vocabularies somehow track better with reality than religious or moralistic ones. The goal of a pragmatist theory of truth, recall, is to be able to account for why Darwin has such a claim on our attention without resorting to a representationalist or correspondentist framework.

With respect to James, Rorty thinks that his idea of the "marriage function" of truth—that ideas "become true" insofar as they function to help us get into satisfactory relationships with other aspects of our experience—runs together linguistic entities with introspective entities. What this means is that James confuses the relationships of justification, which obtain between sentences, with relationships of causation, which obtain between events. Truth cannot float free of sentences, because the only way to make sense of how it could involves a reinstatement of the framework of givenness or of language as the mirror of nature that made intentionality problematic in the first place. But, I have argued, Rorty does not succeed in disabusing us of the problem quite as cleanly as he suspects.

Rorty's failure has to do with a sort of tone-deafness to the nuances of pragmatist metaphysics that James assumes, Dewey waivers in developing, and, I argue in later chapters, the Whitehead develops to full effect. The accusation of panpsychism has to do with this idea of running together relationships of justification with relationships of causation that McDowell argues can be done without a framework of givenness and which I will come back to in the next chapter. Here, however, I would briefly like to examine Rorty's accusation of panpsychism, because this term is often misunderstood in its association with Whitehead's thought.

Rorty's concern is that, when we blur the distinction between the propositional and the non-propositional (the types of relationships that obtain between sentences and the types constituting experiences as introspective entities) it opens the door to thinking of "experience" as non-linguistic, such that a sentient being could "see that" such-and-such is the case without having concepts in any meaningful sense. Dewey does say that sentiency is anoetic, but also that it is the substrate upon which noetic function can arise. But this way of establishing continuity between linguistic animals and other forms of sentient life, Rorty thinks, falls into a sort of infinite regress of attributing proto-intentionality to things like mammals and reptiles, and eventually protein molecules and quarks.[41] The only acceptable alternative, the argument goes, is to construe "thinking" as "simply the use of sentences—both for arranging cooperative enterprises and for attributing inner states (beliefs, desires) to our fellow humans." He concludes, "If we have thinking in this sense—the ability to have and ascribe sentential attitudes—we can see it as something that has nothing in particular to do with 'experience of a non-cognitive sort'."[42] Allow me to put to bed some unfortunate misconceptions about Whitehead's work right away, lest they fester in the reader's mind.

A NOTE ABOUT "PANPSYCHISM"

Many scholars who misunderstand Whitehead's theory of perception—often for the reasons detailed in chapter 1—have associated his theory with the doctrine of panpsychism. This can be an exceedingly misleading title. Donald Sherburne, a notable Whitehead scholar, has written that this term is "the single most confusing, misleading term to be associated with Whitehead's philosophy."[43] I would say that this and the accusations of classical Platonism are both strong contenders for this title, but I share his frustration.

There is fair basis for the attribution of "panpsychism" to Whitehead's thought, even if attributors themselves have misunderstood the nature of that basis. Whitehead does write in *Process and Reality*, "In describing the capacities, realized or unrealized, of an actual occasion, we have, with

Locke, tacitly taken human experience as an example upon which to found the generalized description required for metaphysics."[44] We must consider, in elaboration of this quote, another from *Process and Reality*: "But when we turn to the lower organisms we have first to determine which among such capacities fade from realization into irrelevance, that is to say, by comparison with human experience which is our standard."[45] As Sherburne notes, "The key point here is that what quickly fades into irrelevance as we 'descend the scale' is everything even remotely suggestive of 'psyche', of ordinary human functioning."[46] Whitehead is here, as elsewhere, taking evolution very seriously. He is not trying to account for Darwin's claim upon our attention in relativist terms, as Rorty would have it. Rather, Whitehead thinks that we can wed historicism and scientism by working out a metaphysics that takes as its guiding principles epistemic humility, openness to revision, the relativity and instrumentality of linguistic norms, indeterminism, freedom within constraint, and, above all, the incessancy of growth and creativity converging into the directionality of temporal process. He develops an entire philosophy of the actual entity that puts mind back into nature whilst breaking with the mirror imagery that arose from Cartesian dualism.[47] What Rorty calls a confusion of the relations of justification and the relations of causation, Whitehead calls another dualism. In contrast, Whitehead more deeply[48] appreciates (understands and elaborates on) the reality of causation at every single level of actuality, both efficient and final. This is why his theory of perception rests upon his theory of prehension, to be expanded upon in more detail in the next two chapters.

Whitehead distinguishes the causality of a bodily "taking account of the environment" from the awareness of this causality—the former being what we continue to find as we "descend the scale of being." On the relation between causal relations and knowing relations to one's environment, Whitehead aims to distinguish his position from classical empiricism. To do so, he considers the example of a man blinking in response to an environmental stimulus. He writes,

> He feels that the experience of the *eye* in the matter of the flash are causal of the blink. The man himself will have no doubt of it. In fact, it is the feeling of causality which enables the man to distinguish the priority of the flash; and the inversion of the argument, whereby the temporal sequence "flash to blink" is made the premise for the "causality" belief, has its origin in pure theory.
>
> The philosophy of organism accepts the man's statement, that the flash *made* him blink. But Hume intervenes with another explanation. He first points out that in the mode of presentational immediacy there is no percept of the flash *making* the man blink. In this mode, there are merely the two percepts—the flash and the blink—combining the two latter of the three percepts under the one term

"blink." Hume refuses to admit the man's protestation, that the compulsion to blink is just what he did feel. The refusal is based on the dogma that all percepts are in the mode of presentational immediacy—a dogma not to be upset by a mere appeal to direct experience.

We have here a perfect example of the practice of applying the test of presentational immediacy to procure the critical rejection of some doctrines, and of allowing other doctrines to slip out by a back door, so as to evade the test. The notion of causation arose because mankind lives amid experiences in the mode of causal efficacy.[49]

Whitehead introduces a distinction between what he calls "presentational immediacy" and "causal efficacy," inverting the classical order. Hume's doctrine of perception, for instance, makes causal efficacy dependent upon presentational immediacy.[50] This means that our awareness of the world begins with clearness and distinctness, with fuzziness around the edges. Whitehead holds the opposite; he holds that "taking account" of one's environment begins with constant and incalculable forms of concrete relations to the environment (and within the percipient).

Causal efficacy is the primary mode of awareness that bodies experience in the form of spatial definition. This form of awareness is plagued by vagueness. He writes, "These conclusions are confirmed as we descend the scale of organic being. It does not seem to be the sense of causal awareness that the lower living things lack, so much as variety of sense-presentation, and then vivid distinctness of presentational immediacy." He continues with an example:

> But animals, and even vegetables, in low forms of organism exhibit modes of behavior directed towards self-preservation. This is every indication of a vague feeling of causal relationship with the external world, of some intensity, vaguely defined as to quality, and with some vague definition as to locality. A jellyfish advances and withdraws, and in so doing, exhibits some perception of causal relationship with the world beyond itself; a plant grows downwards to the damp earth, and upwards towards the light. There is thus some direct reason for attributing dim, slow feelings of causal nexus, although we have no reason for any ascription of the definite percepts in the mode of presentational immediacy.[51]

Both causal efficacy and presentational immediacy are modes of feeling (or "prehending," as opposed to apprehending) one's environment. There is no bifurcation, for Whitehead, between the tactile feelings of one's surroundings with one's own hands, and the level of awareness of this feeling that arises with self-conscious (indeed, linguistic) beings such as us. This is part of what it means to attribute "feeling" throughout the actual world. Whitehead's doctrine of prehension is based on "the directly observed fact that 'feeling' survives as a known element constitutive of the 'formal' existence of such actual entities as we can best observe."[52] To use an analogy from physics, Whitehead claims that all physical quantities are vector, not scalar. When describing the motion of an object, a physicist will rely on one of two categories of mathematical representation: scalar or vector.

For example, if I were to describe to you a moving object such as a ball, to tell you how far it has moved without telling you how long it took to get there would not fully describe to you the *motion* of the object. The former would be to give a scalar description of a quantity (e.g., 10 miles), whereas the latter would be to give you a vector description of the object (e.g., 10 miles per 1 second). Numerical quantity is not enough to understand relations in a causal nexus; one also needs directionality. It is the same for Whitehead's theory of actual entities at the most fundamental level, but also for his theory of perception at the highest level of human self-consciousness; if we observe the so-called causal nexus without taking account of the interplay with sense-perception, then we will not fully grasp the way in which the subject is both acted upon by and discriminately receives the objects of its immediate past. It is not enough to understand our experience of "seeing the steam rise off the blacktop" as a clear and distinct presentation, if we do not appreciate the complex substrate of causally efficacious relations and processes upon which that presentational immediacy supervenes.

This is Whitehead's aesthetic ontology; that at the most fundamental level, all actual things are forms of feeling past things. "Taking account" of one's environment operates from the ground up, so to speak. This is what it means to attribute experience to the lowest levels of existence: that everything is at the same time the subject taking account of past objects, and an object for future subjects. It is *not* to attribute "psyche" throughout existence—not if such a term carries with it any trace of the bifurcation of nature. I will now return to the primary aim of this chapter, which is to outline the problem of intentionality as it currently stands in analytic philosophy.

TWO USES OF "TRUE": BRIDGING THE DESCRIPTIVE AND THE NORMATIVE

Recall Brandom's earlier-quoted pronouncement that, "Once the metaphysician renounces the adoption of an exclusionary or dismissive attitude toward non-conforming vocabularies, the project of metaphysics modestly understood represents one potentially useful discursive tool among others for getting a grip on our multifarious culture. This is not an enterprise that the enlightened pragmatist ought to resist."[53] Metaphysics is permissible so long as it has also taken the linguistic turn. This means that the metaphysician must also be a pragmatist in the sense of recognizing relativity without being a relativist, and must operate within a particular cultural starting point, with the conceptual resources presently available, while using those resources to reveal both their own limits and implications. Such a metaphysician will start with this commitment to historicism, but will never let ethnocentrism devolve into relativism, because she will recognize that to be fallible is not the same as to be incapable of approximating better or worse perspectives on the whole.

Consider this conception of metaphysics in conjunction with a quote from Davidson: "The merit of the method of truth is not that it settles such matters once and for all, or even that it settles them without further metaphysical reflection. But the method does serve to sharpen our sense of viable alternatives, and gives a comprehensive idea of the consequences of a decision."[54] On Davidson's own account of the implications of his truth theory of semantics, one can begin to make a case for better and worse methods of metaphysical reflection. This means that, for Davidson, the normative use of "true" *is* combinable with the descriptive use of "true." He writes, "In sharing a language, in whatever sense this is required for communication, we share a picture of the world that must, in its large features, be true. It follows that in making manifest the large features of our language, we make manifest the large features of reality. One way of pursuing metaphysics is therefore to study the general structure of our language. This is not, of course, the sole true method . . . there is [none]."[55] In this statement, the first instance of "true" could be interpreted as descriptive in the sense that Davidson means that we must, in order to communicate, have significant overlap in our practices of truth-takings. However, this first use of "true" could also be normative, insofar as, for Davidson, truth-taking is not a practice that operates independently of causal relations to the world. He is an externalist about semantics, which means that semantical relations are observable practices, not private psychological entities. Mental contents, because they cannot be truth-bearers, also cannot be meaning-bearers. Truth is a three-way affair between our sentences, other speakers, and the world; it is not a four-way affair between sentences, mental contents, the world, and other speakers. Barring mental entities as truth-bearers from the picture at the outset due to inscrutability leaves us in a domain where truth borne by interpreted sentences must be thought about in non-correspondentist terms.

At times, Davidson seems to be saying what Rorty thinks: that the descriptive use of "true" is all we could ever have. After all, Davidson uses Tarski's Convention T to develop a truth theory of semantics in purely extensional terms in order to avoid inflating the concept of truth as correspondence in the classically realist sense, but he also uses this approach to avoid *deflating* the concept of truth to the idealization of rational acceptability in an anti-realist sense. Truth is the most perspicuous concept we have, Davidson thinks, insofar as we all have a much stronger intuitive grasp of it than we do of, say, meaning or reference (or any other concept we might use to explain them). This grasp of truth is exhibited in any particular language by our readiness to accept such trivial expressions like "'Grass is green' is true if and only if grass is green."

At this point, it seems that Rorty's deflationary reading of Davidson is not entirely off base, even if it is exaggerative and misses some nuances of Davidson's later appraisals of his own theory. Though uninformative about what truth is, such trivialities seem unworthy of dispute. Taken together, such undisputed trivialities demonstrate how "is true" works for all the sentences of a language. This is all we could hope of a (purely extensional) definition of truth. It is in this vein that Rorty writes, "the results of interpreting linguistic behavior as Davidson conceives that activity, formulated in theories of truth in the style of Tarski, are 'descriptive', and as such not just to be distinguished from, but not even combinable in a unified discourse with, any way of talking in which 'true' expresses a norm for inquiry and claim-making."[56] And yet, Davidson also speaks about his method of truth in a prescriptive sense, such that it "serves to sharpen our sense of the viable alternatives." The second half of this statement is as follows: "Metaphysics has generality as an aim; the method of truth expresses that demand by requiring a theory that touches all the bases. Thus the problems of metaphysics, while neither solved nor replaced, come to be seen as the problems of all good theory building."[57] By developing a behavior-based theory of truth, and by showing how one implication of this theory is the rejection of scheme/content dualism, Davidson does not, contra Rorty, invalidate the use of truth in a normative sense and thereby invalidate metaphysics. On the contrary, Davidson (with a seconding from Brandom) shows that the postmodern antipathy toward metaphysics depends upon the very dualism we can now do without.

Davidson and Brandom understand something about pragmatism that Rorty does not: that historical situatedness does not mean relativist, that fallible does not mean false, and that contingency does not mean directionless. Rorty's failure to appreciate these distinctions makes him prone to self-contradiction in advocating for his own understanding. It also deprives any ensuing socio-political critique of its teeth. Awareness of one's fallibility and anxiety about one's contingency need not be merely negative features of one's outlook—they can also be positive, constructive, informative aspects.

Particularity (of time, place, problems, and tools) provides freedom both within and because of its necessary constraints. Whitehead's metaphysics, beyond being merely permissible by analytic philosophy, can also disabuse it of certain tacit presuppositions that have prohibited thinkers like Brandom and McDowell from providing satisfactory solutions to the problem of intentionality, despite their commendable strides in this direction.

With respect to Brandom, I believe a limitation is his inability to make enough of the way in which pre-linguistic modes of "taking account of" the world exists not only in non-linguistic entities but also, so to speak, "all the while." He does appreciate the sense in which our social practices are material prerequisites for our making conceptually contentful claims, which is to say, he understands that there are causal and not merely logical presuppositions of our ability to make meaningful statements about the world. This means that norms, or the realm of normativity, are always first and foremost the implications of social practices, never objects themselves or properties of objects.[58] Brandom makes explicit the norms in our linguistic practices, one of which is the ideal of objectivity and idea of speakers as capable of both authorizing and recognizing normative authority, which is to say that one of the ideas implicit in the social practices constitutive of linguistic activity from the start is our ability to hold ourselves accountable as subjects. As Stout writes, "The social practices we engage in both constitute us as the self-committing, responsibility-oriented subjects we are and make possible the various ways in which we hold one another responsible and aim for correctness when addressing [certain] topics and deciding what to do."[59] Brandom's variety of pragmatism aims, like Davidson's, to preserve a robust sense of objectivity without falling prey to the realist/antirealist debates that are always predicated upon representationalist epistemology. At the same time, both Brandom and Davidson make possible a variety of postmodern theorizing in which subjectivity is not inherently metaphysical in the pejorative sense—an effort for which McDowell shares concern.

For the pragmatist who wants to avoid both the narcissism of Rorty and the common pitfalls of realist discourse, metaphysics is not only possible; it is necessary. Far from ignoring contingency (and the positive aspects of epistemic anxiety about fallibility that follow), however, Whitehead develops a metaphysics that can account for freedom and constraint at both an ontological and normative level. Key to his system is his rejection of the bifurcation of nature and its underwriter, substantialist metaphysics.

In what follows, I will argue that this reinterpretation in Whitehead's thought helps us to reassess the problem of intentionality by reframing the discussion about the relationship of rationality to causality and, therefore, also the contrast of the conceptual, the normative, and the mental to nature that persists in analytic discussions.

NOTES

1. Ian Hacking, *The Emergence of Probability: A Philosophical Study of Early Ideas about Probability, Induction, and Statistical Inference* (New York: Cambridge University Press, 1975), 47; Richard Rorty, "Ten Years After," in *The Linguistic Turn: Essays in Philosophical Method with Two Retrospective Essays,* ed. Richard M. Rorty (Chicago and London: University of Chicago Press, 1992), 367.

2. Donald Davidson, "On the Very Idea of a Conceptual Scheme," in *Inquiries into Truth and Interpretation* (Oxford: Oxford University Press, 2001), 198.

3. Rorty, "Ten Years After," 369.

4. Ibid., 369–370.

5. Richard Rorty, "Twenty-Five Years Later," in *The Linguistic Turn: Essays in Philosophical Method with Two Retrospective Essays,* ed. Richard M. Rorty (Chicago and London: University of Chicago Press, 1992), 373–374.

6. Ibid.

7. John McDowell, "Towards Rehabilitating Objectivity" in *Rorty and His Critics,* ed. Robert Brandom (MA: Blackwell Publishing, 2000), 110.

8. Ibid., 111.

9. Richard Rorty, "Solidarity or Objectivity?" in *Relativism: Interpretation and Confrontation,* ed. Michael Krausz (Notre Dame: University of Notre Dame Press, 1989).

10. Ibid., 170.

11. Ibid., 169.

12. McDowell, "Towards Rehabilitating Objectivity," 114.

13. Ibid., 122n25.

14. Ibid., 116.

15. McDowell, *Mind and World,* 152.

16. John McDowell, "The Constitutive Ideal of Rationality" in *Crítica: Revista Hispanoamericana de Filosofía,* Vol. 30, No. 88 (April 1998), 39; Wilfrid Sellars, *Science and Metaphysics: Variations on a Kantian Theme* (London and New York: Routledge & Kegan Paul, 1967), ix.

17. Wilfrid Sellars, *Naturalism and Ontology* (Atascadero, CA: Ridgeview Publishing, 1979), 92.

18. Robert Brandom, *Making It Explicit* (Cambridge, MA: Harvard University Press, 1998), 331.

19. Ibid.

20. Robert Brandom, "Vocabularies of Pragmatism: Synthesizing Naturalism and Historicism" in *Rorty and His Critics* (MA: Blackwell Publishing, 2000), 161.

21. Ibid., 162.

22. Ibid., 161.

23. Richard Rorty, "Response to McDowell" in *Rorty and His Critics,* ed. Robert Brandom (MA: Blackwell Publishing, 2000), 123–124.

24. John McDowell, *Having a World in View Essays on Kant, Hegel, and Sellars* (Cambridge, MA: Harvard University Press), 218.

25. Ibid.

26. Rorty, "Response to McDowell," 124.
27. Ibid.
28. Ibid., 125.
29. Brandom, "Vocabularies of Pragmatism," 166.
30. McDowell, *Mind and World*, 8.
31. Jeffrey Stout, "Radical Interpretation and Pragmatism: Davidson, Rorty, and Brandom on Truth" in *Radical Interpretation in Religion*, ed. by Nancy K. Frankenberry (Cambridge: Cambridge University Press, 2002), 50.
32. Brandom, "Vocabularies of Pragmatism," 166.
33. Richard Rorty, "Response to Brandom" in *Rorty and His Critics,* ed. Robert Brandom (MA: Blackwell Publishing, 2000), 187.
34. Brandom, "Vocabularies of Pragmatism," 181.
35. Ibid., 180.
36. Stout, "Radical Interpretation and Pragmatism," 51.
37. Ibid.
38. Richard Rorty, "Dewey between Hegel and Darwin" in *Rorty and Pragmatism: The Philosopher Responds to His Critics,* ed. Herman J. Saatkamp, Jr. (Nashville, TN: Nashville University Press, 1995), 7–8.
39. Ibid., 4–5.
40. Ibid.
41. Ibid., 7–8.
42. Ibid.
43. Donald Sherburne, "Whitehead, Categories, and the Completion of the Copernican Revolution," *The Monist*, Vol. 66 (July 1983), 376.
44. Whitehead, *Process and Reality*, 112.
45. Ibid.
46. Sherburne, "Whitehead, Categories," 376.
47. Ibid., 376–377.
48. Rorty does not deny that there are causal relations between thinking as a capacity and other entities. He just treats thinking itself, as internalize public discourse, as exhausted by rule-governed uniformities owing solely to social practices. For example, he writes, "To be sure, there is a causal continuity between experience as what Dewey calls 'a matter of functions and habits of what active adjustments and readjustments of coordination and activities', and thinking, but for that matter there is a causal continuity between nutrition and thinking. Such continuity does not require us to find a sort of proto-intentionality in the amoeba." ("Dewey between Hegel and Darwin," 7–8.)
49. Whitehead, *Process and Reality*, 175.
50. Ibid., 176.
51. Ibid., 176–177.
52. Ibid.
53. Brandom, "Vocabularies of Pragmatism," 181.
54. Donald Davidson, "The Method of Truth in Metaphysics," in *Inquiries into Truth and Interpretation* (Oxford, UK: Clarendon Press, 2001), 214.
55. Ibid., 199.

56. Richard Rorty, "Pragmatism, Davidson, and Truth," in *Objectivity, Relativism, and Truth* (Cambridge, UK: Cambridge University Press, 1991), 213–214.
57. Davidson, "The Method of Truth in Metaphysics," 214.
58. Stout, "Radical Interpretation and Pragmatism," 50.
59. Ibid., 50–51.

Chapter 4

The Aesthetics of Experience

INTRODUCTION

My aim here is to provide an in-depth analysis of the nature of perception and judgment, according to Whitehead's ontology. This analysis will stand in contrast to the prevailing account of perception and judgment in analytic philosophy of mind. I have already suggested various ways in which McDowell's commitment to a Kantian conception of judgment limits his attempts to reconnect mind and world. This chapter expands on this critique and develops Whitehead's detailed alternative.

A PROBLEMATIC ASSUMPTION

The conception of a judgment as the basic unit of awareness, while it has served as a springboard for analytic accounts of truth and reference such as Brandom's inferentialism, has limited the effectiveness of such projects. The difficulty of this idea becomes acute when we broach the question of the connection between judgments and intuitions. Recall from the previous chapter McDowell's point that Kant does not associate intuitions with the supposed immediate givens that figure into the classical empiricist depiction of "the framework of givenness." Intuitions, for Kant, are not episodes of sensory receptivity that could so much as operate independently of the understanding. Rather, intuitions, as they factor into the Transcendental Deduction, are episodes of sensory receptivity that are *already* structured by the understanding.

Recall also that, for McDowell, a problematic conception of freedom arises from such a claim. Indeed, if intuitions have the same logical structure as judgments, then in order for intuitions not to be confused, tacit exercises of freedom, we must make a distinction between the different modes in which we actualize conceptual capacities. In order to continue Kant's purported task of vindicating the "objective validity" of the categories, McDowell insists upon the ineliminable sense in which perceptions are not, so to speak, up to us. What we need, on McDowell's appraisal, is a notion of subjectivity or experience that makes room for the distinction between having conceptual capacities drawn into operation, and employing conceptual capacities in judgment. The former accounts for perception in a dominantly causal sense, and the latter accounts for reflection in the dominantly rational sense. It is only in this way, he purports, that we can make sense of our ability to confer or withhold endorsement of empirical observations—for instance, in the difference between "seeing that" something is the case and asserting its merely "seeming" to be the case.

Davidson's solution to the problem of the objectivity of our thought, as explored in the last chapter, maintained the sense in which the world impinges upon us. Yet, while not forthrightly rejecting the world of Peircean Secondness, he ceased to see any way to account for it. The result is that subjectivity and experience cease to have any means of employment, in which case we are forced to understand reference, truth, and "the robust sense of engaging external things" only in terms of our ways of speaking. Furthermore, the category of "experience" is sidelined because the only sense it conceivably could have is that of a "broker" for our in-touch-ness with the world. Davidson sees truth as relative to language, but he also sees language externalistically, as having an "unmediated touch with the familiar objects whose antics make our sentences and opinions true or false."[1] At this point, however, we begin to lose the distinction between intuitions and judgments. It seems to have suffered the same fate as the distinction between language and experience. As McDowell notes, it is precisely this coherentist frame of mind that made the Myth of the Given so tempting in the first place.

McDowell thinks of perceptual experience as having the conceptual form of a judgment, but as not yet an exercise of the understanding. A perceptual experience is a reflective opportunity to make a judgment. This opportunity arises because of the acquisition of mind through the initiation into a natural language.[2] In *Mind and World*, McDowell says that "the feature of language that really matters" is that it "serves as a repository of tradition, a store of historically accumulated wisdom about what is a reason for what." In this way, McDowell thinks that, in "being initiated into a language, a human being is introduced into something that already embodies putatively rational linkages between concepts, putatively constitutive of the layout of the space of reason, before she comes on the scene."[3] In "enjoying an experience," then, we receive *thinkable* content via our initiated conceptual capacity, and so become open "to manifest facts that *obtain anyway* and impress themselves on one's sensibility."[4] This point, according to McDowell, provides "all the external constraint we can reasonably want."[5] These facts can so impress themselves on us because meaning already shapes human life. Indeed, our linguistic practices are as much a part of our natural history as non-linguistic ones (a point that I will elaborate on in chapter 6).

How is it that we can reflect on the adequacy of concepts drawn into operation? How is it, in other words, that we can exercise freedom *even within* the constraints imposed by the conceptual norms available to us? What we need, according to McDowell, is the idea of norms *internal* to thought itself. This is how we can have constraint that can come from outside our thinking, "but not from outside what is thinkable."[6] Implied here is a shared structure between judgments and intuitions, meant to obviate the frame of mind that made it look as if mind could so much as be out of touch with the world. We need to downplay the connection between reason and freedom if we are to "avoid losing our grip on how exercises of concepts can constitute warranted judgments about the world."[7] This is how we avoid, in his terms, "rampant Platonism" and regain a sense of how our thinking can be accountable to the world.

Immediately, however, a problem arises, for not only does McDowell accept Kant's view that judgments are to be taken as the most basic unit of awareness, but McDowell makes the tandem assumption that propositions have the merely logical role of being the content of those judgments. This assumption limits McDowell's account, even after he has replaced "transcendentalism" with "naturalized Platonism." When one makes this tandem assumption, suddenly the very idea of being in touch with "reality" appears as the "confusion between relations of justification, which hold between propositions, and causal relations, which hold between events."[8] We need to be able to make sense of mind as intrinsically related to whatever is not mind.

If, as McDowell does, we attempt to elucidate the nature of thought through a picture of propositions as merely the content of judgments, then the idea of reality as such will continue to look like a creation of the relations of justification. The more promising approach, I think, is to think about how the exercises of conceptual capacities in the form of judgments could arise in the first place. This is to ask the question of what the world must be like in order for traditions of meaning, as exemplified by the natural languages (to which we are initiated in becoming "minded" in the way McDowell understands mindedness), could so much as get up and running in the first place. I argue that a Whiteheadian understanding of judgment as a complex form of feeling can offer critical resources for getting beyond these problematic assumptions.

Such an approach rejects the idea that judgments are primitive units of awareness, with the implication that awareness is first and foremost linguistic and conscious. In brief, Whitehead's approach is to take feeling (or "aesthetics") as the broader genus of which "judgment" and "belief" are a species. On this model, judgment is only one mode of concrete, internal relation to a proposition, and not all such relations involve consciousness. In what follows, I argue that Whitehead's aesthetic ontology can assist us in making sense of how it is that the thinking subject can "have" a world in view.

ONTOLOGICAL TOGETHERNESS

The assumption that judgments are the basic units of awareness presupposes three things: (1) that apart from concepts there is nothing to know, (2) that concepts are the sole possession of conscious thought, and (3) that subjectivity is constructive of objectivity via conceptual employment. These are the premises with which Whitehead takes issue.

Whitehead commends Kant for producing the general idea that an experience is the result of constructive functioning. On Whitehead's account, however, it is objectivity that constructs subjectivity. The problematic understanding of intuitions is rooted in what Whitehead calls Kant's "obsession" with the "mentality of intuition." Working with a bifurcated conception of mind, Kant assumes that consciousness is necessarily involved in intuition. Insofar as McDowell makes the same assumption, about the inseparability of intuitions and consciousness because of a fallacious picture of "conceptual space," his attempt to conceive of intuitions as gaining traction with the world through a passive operation of conceptual capacities will never be able to make sense of how judgment relates a knower to their actual world. I think that it is for this reason that the constructive aspects of his work remain so underwhelming.

Similar to the way that McDowell suspects Kant of taking intuitions as having the same "unity" or structure as do judgments, Whitehead suspects Kant of operating by the "suppressed premise" that "intuitions are never blind."[9] Limited by a tacit metaphysical assumption that spatialized mind, however, this premise remained suppressed. Whitehead's revised subjectivism positions us to understand the perspicuity of intuitions in terms of concrete forms of relation that differ only in degree from those constituting judgments. The key to understanding Whitehead's account is to see ontology as preceding epistemology. For example, we must understand what Whitehead means by "conceptuality" ontologically before we can understand how it relates to human cognition. Ontologically, for Whitehead, the conceptual is to possibility what the physical is to actuality. Epistemologically, then, our ability to consciously entertain possibilities exhibits a peculiar sort of freedom from established fact made possible by ontologically complex forms of relation constitutive of organisms capable of such cognitive capacities.

Insofar as Whitehead's ontology takes concrete relationships (what he terms "prehensions") as the only means of explanation, it follows that there must be different types of relationships or relational complexes generative of different phenomena. In other words, we must be able to explain the difference between the process constitutive of igneous rock and that of the carpenter's cabinetry designs. And we must be able to do this, per chapter 1, without invoking an ontological distinction between the sorts of things constituted by means of causal relations and the sorts of things constituted by rational relations; without, that is, the bifurcation of nature, and, therefore, without the sorts of Platonism about which McDowell worries.

One way in which Whitehead's metaphysics avoids such issues is through the distinction between formal and informal constitution. Keeping this distinction in mind will help readers resist unhelpful metaphysical pictures when interpreting what follows in this chapter. Whitehead wanted to account for how "possibility which transcends realized temporal matter of fact has a real relevance to the creative advance."[10] Matters of fact are "actual entities"— they make up the givenness of the past and are causally efficacious for the future. Possibilities are "eternal objects"—they exhibit the indeterminateness out of which determinateness occurs. Actual entities and eternal objects are only separate in their "formal constitutions," or for the purposes of analysis. Whitehead's system is emphatically not dualistic. Actual entities are the final real things. But while atomistic, his system is not one of vacuous actualities. Actual entities are internally related to one another in (relative) temporal successions, and the manners in which they become, or the qualities or characters they have and contribute to the future, exhibit the realization of some possibility. Informally, then, actual entities and eternal objects are mutually implicative. We never encounter them except as informally constituted—their interplay is Whitehead's way of accounting for the efficacy of both causality and purpose in the world. And he makes explicit this distinction between formal and informal constitution in order to maintain the difference between our ways of speaking for the purposes of metaphysical analysis and reality.

This chapter will demonstrate that we need not invoke a bifurcation of nature in order to maintain that our ways of speaking do not re-present ontological relations, even if we can make sense of truth according to a modified correspondence theory—a modification that will become clearer as we go. Whitehead took issue with the ways in which modern philosophy presumed the correspondence between subject-predicate linguistic formulations and particular-universal ontological ones. He eliminates the possibility of such a presumption by way of his Ontological Principle. He asserts: "no actual entity, then no reason."[11] Actual entities are the "final facts," the "final real things" that make up the world. "There is no going behind actual entities to find anything more real," Whitehead writes.[12] Unlike Aristotelian substance, however, these entities are event-based, described as "actual occasions" or "drops of experience" that are "complex and interdependent."[13] The only reasons for things are "to be found in the composite nature of definite actual entities," such that explanation can make no recourse but to past actual entities internally related to the event in question.

Events are constituted by means of relations converging to characterize a specific duration in space-time, such that to analyze an event is to analyze these relations. The most concrete way to analyze an event is in terms of these component elements, which will hereafter be referred to using Whitehead's term "prehensions." Whitehead's notion of prehensions seeks to correct the extremes in modern philosophy's dualistic ontology, which emphasized physical bodies, on the one hand, and mental substance, on the other. Between physical and mental, Whitehead writes, "the philosophy of organism endeavours to hold the balance more evenly."[14] What this means is that an event-based ontology, in which there is only one final real thing (actual entities), the physical and the mental are not two types of *things*, but two modes of relation.

Actual entities, unlike substances, have real togetherness. They "involve each other," Whitehead writes, "by reason of their prehensions of each other."[15] The real facts of togetherness of actual entities are called "nexus" (sing.) and "nexūs" (pl.). "The ultimate facts of immediate actual experience are actual entities, prehensions, and nexūs," he writes, "[a]ll else is, for our experience, derivative abstraction."[16] As I discussed in chapter 1, if we do not begin with ontological togetherness, we will never be able to achieve the epistemological togetherness that is necessary in order to rejoin propositions and judgments. This is the purpose of the actual entity.

The actual entity is how Whitehead makes sense how of concrete facts relate to one another in constitutive ways without compromising the sense in which they remain individual facts. Each fact participates in various forms in those that succeed it, but these forms of participation do not exhaust it, because it is itself a true individual. If this were not the case, then there would be no genuine novelty, no creative advance. The principle of process is that "the many become one, and are increased by one."[17] The process by which novel forms of concrete togetherness come to be constitutes the cosmic passage. Whitehead assigns the term "concrescence" to this process creative of new forms of ontological togetherness. Any attempt to analyze this process, either in terms of the concrete components or in terms of the general forms of their participation with one another, relies upon abstraction. Abstraction for the purpose of analysis is inevitable simply because of the nature of symbolic reference. It is useful for a certain purpose, but as a form of relation, it introduces other novel forms of togetherness capable of analysis. For this reason, Whitehead concludes, in relating to reality at the most concrete level, "[t]he sole appeal is to intuition."[18] Intuition is a technical term for Whitehead, and its meaning will become clearer after some discussion of the terms involved in its explication.

Whereas we ought to understand actual entities as the final real things, and prehensions as concrete facts of relatedness, Whitehead introduces, for the purposes of analysis, eternal objects as the forms of definiteness that facts can take. Remembering the corrective readings offered in chapter 1, eternal objects are not "real" in the sense of having independent existence—actual entities are the only real things, the only final realities. They are, however, the various forms of togetherness that real things have or can take, considered in abstraction from these specific determinations of fact. It is only because these forms are considered in abstraction from any particular duration within the spatiotemporal extension that Whitehead calls them "eternal" or "pure potentials." In other words, to call them "eternal" objects is not to attribute anything positive to them over and above temporal things; it is, rather, to take something away from them, namely, actuality. Their ontological status is one of demotion or privation, not reification. The actual entity is the *real* becoming of many potentialities, or the *becoming* real of many potentialities. Eternal objects themselves do not "become"; there can be no novel eternal objects. It would be a category mistake to claim otherwise.

PROPOSITIONS

Whitehead uses the term "propositions" to refer to potential matters of fact; that is, to refer to the *particular* forms of definiteness that may or could have occurred. They are specific determinations of fact that remain potential, and so lack both the generality of eternal objects and the determinateness of actual entities. Whitehead calls potential facts "propositions," because they take the form "X is p" in analysis. Unlike eternal object, propositions are not pure potentials, but specific ones concerning potential forms of novel togetherness of real things. Propositions are "the tales that perhaps might be told about particular actualities."[19] They, therefore, concern real potentials, which differ from pure potentials insofar as they are partly composed by the givenness of established fact or the actual world. Whereas an eternal object is devoid of all determination, and thereby devoid of actuality, a proposition is a *conditioned* indetermination, insofar as it is limited to the forms of togetherness that determinate matters of fact may take given the actual states of affairs. It is in this sense that Whitehead sometimes refers to propositions as "theories."[20] We are still not speaking epistemologically.

Propositions involve indeterminateness insofar as they concern potentials in the way of possible predicates, but they involve conditionedness insofar as they concern the potential of specific actualities, or what Whitehead calls the "logical subjects" of the proposition. The logical subjects play the role of "X" in "X is p"; they are the element of sheer givenness or established fact.

It is only because of the aesthetically given that propositions can become true or false—*not*, that is, with respect to conscious judgments, but only, so far, with respect to the determination of novel facts.[21] On this model, unlike on the logicist's model discussed in chapter 1 (of which Russell was expressive), we can make sense of the importance of not only true propositions, but also false ones. "The fact that propositions were first considered in connection with logic, and the moralistic preference for true propositions," writes Whitehead, "have obscured the role of propositions in the actual world."[22] The result has been that propositions have been treated as the accessories of judgments, so much so that some philosophers fail to properly distinguish the two at all.[23] F. H. Bradley, for instance, "does not mention 'propositions' in his Logic. He writes only of 'judgments'."[24] The role of propositions in the actual world exceeds the logical role, in which the "one function is to be judged as to their truth or falsehood."[25] On Whitehead's account, judgments are a species of the larger genus of propositional feelings, where "feelings" (or prehensions) are Whitehead's broader aesthetic substitute for the modern mentalistic treatment of judgment as something that the mind does at a remove from the world. To understand propositional prehension, more needs to be said on prehension as Whitehead's language for real togetherness.

The language of prehension stands to correct the dualism between "sensation" and "reflection" in modern philosophy broadly, particular as it is found in Locke and Hume. This dualism is the result of "two defects," according to Whitehead. The first defect is the confusion of an idea and consciousness of an idea (in Locke's sense); the second is the presumed relationship between the "impressions" of sensation and the "impressions" of reflection (in Hume's sense), where Whitehead reads "impression" as functionally synonymous with "ideas" in the case of both sensations and reflections. These defects contribute to the "sensationalist" doctrine of perception, which presumes that an actuality's awareness of another actuality depends upon the mediation of private sensations. The sensationalist doctrine entails the notion that emotional feelings are derivative from these private sensations. This doctrine bifurcates nature into primary and secondary qualities by way of an implicit theory of "psychic additions."[26]

Whitehead thinks this doctrine is empirically backward: "If we consider the matter physiologically, the emotional tone depends mainly on the condition of the viscera which are peculiarly ineffective in generating sensations."[27] Emotional feelings or "tones," according to Whitehead, are more primitive modes of real togetherness. Only in more sophisticated organisms does sensation "supervene with any effectiveness" upon this more primitive mode of togetherness.[28] Whitehead's term for this real togetherness is "objectification," by which he means that mode of participation in a subject qua object for feeling. Such feelings are, in turn, constitutive of the subject. These two modes of "direct mediation" with other actualities play a foundational role for any understanding of the possibility of perceptual knowledge in Whitehead's thought.

Temporality is central to the doctrine of prehension. Actualities are what they are because of how they prehend actualities in their immediate past. Actual entities are not Leibniz's "windowless monads."[29] It is only because Western philosophy has, for so long, operated upon substance-quality metaphysics that individuals could be thought of in exclusively spatial terms, such that they could be atomized without relation along a line of temporal succession. For such philosophical thinking, Whitehead argues, the relations between these individuals can only amount to "metaphysical nuisances."[30] Such has been the fate of intentional relations.

The doctrines of prehension and objectification are meant to give metaphysical interpretation to a suppressed principle by which Locke operates: that some sort of perception of "particular existents" is possible.[31] It is because of the influence this tacit principle has on Locke's philosophy that makes for his "metaphysical superiority" over Hume. Whitehead provides the following reading of Locke:

> He first (I, I, 8*) explains: "I have used it [i.e., idea] to express whatever is meant by phantasm, notion, species, or whatever it is which the mind can be employed about in thinking" But later (III, III, 6), without any explicit notice of the widening of use, he writes: "and ideas *become general* by separating from them the circumstances of time, and place, and any other ideas that may *determine them to this or that particular existence*." Here, for Locke, the operations of the mind originate from ideas "determined" to particular existents.[32]

Locke is not the only modern philosopher that Whitehead thinks demonstrates a suppressed premise of this sort, one that remains inconsistent with their wider philosophies of experience. Hume exhibits a similar inconsistency when he writes: "As to those *impressions*, which arise from the *senses*, their ultimate cause is, in my opinion, perfectly inexplicable by human reason, and it will always be impossible to decide with certainty, whether they arrive immediately from the object, or are produced by the creative power of the mind, or are derived from the Author of our being."[33] In each instance, Locke and Hume allow tacit affirmations of "the" object, even while neither of them can justify this demonstrative use. When Hume writes, "There is no object which implies the existence of any other, if we consider these objects in themselves, and never look beyond the ideas which we form of them,"[34]

Whitehead reads him as mingling an objectivist principle like Locke's about "the object" with one that expressly contradicts it, namely, the subjectivist principle derived from substance-quality metaphysics.

In the same way that, per chapter 1, Whitehead finds in Kant's "noumena" the ultimate consequence of spatializing mind, he also finds in Kant the ultimate expression of these conflicting premises. Explicitly, Kant presumed the mentality of "intuition" such that consciousness was always consciousness of ideas. This is why intuitions without concepts are "blind." But Kant's explicit principle is contradicted, Whitehead argues, by his own statement that "thoughts without intuitions are empty." What this statement implies, according to Whitehead, is that intuitions are, in fact, never blind.[35]

"'Actuality'," writes Whitehead, "is the fundamental exemplification of composition."[36] The actual entity is composed by its modes of real togetherness with other actualities. It is because actual entities are composites that Whitehead refers to the process of composition as a "concrescing," because it is a biological term for the coalescing or conjoining of what was formerly disjointed. This doctrine of actual entities is the inversion of the one to which Hume gave expression above, when he wrote that, considered "in themselves," objects never imply the existence of other objects.

On Whitehead's account, it is precisely because actuality is fundamentally compositional—is, in principle, real togetherness—that the notion of "a common world" makes any sense.[37] Just how an actuality exemplifies this common world, adding to it in the achievement of this exemplification, is what constitutes it as actual. The possible "hows" in this context are eternal objects qua potentials without respect to any particular determination of fact. Actual entities differ from one another—they are, in a genuine sense, individuals—because of how they realize potentials; "whatever component is red, might have been green, and whatever component is loved; might have been coldly esteemed."[38] Determination occurs by means of incompatible possibilities; something cannot be, in the same way, both red and green, both loved and unloved. There is a principle of limitation evidenced by actuality that must constitute the relations among pure potentials. Whitehead describes this principle ordering among pure potentials as a graded relevance of possibility.

Whitehead refuses to use the classical term "universals" for these modes of determination, because the term, indexed to substance-quality metaphysics, denies the real togetherness of the particulars to which they purportedly apply. Before Whitehead introduces his peculiar vernacular, however, he offers a description of how the old term "universals" might be employed in his revised sense. "Universals" are the terms in which the "definiteness" or determinateness of immediate experience is exhibited. "But such universals," he explains, "by their very character of universality, embody the potentiality of other facts with variant types of definiteness."[39] This is why what is the case always tells us something about what was and may be the case; it is the basis of the continuity of nature presupposed by inductive reasoning.

The ways in which actualities become determinate—the realization of particular relations to actualities in its immediate past—are what Whitehead means by the "ingression" of eternal objects. Ingression is emphatically *not* to be conceived as the transition from non-being into being of the (modernist) Platonic Idea; ingression is, rather, properly conceived as the "evocation of determination out of indetermination."[40] The language of evocation is intentional, because Whitehead is concerned to restore a proper balance between efficient and final causation. The creative advance, the passage of nature, is not the brute efficient causality of McDowell's "bald naturalism." Actual entities, the facts constitutive of the "common world," are not sufficiently explained simply by means of causal relation to the immediate past, but by purposive relation the facts. When temporality is written back into the account of ultimately real things—when individual facts cease to be billiard balls atomically strung together in a temporal extension that bears no internal relation to their constitution—coercion and force cease to be the only expressions of power in the world. Appetition becomes plausible as a mode of the self-determination of actualities.

It is only because of the relevance of pure potentials to actual subjects that appetition can enter the picture as a self-generating power. "Appetition is immediate matter of fact including in itself a principle of unrest, involving realization of what may or may not be," explains Whitehead.[41] Actualities, in their becoming or concrescing, are subjects—this is the broader sense of "experience," so far devoid of consciousness or self-consciousness. To experience is to be the subject prehending objects. All subjects become objects for novel subjects; become, that is, part of the givenness of the actual world: "Actuality in perishing acquires objectivity, while it loses subjective immediacy. It loses the final causation which is its internal principle of unrest, and it acquires efficient causation whereby it is a ground of obligation characterizing the creativity."[42] Efficient causation entails the notion of givenness or determinateness, and such givenness is a requisite of the passage of nature. The logical counter-requisite, however, is the element of *un*rest, the indeterminate that is nevertheless in relation to the actual.

Prehension is an activity, an actualizing. It is not, thereby, something that happens to a subject, but that by which a subject "effects its own concretion of other things."[43] The notion of prehension means that consciousness presupposes experience, but experience does not presuppose consciousness.[44] It thereby resists the "two defects" of Locke and Hume identified earlier, as well as Kant's mentalization of intuition—all of which owe to the spatialization of mind by way of substance-quality metaphysics (per the misreading of Plato and the misappropriation of Aristotle).

So far, however, I have only spoken of past actual entities as possible objects of prehension. Prehensions of past actual entities are termed "physical prehension," where physicality indicates those given elements of the actual world that enter into the physical sciences. Physicality stands in creative contrast with what is indeterminate, thus far referred to as pure potentiality or eternal (because unconditioned by any *particular* terms of exemplification) objects. The element of indeterminateness, unrest, and appetition involved in the composition of an actual entity is termed, in contrast to physicality, "mentality." Whitehead has not reintroduced an ontological dualism here; he has merely reappropriated the formerly dichotomous terms as co-constituents of novel facts. The distinction between formal and informal constitution should be kept in mind.

We need more than physical prehension to account for appetition, because appetition is the yearning for the realization of something not yet realized. The object of yearning is related to by "conceptual" prehension. Conceptual prehensions are "the basic operations of mentality," considered in its formal or "pure" constitution.[45] Informally, however, physical and mental prehensions are "impure" in the sense of being integrated with one another; for instance, "thirst is an immediate physical feeling integrated with the conceptual prehension of its quenching."[46] We return here to propositions, because propositions are those entities forming the datum of an integrated or "impure" physico-mental prehension. As entities, however, they aren't in any place or at any time. This is the wrong way to speak of them. They are nothing other than the datum of a specific form of prehension, together only by means of that prehension, with all the particularity of its time and place.

Physical feelings, on the one hand, introduce no significant novelty. Pure conceptual feelings, on the other hand, do not involve the determination of new facts. But if our goal is to make sense of the sorts of experience like conscious awareness, no account will be complete if it is based solely upon efficient causality or all-determining laws of nature, because error and confusion have no place in such a scheme. The possibility of error or confusion presupposes an element of freedom, and this freedom Whitehead accounts for in terms of aesthetic abstraction.

Conscious awareness is neither perception without interpretation (purely physical), nor perception of the absolutely indeterminate without respect to any particular fact (purely conceptual). The possibility of being "correct" or "incorrect" in conscious perception or judgments requires a different type of entity to be the object of a subject's prehension. This is because truth and falsehood "are always grounded upon a *reason*," (italics mine) and, per the Ontological Principle, actual entities are the only reasons. Eternal objects, in being devoid of all determinacy, cannot be reasons—something isn't red because of redness; something is red because its mode of relation to other real things exhibits redness. But the possibility of *falseness* also means a conscious judgment cannot take the purely determinate (physical) as its object. The possibility of truth or falsehood requires a third entity, other than actual entities or eternal objects, which entails an element of determinateness (some particular actuality or "logical subject") and an element of indeterminacy (something predicated of that subject). These are propositions.

Propositions function beyond the role as objects of conscious judgments. They must be understood ontologically before they can have any meaning epistemologically. The truth of a proposition depends upon the actual world being qualified in the way indicated by the predicate, and, therefore, on a relation involving some degree of conformity, not of substance, but of feeling. For a propositional feeling *qua* integrated physico-conceptual feeling, the objective datum involves, on the one hand, a determinate set of actual entities "indicated by their felt physical relations to the subject of the feeling," and on the other, a potentiality conditioned or restricted by those actual entities constituting the logical subject(s).[47] "The proposition," writes Whitehead, "is the possibility of *that* predicate applying in that assigned way to *those* logical subjects."[48] A proposition can be prehended by a subject in varying ways, only one of which constitutes a judgment of truth or falsity; the judging subject of a proposition is a subset of the prehending subject. In a summary statement of the nature of a proposition, Whitehead writes:

> A proposition shares with an eternal object the character of indeterminateness, in that both are definite potentialities *for* actuality with undetermined realization *in* actuality. But they differ in that an eternal object refers to actuality with absolute generality, whereas a proposition refers to indicated logical subjects. Truth and falsehood always require some element of sheer givenness. Eternal objects cannot demonstrate what they are except in some given fact. The logical subjects of a proposition supply the element of givenness requisite for truth and falsehood.[49]

Because propositions involve logical subjects, and require just those actual entities constituting the logical subjects in order to be *that* proposition, a proposition cannot be prehended by an actual entity (or nexus) if its actual world (its constitutive relations) does not include those logical subjects.[50] Harriet Tubman could not feel the proposition "Barack Hussein Obama was the 44th President of the United States of America" because Barack Obama, as a logical subject, was not part of her actual world. By contrast, Tubman could feel the proposition "Abraham Lincoln was the 16th President of the United States of America," but her subjective form of this propositional feeling may have been one of affirmation, negation, or indifference. Whereas the proposition is true, it is how she relates to it that renders its truth or falsehood significant—that is, efficacious—for the world. The efficacy of this relation could not be explained by an analysis of propositions in purely logical terms.

What this aesthetic reappropriation of classically epistemological terms affords us in the way of analysis is the ability to depict propositions, intuitions, and judgments in ontological terms prior to any epistemological problems. This move is in keeping with Whitehead's conviction that the concrete must explain the abstract, and not vice versa. Insofar as aesthetic relations are the most concrete, Whitehead relies upon them to explain how we get logical ones. Rationality is a subdivision of aesthetics. What this means is that we must be able to explain rationality in terms of aesthetics, the latter being the more concrete. When we attempt this, however, we are dealing at a higher level of abstraction and, therefore, lose an element of exactness. "Language," writes Whitehead, "is always ambiguous as to the exact proposition which it indicates." He continues, "Spoken language is merely a series of squeaks."[51]

Inverting the approach of much modern and analytic philosophy, therefore, Whitehead insists that perception and judgment, qua varieties of propositional prehensions, require concrete aesthetic description as a precursor to logical description. Furthermore, as a precursor to accounting for the types of experience we specify with language, we need something capable of consciously "taking account" of the world.

ORDER AND ORGANISM

Organisms emerge through the complexity of a certain type of order among groups of actual entities, what Whitehead calls a "personally ordered society." We ought not conceive this "group" as a unit in space alone, because since actual entities are what they are by how they prehend preceding actualities, there can be no internal relation to exact contemporaries. Contemporaries can be related only genetically. This means that to be a group of actual entities that functions *organismically*, the personal order obtains spatiotemporally. This is why Whitehead refers to organisms as "enduring objects with personal order," and refers to the prehended objects constitutive of this society as its "historic route."[52] Enduring objects *without* personal order would be aggregate actualities that do not function organismically, namely, inorganic things.

"Order" is a technical term. It is differentiated from mere "givenness." Actual entities and nexūs attain various measures of order out of their actual world (where "actual world" is also a technical—and relative—term, meaning those past actual entities serving as the subject's objective datum). Order exhibits givenness adapted for the "attainment of an end."[53] The attainment of this end is the exhibited order. Biological order, for instance, exhibits the means for the attainment of an aim specific to that individual. "It is notable," writes Whitehead, "that no biological science has been able to express itself apart from phraseology which is meaningless unless it refers to ideals proper to the organism in question."[54] This is different than saying that there is some "ideal" cow to which all cows biologically aspire. Such a claim falls back upon classical notions: "The notion of one ideal arises from the disastrous overmoralization of thought under the influence of fanaticism, or pedantry. The notion of a dominant ideal peculiar to each actual entity is Platonic," where "Platonic" means the Plato of Taylor and Whitehead.[55] The dominant aim or ideal of an actual entity or nexus is what makes it an ordered thing, something that makes it subjectively unified, rather than a chaotic collection of things.

The degree of order within a society is equivalent to the degree to which it is capable of self-sustenance, where something is self-sustaining if it can provide its own grounds for endurance. This counts as "self"-sustenance insofar as the sustenance derives from a "personally" ordered society of actual entities. A society is different from a class because "order" here means something more than it does in mathematics; a society is a group of actual entities, all of to whom a particular class-name applies "by reason of genetic derivation from other members of that same society."[56] The societal nature of each member has to do, in short, with the fact that they serve as the conditions, the reasons or objective datum, for the likeness of future members. What makes my life *mine*, for example, is the fact that my dominant datum for experience in this moment derives from the datum a moment prior to that, and so on along "my" historic route until the organic order necessary to sustain consciousness diminishes to a negligible amount. The point at which this negligible amount is reached is what is at stake in any definition of "life" or "death."

Order is always achieved in greater or lesser degrees of intensity. "Perfection," when applied to actual order, can, therefore, only be a category mistake. It either implies a moralization of order or it implies a classical notion of staticity, which can only mean out of relation and, therefore, incapable of change. Societies are no more vacuous actualities than anything else in Whitehead's metaphysics and, indeed, there are societies within societies. It is the nature of an environment to be a larger society.[57]

The relations between societies have social, rather than personal, order. What constitutes the "order of nature" or "physical laws" has to do with the characteristics applicable to all actual entities forming the "cosmic epoch"[58]—the most general characteristics attributable to the ordering and disordering of societies. For example,

> This epoch is characterized by electronic and protonic actual entities, and by yet more ultimate actual entities which can be dimly discerned in the quanta of energy.... [E]ach electron is a society of electronic occasions, and each proton

is a society of protonic occasions. These occasions are the reasons for the electromagnetic laws; but their capacity for reproduction, whereby each electron and each proton has a long life, and whereby new electrons and new protons come into being, is itself due to these same laws.[59]

What these laws are at any moment is arbitrary, whether they are those of electromagnetism, the dimensionality and measurability of the spatiotemporal continuum, geometrical axioms, and so on. And they could be otherwise, as the presence of disorder or chaos indicates. "Thus a system of laws determining reproduction in some portion of the universe," writes Whitehead, "gradually rises into dominance; it has its stage of endurance, and passes out of existence with the decay of the society from which it emanates."[60] There is disorder to the extent that there are failures of reproduction, whereby new types of order gradually emerge to dominate older ones. Disorder is, thus, a term of nonrelation or, better, privation; there is disorder when the dominant characteristics of the societies in question exercise a trivial degree of influence upon one another.[61] In this case, those "disordered" societies contribute nothing to the general characteristics of a cosmic epoch making up natural law or the order of nature.

The reason why those philosophies against which Whitehead pits his own conceived of "natural laws" without sufficient appreciation of contingency is because they understood extensiveness in terms of spatiality alone. Whitehead, whose concern was always the *applied* nature of mathematics, was able to indicate the ways in which the logical and mathematical investigations of the eighteenth and nineteenth centuries were relevant to philosophy, in the way "the cosmological theories of Descartes, Newton, Locke, Hume, and Kant" were unable to do. He argues that, in fact, the Plato of the *Timaeus* "seems to be more aware of [this significance] than any of his successors, in the sense that he frames statements whose meaning is elucidated by its explicit recognition."[62] That is to say, on Whitehead's (and Taylor's) reading, Plato's cosmology is such that it is helped, not hindered, by these new discoveries.

Having been uninfluenced by Semitic ideas of absolute transcendence, Plato's *Timaeus* is more metaphysically sound than Newton's *Scholium,* Whitehead purports, insofar as Newton's cosmology was predicated upon a concept of the world as "externally designed" and "obedient," and, therefore, provided no hint of the limits of its own applicability. For Newton, "nature is merely, and completely, *there.*"[63] Consequently, there was no room for nature *naturing.* Despite its naïvete when read as a statement of scientific exactness, the *Timaeus* at least lends itself to an allegorical reading open to notions of self-production and the sociality of order. "The full sweep of the modern doctrine of evolution," Whitehead says, "would have confused the Newton of the *Scholium*, but would have enlightened the Plato of the *Timaeus*."[64] Order is a product of sociality, emerging from the ground up; it is not a product of cosmic coercion or divine fiat. Modern science expresses its understanding of the social nature of order in terms of genetics and statistics.[65]

Organisms capable of perception exhibit a more complex social order than those that are merely reactive to an environment. Water molecules excite with changes of barometric pressure. We can appropriately speak of melting ice as a reaction insofar as the events involved can be characterized by the physical transference of energy throughout a given environment. When a cedar stump rots, however, the event may be considered not merely reactive but, in some sense, *motivated,* because it is the effect of the metabolic process of a type of multi-celled organism whose dominant characteristic is its growing by decomposing other things. Growing fungi exhibit the workings of more complex social order than does melting ice. The gestation of a human fetus is more complex yet, involving the personal ordering of innumerable subordinate societies called "living cells" that interrelate so as to support an enduring personal order that we can eventually identify as "me" or "you." Billions of human organisms have exercised greater degrees of freedom from mere physical inheritance, like the reaction of the water molecules, and such exercises have significantly altered the character of the world, such that we have come to describe this geologic age as the Anthropocene.

We must resist the temptation to think of freedom as floating in from beyond real relations with actual entities—it does not. The freedom to realize potential is never absolute; actualizable potential can only be real potential, or potential by reason of other actual things. Actual entities are the only reasons, which means that the character of a subject depends entirely upon the objects that constitute its datum. "[W]hatever be the freedom of feeling arising in the concrescence," Whitehead reminds us, "there can be no transgression of the limitations of capacity inherent in the datum. The datum both limits and supplies."[66] There are no ontological breaks, no hard-and-fast divisions; all categories of existence are mutually implicative for Whitehead. There are, however, watershed moments—occasions of terminal velocities and critical capacities that issue in the intensification or attenuation of types of social order. Intensifications of social order can create novel entities, whereby a community of individuals creates something beyond the sum of its parts. The primary way to analyze these processes is in terms of the most concrete relations of which we can speak, which are aesthetic ones for Whitehead.

Whitehead thereby relies on aesthetic relations to inform how we understand epistemological ones. He analyzes the creative advance or cosmic passage—the one from reactions of water molecules to technological innovations of human collaboration—in terms of various and multitudinous prehensive phases constituting the extensive continuum of events.[67] Physical relations to other actual entities dominate the coalescence of simpler actual occasions, which means that their inheritance from the past is aesthetically more direct.

Directness of prehension should be understood, as Whitehead uses it, in terms of the vector-theory of physics, rather than in terms of modern epistemology and the problematic "Given." When A directly perceives B, A receives from B a definite transfer of energy—or, rather, the transfer of energy *is* the nature of perceiving. The transfer is the objectification of the past in the subject, and this objectification, when direct, counts as a low-grade perception from the point of view of a subject. A direct perception, as the simplest form of perception, is more of a reception. The degree of receptivity is proportional to the degree of directness. What A receives from B is a "quantitative emotional intensity."[68] The quality of this energy, apart from its sheer quantity, is termed the "specific form of feeling." This specific form, the qualitative aspect of this reception, is the subjective element of this occasion. In physics, a transfer of energy is not exhaustively described only in scalar terms, which are akin to the quantity of energy. What a full description requires in addition is the quality of the transfer, or a description in terms of its being a vector. I have not told you very much about a race if I say that the winner ran 17 miles—so did everyone who finished. What you really want to know is how fast she ran—say, 17 miles in 2 hours and 49 minutes. Saying that the winner averaged a six-minute mile, and that that was the fastest of any other average achieved in relevant proximity, describes the nature of a race in a way that the sheer distance does not. Speed entails distance in a way that distance does not entail speed. The speed is analogous to the subjective form; it is the full measure of energy from the point of view of the subject. The runner experiences speed; she does not experience 17 miles separately from the 2 hours and 49 minutes. In aesthetic terms, the subjective form is how the experience feels the datum at the most concrete level. It is what Whitehead calls "sensa." Sensa are forms of subjective experience or emotion, in the technical sense of the specific quality of agitation or excitement of a subject. When Whitehead describes actual entities as vector-like, he means to correct the scalar descriptions of experience prevalent in thinkers like Locke and Hume, whose metaphysics denied actualities the real togetherness necessary to account for the objective elements of perception.

The interpreter of Whitehead must appreciate the technicality of his vocabulary, for he is not approaching the subject of perception and judgment in modern epistemological terms that treat sense perception as a primitive mode of experience, but as a mathematician and theoretical physicist for whom sense perception is a highly complex phenomenon. This is how he intends to correct the "two defects" found in Locke and Hume that arise from the conflation of ideas and impressions with consciousness. One consequence of this conflation is not only the "mentalization" of intuition, discussed earlier, but also of emotion. Considered apart from the dualism of substance-quality metaphysics, however, emotions are not fuzzy psychological phenomena, but are the specific forms of excitation resulting from the real relatedness (prehension) between actual things. As such, they are entirely independent from consciousness.

Translated into the language of Lockean epistemology, Whitehead's account of direct perception "describes how the ideas of particular existents are absorbed into the subjectivity of the percipient and are the datum for its experience of the external world."[69] Here we understand "ideas" as earlier characterized, without the dualism between sensation and reflection. Whitehead critiqued Locke's confusion of an "idea" with "consciousness of an idea," and Hume's dichotomy of "impressions of sensation" and "impressions of reflection." Whitehead's theory of prehension dissolved this dichotomy, analyzing experience in terms of two phases of perception: the first, sense-reception; the second, sense-perception. When sensa are perceived rather than received, the element of directness is lost, and this introduces the possibility of error. This loss of directness manifests in several ways, the initial way being in terms of his "Category of Conceptual Reversion."

Conceptual reversion is a technical term for what might be simplistically described as a feeling of a feeling. When A directly perceives B, A receives a definite transmission of energy or emotional intensity. How this definite transmission is received is the "specific form of feeling" and this form is, as above, the subjective form of the transmission. Since Whitehead is accustomed to speak of these forms, potential before realized, as "eternal" objects, which are the objects of "conceptual" (because not physical-qua-actual) prehension, he is inclined to describe direct perception (or sense-*reception*) in terms of a direct reproduction of form. This is his "Category of Conceptual Valuation," appropriately understood as the category of conceptual reproduction. Conceptual reversion is indexed to this prior category. Whereas the direct reproduction of form constitutes endurance, a reversion alters this direct inheritance, introducing novelty. Whereas a rock endures for a time as a self-same entity of varying degrees, something is living when it is capable of novel responses to established fact. When some measure of an organism's response is "inexplicable by *any* [that is, to any one] tradition of pure physical inheritance," to that degree the organism is "alive."[70] To be alive is to be capable of originating, to some degree, one's response to the past. This origination is an introduction of novelty, or something nonactual, into actuality, and thereby qualifies in Whitehead's vocabulary as a conceptual feeling, but this time, it is a conceptual feeling responding to the form of a direct perception, and is therefore a sort of reversion.

The degree to which conceptual reversion is possible for an organism is the degree to which novelty is possible. More simply, the degree to which an organism's responses are indeterminate is the degree to which that organism is alive. The human standard for such indetermination or freedom is the capacity for imagination. Imaginative freedom can never be absolute, because an actual entity or society only possesses freedom of conceptual production to the extent inherent to the real potentiality available to it by way of the relations constitutive of its actual world. There are no absolutes for Whitehead, because his aesthetic ontology prohibits vacuous actualities that lack real relatedness; absolute could only mean absolutely relative. Freedom is, therefore, a term of relation that presupposes others and stands with them in terms of mutual limitation. Freedom is freedom from something given and freedom for some conditioned range of potentiality.[71] The human standard for such freedom is exhibited most intensely by means of our intellectual capacities.

CONSCIOUSNESS AND THE POWER OF ABSTRACTION

So far I have considered how Whitehead accounts for the real relatedness of an actual entity to its actual world, how this relatedness involves objectification and subjective experience, and how groups of actual entities achieve varying degrees of order. None of these things is enough to give us an account of the type of complex sociality of things capable of explaining consciousness.

Whitehead does not equate mentality with consciousness. The former is a fundamental aspect of all becoming; the latter depends upon prior phases of experience and arises only at a sufficiently high degree of abstraction to produce a unified sense of things. The real relatedness capable of such abstraction occurs through a process Whitehead calls "transmutation." "Transmutation," Whitehead explains, "is the way in which the actual world is felt as a community, and is so felt in virtue of its prevalent order."[72] When we are conscious of the world, we are not conscious of every event constituting each cell of our body and its relevant environment. Rather, when we are conscious of the world, we are so by attending to it propositionally—that is, in terms of a determinate set of actualities characterized (rightly or wrongly) in a particular way. In short, consciousness depends on *some* quantity with *some* quality. This focus of the many into one occurs when the simple physical feelings for many actualities become a single complex physical feeling of a nexus in terms of what unites rather than what differentiates its members.[73] Whitehead introduces this new category of existence—the transmuted feeling—to account for how this derivative feeling of a nexus functions as a novel (more complex) entity. Without the new category, the communal feeling would amount to nothing more than the sum of its components, and would be counted as inefficacious in the world. This was precisely what Whitehead took to be Leibniz's problem in the *Monadology*.

A transmuted feeling arises by reason of the "analogies" between the members of a particular group of actualities. "Analogy" is another technical term for Whitehead, as it here describes an ontological reality rather than linguistic device. It describes the shared character of experience between constituents of a group that, once isolated from their discrepancies, amounts to something like a dominant characteristic or quality of the group. The analogies are felt by means of a conceptual prehension; that is, in terms of the single eternal object or quality exhibited by each of the members conjointly. If the multiple simple physical feelings amounted only into a single complex physical feeling, this would merely be an instance of causal efficacy involving no transmutation, and no new category of existence would be necessary.

A transmuted feeling, however, is a single direct feeling by a nexus-qua-subject of the analogy among its constituents. The constituents are analogous insofar as they exemplify the same eternal object, and thus share a quality of determinateness. The emergence out of multiplicity of one dominant conceptual feeling with adequate intensity to constitute a new entity is the occurrence of transmutation. This transmuted feeling of the nexus introduces novelty; the novelty is a new subject which prehends the nexus in a single physical feeling that takes the mutually exemplified eternal object as its datum. A transmuted feeling is thereby a "definite physical fact."[74] It is a new actual occasion of greater complexity and intensity of experience. A novel subject achieves this greater intensity by aesthetic emphasis upon similarity and elimination of discord, such that the novelty is at once dependent upon real relatedness and abstraction—it is a concrete abstraction.

Those aspects emphasized in a transmuted feeling constitutive of a subject are ontologically amplified in the novel entity. Whitehead calls this process, whereby there is analogy between the objective data and the subjective form of a physical prehension, "adversion." He contrasts it (somewhat confusingly) with "aversion," which is the process whereby the intensity of certain aspects in the objective data is attenuated.[75] Adversion and aversion are types of decision, ways in which a subject becomes actual by foreclosing certain possibilities about how it could have become, how it could have prehended the objective datum of its immediate past. Adversion and aversion are determined by how the subject prehends and are, therefore, determined by the conditioned freedom available to (or constitutive of) the subject. There is such an availability because of the real relatedness of a graduated range of eternal objects—the real potential—that the subject conceptually prehends.[76] This conceptual feeling may be properly understood as the subject's purposiveness, insofar as it is the decision that will be causally efficacious for future subjects taking it as their objective datum.[77] (Whitehead calls this aspect of an emergent actual entity, the aspect that has instrumental value, the superjective nature. All subjects are really subject-superjects. "Superjection" is an antiquated term deriving from the Latin superiectiō. Whitehead uses it to speak of the character of a subject that has relevance beyond itself, becoming part of the causally efficacious past. Superjection is the subjective form of a subject becoming object, but prior to objectification, at which point its subjectivity gives way to "objective immortality."[78])

Adversion, aversion, and transmutation are only important for high-grade organisms. For the same reason, they provide the conditions for "intellectual" mentality (Whitehead also calls this "intellectuality"), which is the sort of mentality that can support consciousness (though it need not do so). For our purposes, it is important to notice that this approach to intellectuality "consists in the gain of a power of abstraction."[79] Whitehead explains with unusual clarity:

> The irrelevant multiplicity of detail is eliminated, and emphasis is laid on the elements of systematic order in the actual world. In so far as there is trivial order, there must be trivialized actual entities. The right coordination of the negative prehensions [aversions] is one secret of mental progress; but unless some systematic scheme of relatedness characterizes the environment, there will be nothing left whereby to constitute vivid prehension of the world.[80]

Vividness is the product of emphasis, where emphasis is the dominant relevance that a multiplicity has for the future; dominant because order is relevant in a way that disorder in principle is not. Whitehead continues to illustrate the nature of emphasis in terms of physical energy:

> The low-grade organism is merely the summation of the forms of energy which flow in upon it in all their multiplicity of detail. It receives, and it transmits; but it fails to simplify into intelligible system. The physical theory of the structural flow of energy has to do with the transmission of physical feelings from individual actuality to individual actuality. Thus some sort of quantum theory in physics, relevant to the existing type of cosmic order, is to be expected. The physical theory of alternative forms of energy, and of the transformation from one form to another form, ultimately depends upon transmission conditioned by some exemplification of the Categories of Transmutation and Reversion.[81]

In physics, energy is the capacity for doing work. It can exist in many forms: potential, kinetic, thermal, electrical, chemical, nuclear, and so on. This is to what Whitehead is referring when he names the "physical theory of alternative forms of energy." The "transformation from one form to another" can either be one of "transmutation" or "reversion," by which I take him to be giving metaphysical expression to the physical theory of energy in the process of transfer from state to state, or "body to body." "Energy" is not itself "a thing"; it is the work done between actual occasions. Thermal energy is what we call transferred heat. Whitehead generalizes this transfer in terms of prehension, where "heat" exhibits the emotional tone of the subject—how it "feels" the object in simple physical prehensions. Emotional tone is not to be read as "qualia"; not only are we not yet talking about consciousness, but we are rejecting the picture of subjecthood that describes "private experiences" in this way. Prehension is more like radiance than the handoff of an object. Emotional tone is how the object radiates by some particular account, or how a subject objectifies it. The radiant-ness is akin to the superjective nature of the now-objectified occasion.

When there is a simple, physical, direct transfer of emotional tone, this is sense *re*ception. For the passage to involve sense *per*ception, the transfer must be more complex. What this complexity affords is greater vividness, and what it costs is directness. Sense perception differs from sense reception in that it involves aesthetic emphasis upon the systematic elements of the world and the disregard of chaotic ones. Again, this "emphasis" and "disregard" are not mysterious; they are concrete forms of relation, partially analogous to the varieties of forms of energy in physical theory. The limits of the analogy has to do with the sorts of phenomena which the physical sciences are methodically designed to exhibit, and the ways in which the history of science relies upon tacit metaphysical assumptions about matter and form—assumptions significantly challenged by quantum theory. Whitehead's actual entities are more like "quanta" than billiard balls, but involve not only quanta but quanta-qualia. "Qualia" in this sense entails a very different metaphysics of experience than it does for its more standard uses in Western philosophy of experience.

Just as a theory based on quanta instead of substances entails degrees of indeterminism for which classical notions of efficient causality cannot account, Whitehead's description of the phases of experience are intended to do justice to the degrees of indeterminacy involved in the creative passage. He does so without bifurcating nature or introducing ontological dualisms. For Whitehead, sense perception or experience "in the mode of presentational immediacy" (for which causal efficacy in the mode of sense reception is ingredient) remains a mode of real relatedness to the world, albeit one that loses some element of directness to the facts by virtue of enabling discrete attention. Indirectness, however, is emphatically *not* synonymous with out-of-relation; it is a different form of relation that involves emphasis by way of disregarding "irrelevant" detail.

Narrowness of attention is the condition of the sort of awareness we would count as consciousness. This is why Whitehead can say that the negative prehension, the ability to disregard the chaotic elements of an environment, is an achievement of understanding, or making intelligible. "Triviality," he writes, "arises from excess of incompatible differentiation."[82] The differences among the actual entities of the nexus, pushed into irrelevance, constitutes the vague background against which a dominant characteristic (or an intensity of quality or forms of energy) can be communally reinforced; "By reason of vagueness, many count as one."[83] Vagueness is the cost of narrowness; the price of consciousness is a loss of directness. But what narrowness achieves is an abstracted simplicity—what Whitehead calls, again technically, a "massive simplicity"—that makes intelligibility possible. Without abstraction by way of transmuted feelings, what we commonly refer to as "mind" would not be possible, where "mind" is not a separate thing, but a process or mode of relativity achieved by a personally ordered society of actual occasions, or a community of atomic parts, living cells, organs, body, microbiome, ambient environment, and so on. "Mind" is the form of relation acquired by certain elements in this bodily society, which can be achieved to greater and lesser extents, as in the case of gestational, sleeping, or traumatized states, among others.

In sum, Whitehead characterizes the possibility of consciousness in terms of the possibility of deriving more abstract and unified feelings out of simpler, more disparate ones. This is where the Categories of Conceptual Valuation (Reproduction) and Reversion (Diversity) enter into the Category of Transmutation. Consciousness is decisive and evaluative; it filters out trivial detail and focuses by attending to specific forms of determination that are felt as important. "Importance" should be understood also in technical terms as "being of consequence" as much in terms of "importing" as "importance."

Transmutation of feeling is how Whitehead describes the way in which a unified feeling can be abstracted from a community of somewhat identical and somewhat disparate experiences. Aesthetic abstraction is elimination of difference through the emphasis upon a dominant characteristic within a community. It is only by way of transmutation that our intellectual capacities operate (or, rather, transmutation is an intellectual operation), because transmutation makes generality possible in a concrete sense, and this is the very generality entailed in the pragmatics of "meaning."

FROM GIVEN TO NOVEL SENSA

Whitehead's aesthetics of experience provides a way to account for how the givenness of history gives way, so to speak, to novelty. It does not give way eventually, but on every occasion, to great and lesser degrees. What is necessary for our ability to entertain ordinary propositions like "The air is thin" or "The sky is grey" is the concrete (as opposed to classically epistemological) discrimination of details, such that some details of ontological relevance are intensified and others are diminished. This intensification and this diminishment are not mystical; they are the creative interplay between established facts and real potentials. Established fact both "limits and supplies." There is nowhere else for potential to "be" except among actual entities. The individual essence of an actual entity just is its relational essence, and vice versa, but in order for this to be the case, the two must never be conflated. The many do not only become one, but they are increased by one—this is Whitehead's Principle of Process. The "one" by which the many are increased differs functionally from the "one" that becomes of the many. This is why there is a difference between an ordered community and a disordered one; the former is creative, and the latter is mere chaotic proximity.

Whitehead insists that order and chaos presuppose one another as metaphysical principles, as do vagueness and clarity. He thinks we can only epistemologically discriminate between relevant and irrelevant detail, such as to see a "grey sky," if we have for the occasion ignored all other possible loci of attention. The ignored data forms the vague background of irrelevant detail or "massive uniformity" against which positively prehended data come to the fore. This "coming to the fore" is explained in terms of the concrete emergence of "transmuted feelings." It is only when the ordered relations among a particular group of actual entities is adequately complex and patterned that communal characteristics can be felt with adequate intensity to occasion a "sense" of a broader range of relations—a larger "world," the world of a person as opposed to a cell.

The responsiveness to the past exhibited by a person involves a great deal of sense reception by way of the endurance of form (what Whitehead calls conceptual reproduction). This endurance is the basic conformity of the body from one occasion to the next, such that it counts as an enduring object. But the rock has this, too. What the person has in addition is the adequate complexity of pattern to support a higher stage of experience, which is sense perception or indirect perception. This indirectness enables greater discrimination of detail, and, therefore, broader forms of taking account of one's environment. It is how we get from William James's "blooming buzzing confusion" to the "grey sky." The "blooming buzzing confusion" is the non-discriminating reception of all real relations; the "grey sky" is the achievement of abstraction, whereby some real relations contribute a "general character" capable of serving as a datum in itself (the one that becomes of the many) for a novel, more complex entity (the one that increases the many). This latter "one" becomes the possibility of a novel, as opposed to merely given, sensum.

This sensum is novel rather than given because there has been a decision about which details ought to be relevant and which ought to be trivial. "Decision" does not imply consciousness, but has a technical definition for Whitehead's aesthetic ontology. It is a "cutting off" or decisiveness that is not fully determined by the past. There can be no decision when there is no diversity of possibility. The indeterminism of decision means that we cannot explain it in terms of classical notions of efficient cause. Whitehead attributes it, rather, to an element of "appetition." Indeed, one cannot account for the growth of an organism strictly in terms of the limitations imposed by the past; one also needs a principle of unrest luring toward the future in the form of an ideal aim—"ideal" only in the sense of non-actual, not in any moral sense.

Whitehead calls the novel sensum created by a community exhibiting a general character a "contrast." Specifically, it is "the nexus, as one, in contrast with the eternal object" constituting its general character.[84] The key point here is that generality of character does not mean, for Whitehead, a single universal predicated of many particular substances. In classical metaphysics, the universal is only ever externally related to the particular, while the particular is internally related to the universal. On the classical model, the horizon at dawn is crimson, but crimson is what it is regardless of what it characterizes. One cannot simply substitute eternal objects for universals in the foregoing, because an eternal object is only conceivable qua exhibited by relata, and therefore determinately. They are potential manners of real relation. When a manner of relation obtains, it obtains only by way of the particularity of togetherness among non-repeatable actualities.

This particularity of togetherness is its own category of existence—a contrast—which is "a complex unity with this individual definiteness, arising out of determinateness of eternal objects."[85] This emphasis on the particularity intrinsic to a contrast indicates the inextricability of the contrast from its contrasted relata. What this means is that, although the contrast itself serves as a novel entity in and of itself, capable of objectification by future subjects, it carries within it the particularity of its past. It is, therefore, unlike a universal, because it is unrepeatable. The transmuted feeling that makes possible sense perception by way of novel sensa is the introduction into experience of a contrast. Insofar as it relies upon an abstraction, it also introduces the possibility of accounting for the origination of "confusion" in concrete terms—something Whitehead doesn't think Leibniz was able to do.[86] The capacity for confusion or mistaken perception goes hand in hand with the capacity for abstraction.

JUDGMENT QUA PROPOSITIONAL FEELINGS

The running theme of this chapter has been that ontological togetherness is sufficient to achieve epistemological togetherness. The actual entity is how Whitehead accounts for the real togetherness of propositions and judgments, insofar as both are explainable in terms of actual entities. The only reasons are other actual entities, which means that "a reason is always a reference to determinate actual entities."[87] Propositions are the reasons why judgments can be true or false—they either do or do not reference determinate actual entities. Propositions are potential facts about actual entities. True propositions are facts; the logical subject actually exhibits the predicative pattern constituting the proposition. False propositions are unrealized or foreclosed potentials; the predicative pattern does not characterize the logical subjects. It is not accurate to say that we make true or false judgments about propositions; it is accurate to say that we judge true propositions or we judge false propositions.

Distinguishing himself from Descartes, Whitehead writes: "Descartes in his own philosophy conceives the thinker as creating the occasional thought. The philosophy of organism inverts the order, and conceives the thought as a constituent operation in the creation of the occasional thinker. In this inversion we have the final contrast between a philosophy of substance and a philosophy of organism."[88] Thinking constitutes a thinker; a thinker doesn't construct thoughts. Likewise, knowing is not something knowers do, it is a form of relation that constitutes a knower. The capacity for judgments is prerequisite for the sort of relations by which an enduring, personally ordered society of actual entities could be said to know its world—or rather, to "have" it.

Judgment is a complex form of prehension, different from and more complex than perception because of the element of indetermination involved. Sense reception accounts for the continuity of objects from moment to moment. Sense perception accounts for the diversity of response to the past that entities can achieve. The latter presupposes the former, but is distinct from it. Likewise, judgment presupposes perception in its various modes and yet differs from it.

The guiding conviction of this chapter is that the mentalizing and spatializing tendencies of modern philosophical accounts of experience have hindered efforts to vindicate the objective purport of perceptions. These tendencies have also hindered efforts to account for the relationship between epistemology, logic, and ontology, because the three are pictured as three distinct locations ranging from intimate to remote with respect to the human knower. The very premise of much modern epistemology is that there is a lack of ontological togetherness between knower and known. Upon such a premise, logic is either seen as a tool that links the knower to the real by revealing ontological necessities, or it is seen as merely the formalization of our ways of knowing. Bertrand Russell and early analytic philosophers exhibit the former position, and Kantians who maintain the hard gap between phenomena and noumena exhibit the latter. A system built upon the tacit metaphysics of modern epistemology will never take subjective experience to reveal reality in its most intimate mode of self-expression.

The early Russell worried about the "existence" of propositions. After reading a draft of his work on the subject, Whitehead wrote in a letter to Russell on May 5, 1906: "I have read over your ms on propositions three or four times with the greatest care. . . . False propositions are a great difficulty to me. You say—and this seems sense—there is only the fact that Caesar is dead, and there is not in addition . . . the true proposition, 'Caesar is dead'. But then what the devil is there in respect to 'Caesar is not dead'?"[89] The early Whitehead worried about how to account for the availability to judgment of negative propositions, and struggled with Russell to maintain the distinct between propositions and judgments. We see him conflate propositions to judgments—the very tendency in modern philosophy that he critiques in *Process and Reality*—when he says that true propositions are not actual things like facts. Judgment does not mean here what it means in *Process and Reality*; it is the judgment of formal logic and mathematics, not of metaphysics. In chapter 1, I mentioned that the scholarly collaboration between Whitehead and Russell remained within the strict bounds of mathematics and logic. Any venture into the philosophy of mathematics or the relationship of logic and ontology would have led them in very different directions. We see this tension beginning to build in the 1906 letter, in which propositions become a problem that requires metaphysical investigation.

By 1928, it is clear that Whitehead understands why negative propositions had so bedeviled him. It was because "proposition" referred, in the context of this bedevilment, only to something that figures into judgments—there is "only the fact" that P and not in addition "the true proposition" that P. This language no longer makes sense according to Whitehead's later philosophy, according to which "the fact" and the "true proposition" are redundant not because the latter refers in some mysterious intentional relationship to the former, but because a "proposition," when true, exhausts the meaning of a fact and, when false, exhausts the meaning of fiction. When speaking of "facts," we are speaking of "true propositions." But we can also speak of fictions, or mistake fictions for facts, and when we do we are dealing with false propositions. Propositions, therefore, are not facts, but facts are true propositions. Propositions are "potential" facts. This is not an oxymoron. Facts are constituted by past actual entities, and since these actual entities relate with elements of indeterminacy to subjects, there are many potentials for how facts can be prehended. If these prehensions involve elements of confusion, introduced by reversion or transmutation, then the prehensions can be nonconformal. The nonconformal prehensions are prehensions of false propositions. There is therefore a necessary distinction between propositions and facts, without which there would be no accounting for the intellectual capacity to be wrong.

Judgments "realize" propositions, but qua realized, the proposition only *is* (does work) by way of the outcome of the judgment. A subject judges truly if the actual entities taken as the logical subjects do, in fact, exhibit the character taken as the predicative pattern. If the predicative pattern is mistaken, then the judging subject stands in a non-conformal relationship to those facts. It is only on the basis of conformal relations, Whitehead insists, that induction is possible.[90] Inductive reasoning is possible only insofar as it is "the derivation of some characteristics of a particular future from the known characteristics of a particular past."[91] Conformal relations require the ontological togetherness of actual entities, and thus Whitehead thinks that the substance-philosophy of Descartes cannot account for the possibility of inductive reasoning. Actual entities, qua survivals of order, exhibit something of the general character of the universe; discrete substances can tell us nothing of this general character, which is to say that their environment is unknown.[92]

So long as "actuality" means "a substance with inhering qualities," to say that it has "knowledge" of other actual entities will never involve real relations and, accordingly, intentionality will always be a "problem." If "actuality" means a "percipient occasion" emerging as unity (novel event) out of multiplicity (many past events), then an event evidences the actual world essential to its composition.[93] In substance metaphysics, a subject is ontologically distinct from an object. For Whitehead, there are only actual entities. What constitutes the subject-hood of an actual entity is the object-hood of other actual entities in its immediate past; objectification is the means of becoming, whereby what becomes, while it becomes, is the subject, but once it has become, is an object constituting the immediate past of further becomings.

Subjectivity is, therefore, a mode of internal relation to the givenness of the past and the real potentials for the future. Subjects are the moments when causal efficacy encounters final causation; when fact and ideal meet as mutual instruments of creativity constituting conditioned freedom. For Descartes, experience could only mean the "'self-enjoyment, by an individual substance, of its qualification by ideas'." For Whitehead, experience means the "self-enjoyment of being one among many, and of being one arising out of the composition of many."[94] Experience, for Whitehead, is ontologically perspicacious.

Of course, to say that experience is ontologically perspicacious is to rely in large part upon metaphor. Experience need not involve consciousness on this definition, and it need not involve ocular sensation. But the level of experience involved in our ability to have conversations about it is the human standard. Only the higher phases of experience involve consciousness, but not necessarily and not for all occasions constituting the historic route of an enduring, personally ordered society. To account for the sorts of conscious judgments that are what analytic philosophers have in mind when they use the term requires a further study of Whitehead's aesthetic ontology.

CONSCIOUS PERCEPTIONS VERSUS INTUITIVE JUDGMENTS

A propositional feeling is any prehension that takes a proposition as its object. A judgment is only one species of this genus, and there is also diversity in the nature of judgment. Whitehead at times refers to propositional feelings as "intellectual" feelings, because of the role they play in the emergence of intellectuality of the sort commonly taken as sapience.

Whitehead describes two species of intellectual prehension: conscious perceptions and judgments. Judgments can also be intuitive or inferential. Intuitive judgments can be affirmative or negative, but there are also suspended judgments that provide occasion for inference. Inference is here understood as the work of derivative judgments. It is the suspended judgment, Whitehead thinks, which is the primary tool of scientific progress.[95] Alternatively, it is the first type of judgment that is most nearly analogous to conscious perceptions, insofar as it is dominated by an indifference to truth or falsehood, and is, like conscious perception, merely "the feeling of what is relevant to immediate fact in contrast with its potential irrelevance."[96] No strict boundary can be drawn between conscious perceptions and intuitive judgments. They are prone to the same error, which is the definition of the nexus (a mere fragment of the actual world of the logical subjects) by the observed predicate (which is the eternal object)—in short, the proposition entertained may be nonconformal, that is, false.[97]

Whitehead understands the difference between the two types of propositional feelings, conscious perceptions and intuitive judgments, as the difference between "perceptive feelings" and "imaginative feelings" (soon to be explained). What makes something a perception as opposed to a judgment is ultimately the complexity of its origination. Conscious perceptions and intuitive judgments are different in degree, not kind—in manner, not matter. A conscious perception is the result of a felt contrast (a "comparative feeling") between a physical feeling and a propositional feeling. The physical feeling supplies the "logical subjects" of the proposition. If the proposition is true, the perceiving subject has achieved a conformal relationship to those actual entities serving as the logical subject(s).

An intuitive judgment involves a third element, insofar as the logical subjects and predicate ("predicative pattern" issuing in a particular emotional tone) originate from two different physical feelings. The success of an intuitive judgment is not dependent upon the strict conformity between the felt character of the proposition and the felt character of the actualities supplying its logical subject. The intuitive judgment is composed of (1) a logical subject derived from one physical feeling (feeling of the immediate past), called the "indicative feeling," (2) a predicative pattern derived from a second physical feeling, called the physical recognition or "predicative feeling," and (3) the proposition, which is the unique compound of the two. The indicative feeling is "indicative" because it is the indication of particularity, the concrete inheritance by the subject of an object of consciousness, or the physical provocation of attention. The physical recognition is the element of recollection, the importation or associative abstraction of some character from past experience. The physical recognition is also the "conceptual imagination" or "predicative feeling"—the prehension supplying (functioning as) the predicate. Both the indicative feeling and the physical recognition are essential to consciousness. I am not just conscious of the "the mountain"; I am conscious of the mountain *as* P—or better yet, I am conscious because "mountain-as-*P*" is the form of relation constituting "me" in that moment.

On this point, Whitehead finds agreement (with some interpretive liberty) with Plato:

> Whenever there is consciousness there is some element of recollection. It recalls earlier phases from the dim recesses of the unconscious. Long ago this truth was asserted in Plato's doctrine of reminiscence. No doubt Plato was directly thinking of glimpses of eternal truths lingering in a soul derivate from a timeless heaven of pure form. Be that as it may, then in a wider sense consciousness enlightens experience which precedes it, and could be without it if considered as a mere datum.[98]

Plato, thinks Whitehead, understood that what exhibits consciousness is an element of the abstract in the concrete. The synthesis constitutive of consciousness is the synthesis of determinateness and indeterminateness, of physical and mental operations. It would otherwise be mere physical receptivity. Of course, the language of forms that "linger" in actuality and that are "derivate" from a "timeless heaven of pure form" is, while ripe for sophistication, lacking as a matter of scientific detail. For the contemporary reader, it can read, as it has read for much of modern and analytic philosophy, as a reinstatement of the bifurcation of nature with too strong an emphasis on the enchanted realm of eternality.

The opposite is the case for Hume, whose limitation indeed was the presumption of bifurcation, but by way of an emphasis on the disenchanted realm of brute happenings. Nevertheless, Whitehead sees the same understanding about consciousness in his thought:

> [Hume] maintains that we can never conceptually entertain what we have never antecedently experienced through impressions of sensation. The philosophy of organism generalizes the notion of "impressions of sensation" into that of "pure physical feelings." Even then Hume's assertion is too unguarded according to Hume's own showing. But the immediate point is the deep-seated alliance of consciousness with recollection both for Plato and for Hume.[99]

By substituting "pure physical feelings" for Hume's "impressions of sensations," Whitehead corrects that "defect" in Hume's thought, according to which the causal efficacy of the past entails no real relation to the abstractive generalities employed in perception and judgment. When Hume "remembers to speak in terms of this doctrine" of recognition or recollection, he understands an "impression" in terms of a conscious apprehension of a universal. In such instances, Hume says things like: "That idea of red, which we form in the dark, and that impression which strikes our eyes in sunshine, differ only in degree, not in nature."[100] But if it be the case, as it appears to be according to Hume, that an "impression" of red is only a more vivacious version of our "idea" of red, then we have no means of distinguishing a percept from a concept. This is Whitehead's worry. What Hume lacks is a doctrine of real togetherness that actual entities supply and substances withhold. He thereby denies the real presence of the past in the present.[101]

The indicative feeling introduces a sub-contrast to the physical feeling involved in a conscious perception, diversifying its origination. When this diversity is present, more distance opens up between the actual entities considered by the proposition, and this space, created as it is by the lack of directness or physical determination, may be positively described in terms of an increase of "imaginative freedom"—a phrase only superficially similar to Hume's own.[102] The greater the diversity between the origin of the logical subject and the origin of the predicate, the more the proposition becomes an "imaginative notion" that, when felt, become the object of an "imaginative feeling." In this way, the difference between a conscious perception and an intuitive judgment (or the defining point of a judgment evolving from a perception), is the element of imagination. In simple terms, an imaginative notion differs from a perceived notion when the things it brings together are sufficiently distinct from one another. This is why the risk of a proposition, thus constituted, being false is so much higher. The prehensive capacity to entertain such a high risk of error is what Whitehead calls "imagination." Imagination is the capacity to entertain falsehoods, falsehoods that can bring great enjoyment in art. It is in this way that Whitehead shows how the role of propositions in judgment—in belief, disbelief, or research—fails to exhaust the importance of propositions, specifically *negative* propositions.

It is precisely because, in a conscious perception, the indicative feeling and the physical recognition are prehensions of one and the same set of actual entities, that they involve greater restriction to the facts. The other side of this point is that, because in intuitive judgments there is greater diversity of origination, there is both the chance of greater synthetic capacity and the greater risk of error. The more actual entities, and the greater the genetic differences between them, involved in the initial physical prehensions or givenness of awareness, the greater the possibility of confusion. The possibility of novel syntheses, of greater breadth of awareness, goes hand in hand with the risk of confusion.

This account of propositions thereby entails a "correspondence" theory of truth, but not of the sort supported by substance metaphysics. Whitehead defines truth as "the absence of incompatibility or of any 'material contrast' in the patterns of the nexus and of the propositions in their generic contrast."[103] It is the indicative feeling originative of the intuitive judgment that, because it can be relatively disconnected in its origination from physical recollection, may have involved conceptual reversion—or conceptual diversity rather than reproduction. What conceptual diversity means is diversity of origination. If the physical feelings ingredient in an intuitive judgment do *not* involve reversion, then "from each physical feeling there is the derivation of a purely conceptual feeling whose datum is the eternal object determinant of the definiteness of the actual entity, or of the nexus, physically felt." The indicative feeling involving only conceptual reproduction entails a lower risk of there being a material incompatibility between the proposition and the character of the actual world which it takes as its logical subject. If, however, one of the physical feelings involved in an intuitive judgment involves reversion, then the likelihood of incompatibility or the frustration of the synthesis increases.

It is likewise with conscious perceptions, although the number of physical feelings at risk of involving conceptual reversion is effectively half. Conscious perceptions thereby originate through a process that guarantees the closest possible restriction to the facts, whereas intuitive judgments involve a secondary origination of conceptual feeling. In both situations, truth is defined in terms of correspondence, and correspondence is valuable because it is efficacious. If I have consciously perceived the rope as a rope, my relation to it qua rope will be more efficacious (skillful, appropriate to the facts) than if I perceived it as a snake.

When we define truth aesthetically before we define it epistemologically, we can also account for the possibility of error at a more fundamental level. In both conscious perception and intuitive judgment, error "arises by reason of operations which lie below consciousness, though they may emerge into consciousness and lie open for criticism."[104] What we have is, in a way, a metaphysical basis for immanent critique.

The subjective form of a judgment is not always one of belief, nor of disbelief. Whitehead provides three possible cases: definite belief, definite disbelief, and suspension of judgment. If the felt proposition is true (if complete conformity obtains), the subjective form of the judgment is belief. If the felt proposition is false (if no conformity obtains), the subjective form is disbelief. Complete conformity and complete nonconformity are, predictably, rare instances. What is overwhelmingly the case is partial conformity or partial nonconformity. Only derivative judgments, constitutive of the inferential process, can eventuate belief or disbelief in the case of a suspended judgment.

What Whitehead calls an affirmative intuitive judgment (definite belief) and a negative intuitive judgment (definite disbelief) are, along with conscious perceptions, akin to what Locke calls "knowledge" when he writes, "Thus the mind has two faculties conversant about truth and falsehood,— First, Knowledge, whereby it certainly perceives, and is undoubtedly satisfied of the agreement or disagreement of any ideas." Moreover, what Whitehead calls an "inferential judgment" is what Locke calls "judgment."[105] Locke writes, "Secondly, Judgment, which is the putting ideas together, or separating them from one another in the mind, when their certain agreement or disagreement is not perceived, but presumed to be so; which is, as the word imports, taken to be so before it certainly appears. And if it so unites or separates them as in reality things are, it is right judgment."[106] Whitehead's broader use of "judgment" owes to the ontological togetherness of actual entities, which occasions judgment by way of an extension of the same kind of processes involved in sense reception and sense perception. Whitehead's use, therefore, entails the possibility of intentional relations.

PERCEIVING PARTICULARS

I have attempted to show in this chapter how Whitehead's aesthetic ontology enables an account of perception and judgment that vindicates their objective purport. Moreover, I have argued that it does so in a way unencumbered by the tacit assumptions that continue to problematize intentionality in analytic philosophies of mind. The confusion between percept and concept in modern philosophy, so evident in Hume's writings, made the concept of "experience" highly suspicious for philosophers having taken the so-called linguistic turn.

The problem occurred when the conflation of percepts with concepts issued in the extension of the "truism that we can only *conceive* in terms of universals" to the belief "that we can only *feel* in terms of universals."[107] Whitehead's aesthetic ontology argues, to the contrary, that we do, in fact, perceive particular existents. Our judgments, as complex evolutions of perceptions, retain the real relatedness demanded by Whitehead's Ontological Principle. In the next chapter, I will examine in greater detail the relevance Whitehead's metaphysics of experience has to McDowell's efforts to make sense of how perception can provide rational constraints upon our thinking.

NOTES

1. Donald Davidson, "Radical Interpretation," in *Inquiries into Truth and Interpretation* (Oxford: Oxford University Press, 2001), 198.
2. McDowell, *Mind and World*, 126.
3. Ibid., 125.
4. Ibid., 29.
5. Ibid., 28.
6. Ibid.
7. Ibid., 5.
8. Ibid., 61.
9. Whitehead, *Process and Reality*, 139.
10. Ibid., 31.
11. Ibid., 19.
12. Ibid., 18.
13. Ibid.
14. Ibid., 19.
15. Ibid., 20.
16. Ibid.
17. Ibid., 21.
18. Ibid., 22.
19. Ibid., 256.
20. Ibid, 22.
21. Ibid., 258.
22. Ibid., 259.
23. Ibid.
24. Ibid., 184.
25. Ibid.
26. See Whitehead, *Concept of Nature*, 43.
27. Whitehead, *Process and Reality*, 141.
28. Ibid.
29. Ibid., 48.
30. Ibid., 137.
31. Ibid., 138.

32. Ibid., 138.
33. Ibid., 139.
34. Ibid.
35. Ibid.
36. Ibid., 147.
37. Ibid., 148.
38. Ibid., 149.
39. Ibid., 14.
40. Ibid., 149.
41. Ibid., 32.
42. Ibid., 29.
43. Ibid., 52.
44. Ibid., 53.
45. Ibid., 33.
46. Ibid., 32.
47. Ibid., 257.
48. Ibid., 258.
49. Ibid.
50. Ibid., 259.
51. Ibid., 264.
52. Ibid., 99, 90.
53. Ibid., 83.
54. Ibid., 84.
55. Ibid.
56. Ibid., 89.
57. Ibid., 90.
58. Whitehead defines a "cosmic epoch" as "that widest society of actual entities whose immediate relevance to ourselves is traceable." Ibid., 91.
59. Ibid.
60. Ibid.
61. Ibid., 92.
62. Ibid., 91–92.
63. Ibid., 93.
64. Ibid.
65. Ibid., 92.
66. Ibid., 110.
67. Ibid., 117.
68. Ibid., 116.
69. Ibid., 117.
70. Ibid., 104.
71. Ibid., 133.
72. Ibid., 251.
73. Ibid., 251.
74. Ibid., 253.
75. Ibid., 253–254.

76. I will discuss this subject in greater depth in the Epilogue.
77. Ibid., 254.
78. Ibid., 32. Whitehead here describes the "objective immortality" of actual entities as the "function of creatures" by which "they constitute the shifting character of creativity."
79. Ibid., 254.
80. Ibid.
81. Ibid.
82. Ibid., 111.
83. Ibid., 112.
84. Ibid., 27.
85. Ibid., 228.
86. Ibid., 27. Leibnizian monads lack the internal relatedness requisite for the possibility of real contrasts, and, therefore, of the complex unity requisite for complex entities capable of perceiving a particular conjointness instead of a disjointed many.
87. Ibid., 256.
88. Ibid., 151.
89. Lowe, *Alfred North Whitehead*, Vol. 1, 280–281.
90. Whitehead, *Process and Reality*, 200–201.
91. Ibid., 204; Whitehead is here quoting his own *Science and the Modern World*, 44.
92. Ibid., 205.
93. Ibid., 145.
94. Ibid., 145.
95. Ibid., 275.
96. Ibid., 268.
97. Ibid., 270.
98. Ibid., 242.
99. Ibid.
100. David Hume, *A Treatise of Human Nature,* bk. 1, pt. 1, sec. 1, lines 31–33; Whitehead, *Process and Reality*, 242.
101. Whitehead sees this as a violation of his Principle of Relativity, or the Fourth Category of Explanation. Ibid., 243.
102. Ibid., 132–133.
103. Ibid., 271.
104. Ibid., 272.
105. Ibid., 274.
106. John Locke, *An Essay Concerning Human Understanding*, ed. Kenneth Winkler (Indianapolis, IN: Hacket Publishing, 1996), 302; Whitehead, *Process and Reality*, 274.
107. Ibid., 230.

Chapter 5

McDowell and the "Connivance of the World"

INTRODUCTION

In the previous chapter I presented some of the more technical aspects of Whitehead's philosophy of experience, with specific focus on the aesthetics of perception and judgment. The demands of following Whitehead through his revised account of subjectivity are rewarded when intentional relations come to be seen as presupposed rather than constructed by the subject. As I said at the outset of that chapter,[1] Whitehead's revised account of subjectivity positions us to understand the perspicuity of intuitions in terms of concrete forms of relation that differ only in degree from what we might call judgments. McDowell also wants to reconceive intuitions in a way that can vindicate their objective purport, something I discussed in chapter 3 as well.

However, I have been arguing all along that McDowell's constructive work remains underwhelming insofar as he remains committed to a mentalizing of experience; that is, to a picture of exclusively conscious subjects as "having" a world by means of (a revised, Kantian notion of) "intuitions." McDowell remains limited, in short, by the same tacit assumptions as Kant, namely, the related assumptions (1) that subjectivity presupposes consciousness, rather than vice versa; (2) that intuitions are inseparable from consciousness; and (3) that intuitions gain traction with the world through a passive operation of conceptual capacities, capacities actively employed in judgment. On the basis of these three assumptions, McDowell commits himself to a metaphysics of experience that will continue to leave him empty handed when trying to account for the ontogeny of subjectivity in general, and of linguistically equipped subjects in particular.

The purpose of this chapter is to demonstrate this empty-handedness, while also demonstrating the remarkable similarity of McDowell's epistemological concerns to Whitehead's own. To begin this task, I will compare their respective readings of Kant on the contentfulness of intuitions. I will then unpack McDowell's theory of perception as a capacity for knowledge in detail, specifically as he works it out in contrast to Brandom's inferentialist account, in order to show the promising but ultimately encumbered nature of this theory.

KANT AND THE FORMED-NESS OF INTUITION

While Whitehead contrasts his account of experience with Kant's, he does not think the contrast is complete in all respects. The reason why Whitehead positions himself in conversation with Locke and Hume more often than with Kant is because the "defects" in the latter's thinking are responsible for many of the philosophical premises that Whitehead finds problematic in Kant—specifically, the disconnection between substances (particular existents/things-in-themselves) and data (sensa/impressions/intuitions). But just as there are elements of Locke and Hume's accounts of experience that remain consistent with or receive emphasis by the philosophy of organism, there are likewise moments in Kant's first *Critique* where Whitehead sees Kant struggling to introduce the real connectedness between phenomena and things-in-themselves otherwise denied by his system.

What is important for my purpose here is to point out the similarity between what Whitehead identifies as such moments in Kant's first *Critique* with what McDowell identifies as Kant's commitment to the formed-ness of intuitions and, therefore, to the logical continuity between intuitions and spontaneity. If I am correct about this similarity, it will make all the stronger my case for the relevance of Whitehead to analytic debates about mind and world in general, and about the problem of intentionality in particular.

Whitehead's critique of Kant thus far has concerned the way Kant "mentalizes" intuition and thereby schematizes "experience" as being the product of the more sophisticated modes of cognitive functioning. The real ontological relatedness between one's intuitions and their purported objects thereby becomes problematic because experience is taken as a mode of thought, and thought is understood on the substance-quality model of reality. On this model, the subject is already ontologically *un*related to objects, and no amount of epistemological construction upon this ontological basis will be able to establish real togetherness. But Kant does not mentalize experience in every instance: "The exception is to be found in Kant's preliminary sections on 'Transcendental Aesthetic', by which he provides space and time."[2] If Kant had based his *Critique* around the "Transcendental Aesthetic," such that it would have been the *Critique of Pure Feeling* rather than the *Critique of Pure Reason*, then Kant may have anticipated by many years Whitehead's philosophy of organism. It was because Kant followed Hume in assuming "the radical disconnection of impressions *qua data*" that this never occurred. Rather, for Kant, the "Transcendental Aesthetic" amounted to nothing more than "the mere description of a subjective process appropriating the data by orderliness of feeling."³ For Kant, however, the orderliness of feeling did not, on Whitehead's reading, have any ontological togetherness with the datum. This Kant shared with Hume.

Whitehead understands his alternative, whereby the datum is intrinsically, because constitutively, interconnected with that for which it is datum, to have more affinity with Locke's secondary use of "ideas," exhibited in the later portions of his *Essay*. As earlier explained, this secondary use exhibited according to Whitehead's interpretation is Locke's "suppressed principle" that allowed for perception of *particular* existents. Locke "speaks of the ideas in the perceived objects," Whitehead explains, "and [he] tacitly presupposes their identification with corresponding ideas in the perceiving mind."⁴ The tacit admission of some ontological togetherness between ideas "in" particular existents and the ideas "in" the perceiving mind introduced an inconsistency that keeps Locke's philosophy of experience at least apparently plausible. The inconsistency was not adopted by Hume, and for this reason ontological togetherness, accounted for only by an ontology based upon causal efficacy, as a fundamental mode of becoming, was almost entirely absent. Instead, Hume spoke of "habits" of "constant conjunction," and provided at best only rhetorical solutions to account for their nature and possibility (after all, why are "habits" any less problematic than "causes"?).

Locke's "ideas" in this secondary sense are analogous to Whitehead's "ingression" of eternal objects, that is, to Whitehead's account of how quality can be genetic. "[T]he first stage of the process of feeling," he writes, "is the reception into the responsive conformity of feeling whereby the datum, which is mere potentiality, becomes the individualized basis for a complex unity of realization."⁵ This conformity is concrete conformity, grounded in real togetherness. Only on the basis of this real togetherness can any account of the process by which experiential unity is attained avoid epistemological problems.

The difference between Whitehead and McDowell's assessment of the Transcendental Aesthetic lies in the fact that, while Whitehead sees it as an inconsistency and a missed opportunity, McDowell sees it as the "clue" to understanding what Kant really wanted to achieve—namely, a defense of the objective purport of our intuitions.⁶ In fact, McDowell's insistence upon this understanding of the Transcendental Aesthetic was the basis of his critique of Sellars's variations on Kant in *Science and Metaphysics* (1963). McDowell writes, "Sellars thinks Kant is misstepping by his own lights in failing to discuss forms our sensibility can be taken to possess in isolation from its cooperation with understanding." He continues,

> But this is hard to square with some striking remarks in the second-edition version of the Transcendental Deduction. There Kant explicitly insists on the very feature of the way he handles the *formedness of our sensibility* [italics mine] that Sellars thinks is a mere slip. He insists that our sensibility is not to be seen as having its forms independently of its interaction with understanding. As Kant in effect acknowledges, one might have gathered from the Transcendental Aesthetic that he takes the formedness of our sensibility to be intelligible before we bring the understanding into the picture (B160n.) This is just what Sellars thinks Kant's line ought to be. But in the second half of the B Deduction, Kant makes it clear that he wants us to realize the Aesthetic was not to be read as offering a self-standing account of the forms of our sensibility.[7]

Sellars is wrong, McDowell thinks, to read Kant as saying that intuitions can function independently of the understanding, and so involve a sort of "sheer receptivity," the structure of which owes nothing to the categories of the understanding.[8] Sellars thinks that this is the second of two ways in which sensibility "figures in" to an "authentically Kantian account of empirical cognition," the first being the way intuitions are "already shaped" by the structure of the understanding.[9] What Sellars thinks we need is a way to account for how intuitions are constrained by a reality outside the mind, in order to vindicate their objective purport and so defend any robust account of empirical cognition. But Sellars's conclusion is not, therefore, that the objects present to consciousness in perceptual intuitions are, therefore, "real" objects. Rather, they are phenomenal objects. This is Sellars's Scientific Realism, according to which the merely apparent ordinary objects of perceptual intuitions correspond to, and are constrained in their manifestation by, the real objects of the scientific image.

Sellars promotes Scientific Realism as the authentically Kantian account of the external constraints reality exercises upon empirical cognition. His constituents of the "manifest image" are "Kant's" phenomenal objects, and his constituents of the "scientific image" are "Kant's" things-in-themselves. The warrant for such claims to authentic Kantianism, Sellars argues, comes from what Kant ought to have concluded by his own lights from the Transcendental Aesthetic, namely, McDowell surmises, "that our sensibility brings its own forms, spatiality and temporality, to its cooperation with the understanding."[10] But McDowell thinks Sellars is wrong to claim that the external constraint upon our intuitions can or must only come by way of sensibility operating independently of the understanding.

For McDowell, what Kant says about the Transcendental Aesthetic in the second-edition version of the Transcendental Deduction renders Sellars's argument unintelligible:

> Space, represented as **object** (as is really required in geometry), contains more than the mere form of intuition, namely the **comprehension** [*Zusammenfassung*] of the manifold given in accordance with the form of sensibility in an **intuitive** representation, so that the **form of intuition** merely gives the manifold, but the **formal intuition** gives unity of the representation. In the Aesthetic I ascribed this unity merely to sensibility, only in order to note that it precedes all concepts, though to be sure it presupposes a synthesis, which does not belong to the senses but through which all concepts of space and time first become possible. For since through it (as the understanding determines the sensibility) space or time are first **given** as intuitions, the unity of this *a priori* intuition belongs to space and time, and not to the concept of the understanding.[11]

McDowell takes Kant at his word in insisting that space and time are not forms of intuition that sensibility has prior to any cooperation with the understanding, but only that these forms precede all concepts, even while they presuppose the understanding. Sellars, in contrast, thinks that Kant needed to maintain the independence of the forms of intuition in order to vindicate their objective purport.

As I read him, McDowell doesn't see why "phenomenal objects" need be "merely" phenomenal if we assist Kant with a notion of "second nature." McDowell thinks this notion was not a live option for Kant, as I discussed in chapter 1, because of the influence of Platonic "idealism" (a phrase that would have confused Whitehead and Taylor). In *Mind and World,* McDowell writes, "From the thesis that receiving an impression is a transaction in nature, there is no good inference to the conclusion drawn by Sellars and Davidson, that the idea of receiving and impression must be foreign to the logical space in which concepts such as that of answerability function."[12] Once we have rejected the bifurcation between mind and nature, the space governed by rational relations and the space governed by causal ones, by way of the idea that rational relations are sui generis and yet coextensive with nature, we can no longer associate "nature" with some disenchanted realm of brute causality. When this association can no longer be plausibly made, then conceptual capacities, McDowell concludes, "can be operative not only in judgments—results of a subject's making up her mind about something—but already in the transactions in nature that are constituted by the world's impacts on the receptive capacities of a suitable subject; that is, one who possesses the relevant concepts."[13] In effect, McDowell is saying that intuitions and judgments are two sides of the same coin, conceptual capacities can be both passively elicited and actively employed.

Per chapter 1, Whitehead could not read Kant in this way because he never read Plato and Aristotle in McDowell's way. The bifurcation of nature isn't to be solved by way of an Aristotelian innocence expressed in the notion of "second nature," because any such appeal to Aristotle would only reinforce the substance-quality metaphysics that was the source of the bifurcation. For Whitehead, the objective purport of our intuitions was always already vindicated by way of ontological togetherness. This is why he reads the Transcendental Aesthetic as Kant's struggle to establish this real togetherness by way of epistemological togetherness. When Kant postulates spatiality and temporality as forms of intuition, Whitehead thinks he is letting good sense, rather than systematic coherence, inform his thinking.

Whitehead, therefore, anticipated McDowell's appreciation of the Transcendental Aesthetic and its potential for addressing the problem of intentionality by many decades. Not only did he recognize the longings within modern philosophy for a real togetherness to repair the epistemological rupture with the world—for example, in Kant's speaking of the formed-ness of intuitions—but Whitehead offers a fuller solution to this problem. Unfettered by the suppressed Aristotelianism that informed Kant's "mentalizing" of intuitions by way of the disconnection of substance and data, Whitehead exhibits the necessary ontological togetherness involved in the various phases of experience, from the simply conformal to complex originative phases, in terms of aesthetic rather than rational relations, and thereby explains the more abstract by way of the more concrete.

I take McDowell to be unable to achieve this togetherness despite his repeated attempts to rethink experience beyond the dualism of subject and object, both in its classical and contemporary iterations. The point of the remainder of this chapter is twofold: (1) to examine these attempts in more detail, specifically McDowell's attempt to defend "the connivance of the world" in constituting knowledge; and (2) to show how something as radical (to modern ears) as Whitehead's aesthetics of experience, with its revised theory of subjectivity, is necessary to allow the full sweep of assumptions complicit in the bifurcation of nature to stand in relief—including those remnant in McDowell's own efforts to rehabilitate Kant's notion of intuition.

MCDOWELL ON PERCEPTION AND ENTITLEMENT

In 2011, McDowell gave The Aquinas Lecture at Marquette University on "Perception as a Capacity for Knowledge."[14] He is concerned in this lecture, as he has been for many decades, with defending a theory of knowledge in general, and a theory of justification in particular, according to which observational reports can serve as a warrant for belief. More specifically, he is concerned to defend a theory of justification that includes non-inferential forms of entitlement without succumbing to a problematic form of Givenness. Such a theory would make sense, in a way McDowell thinks Brandom's inferentialism cannot, of observational knowledge.

To speak of observational *knowledge*, for McDowell, means that one is *not* simply speaking of situations in which objects display reliably responsive dispositions to stimuli (e.g., thermostats); they must do so in a somewhat self-conscious way. He follows Sellars definition from *Empiricism and the Philosophy of Mind* on this point: "The essential point is that in characterizing an episode or a state as that of *knowing*, we are not giving an empirical description of that episode or state; we are placing it in the logical space of reasons, of justifying and being able to justify what one says."[15] McDowell and Brandom read this passage quite differently, as I'll discuss later on. For now, note that McDowell reads Sellars here as arguing simply that we only attribute observational *knowledge* to someone who has made it explicit by means of linguistic moves, which we call observational *reports*.[16] This claim, of course, rests on a prior assumption of Sellars's that "to be a rational animal is to be a language-using animal."[17] McDowell does not find this claim liable to "human chauvinism"[18]; he merely reads Sellars as saying that an "instance of knowledge" of the sort he is concerned with must be understood as "an act of reason," and someone capable of such an act must be "self-conscious" of her credentials for it. In short, one can only occupy a position in the "space of reasons" insofar as one is "able to justify what one says."[19]

This is how McDowell gets to his topic of perception as a *capacity* for knowledge. It is not that *all* knowledge is "self-conscious rationality at work"—such that non-linguistic animals or pre-linguistic infants would be disqualified as knowers *tout court*. Rather, it is that the species[20] of knowledge about which Sellars and McDowell are talking when they speak of *perceptual* or *observational* knowing is the sort that is attributed to one upon linguistic articulation ("reports"). Moreover, McDowell will argue that it is also the sort of standing in the space of reasons *available* to one in the first place because of one's initiation into linguistic practice (what has been referred to in earlier chapters as McDowell's "second nature"). The point, as he sees it, is that a linguistically initiated perceiver is capable *not* merely of claiming that things *seem* or *appear* thus-and-so, but, when all goes well, that things *are* thus-and-so. This amounts to saying that a perceptual experience, when had by a linguistically initiated subject, can provide *indefeasible* warrant for believing that what seems to be the case actually is the case. A linguistically initiated perceiver, in short, is *capable* of non-inferential[21] *knowledge*, and not merely of justified belief. There are, of course, no guarantees, but as a rule, success must be possible to make sense of error in perception.

Sellars's requirement of self-consciousness, such that a candidate knower must be aware of her ability to give reasons for her claim, can be understood as his "internalist" requirement by virtue of the fact that it demands that a potential knower must have cognitive *access* to the warrants for that belief. One cannot, on this account, *be* justified without *being able* to justify oneself. But this is only *problematically* internalist, McDowell thinks, if we have an inadequate picture of what constitutes cognitive access to warrants—or, rather, of what constitutes justification.

Tyler Burge worries about the internalist criteria. His concern is that requiring a candidate knower to have conceptual access to the reasons for her belief is guilty of being excessively intellectualist. Rather, he argues, an individual can be fully entitled to a belief (justified) even without being able to explain (to justify) her entitlement. He writes, "The individual need not have the concepts necessary to think the propositional content that formulates the warrant."[22] Burge, in short, thinks that the internalist requirement denies knowledge of any kind to anyone or anything other than linguistically able adult human beings. On this assumption, he argues, "A viable conception of warrant and knowledge must include both primitive and sophisticated types."[23] But McDowell thinks Burge's assumption is misguided; in fact, it is precisely the one he tries to avoid by speaking of Sellars's definition of knowledge (qua self-conscious rationality at work) as only a species of knowledge (see my footnote 20). Moreover, he argues that Burge's worry about excessive intellectualism depends on another (equally problematic) assumption: namely, "that the warrant a perceptual state provides for a belief cannot guarantee the truth of the belief."[24] Burge's accusation, McDowell argues,

> depends on supposing that everyone, including Sellars, would accept that the warrant provided by a perceptual state cannot be conclusive. But the Sellarsian idea makes room for a conception of perceptual states on these lines: when all goes well in the operation of a perceptual capacity of a sort that belongs to its possessor's rationality, a perceiver enjoys a perceptual state in which some feature of her environment is *there* for her, perceptually *present* to her rationally self-conscious awareness.[25]

In order to make sense of perceptual error, we might read McDowell as saying, we must first be able to make sense of perceptual success. And perceptual success must amount to more than a justified *seeming* thus-and-so in order to count as such, namely, where success is, according to our ordinary expectations, defined not as achieving merely justified beliefs, but as achieving *true* beliefs non-accidentally. But this means, according to McDowell, that perceptual states must be able to provide warrants that cannot be undermined,[26] at least in ideal circumstances. "When all goes well," therefore, perceptual states must be understood as making some features of the world (rationally, self-consciously) "present" to one. He goes on,

> This presence is an actualization of a capacity that belongs to the subject's reason. Reason is at work, that is, in the perceptual presence to rational subjects of features of their environment. And if a perceptual state can consist in a subject's having a feature of her environment perceptually present to her, that gives the lie to the assumption that a perceptual state cannot warrant a belief in a way that guarantees its truth.[27]

This last statement will be particularly pertinent when we turn to McDowell's contention with Brandom on observational states. McDowell is saying that, in the case of perception by means of a linguistically initiated subject, that subject can have non-accidental true beliefs about her environment simply by virtue of having a perceptual experience which the rational, self-conscious subject knows to be reliable by virtue of her general acquaintance with the world. This general acquaintance with the world is, for the linguistically initiated subject, replete with knowing many things, but not in the sense that her perceptions are, therefore, somehow inferentially derivative of this knowledge, but rather in the sense that those knowings are integrated with her mode of subjectivity, such that they are, *pace* Wittgenstein, as much a part of her natural history as anything else.

I will discuss the ways in which McDowell thinks language creates individuals capable of new sorts of experience in the next chapter, particularly in conversation with Whitehead's own take on the difference language makes. For now, it is helpful to focus on the distinction McDowell is making (pace his reading of Sellars) between non-rational and rational perceptual capacities, the latter being the sort that can non-inferentially position one in the space of reasons—that is, can position one to give reasons for how they *know* "that P." McDowell explains, "on this picture it is a perceptual state *itself* that warrants one in a belief that counts as knowledgeable by virtue of having such warrant."[28] Nothing is *added*, in other words, to the perceptual experience in order to make it count as a warrant. He continues, "When one knows something to be so by virtue of seeing it to be so, one's warrant for believing it to be so *is that one sees it to be so*—not one's *believing that* one sees it to be so, which would raise the question of what warrants one in *that* belief—the question Burge exploits in order to argue that the Sellarsian picture falls into an excessive intellectualism."[29] Again, this insistence that nothing need be added to the perceptual state to justify one in claiming true belief plays a role in McDowell's critique of Brandom's inferentialist alternative. Here, this insistence serves to discredit the assumption upon which McDowell takes Burge's critique to depend; again, the assumption "that the warrant a perceptual state provides for a belief cannot guarantee the truth of the belief."[30]

What is at stake here, as in McDowell's earlier works, is the ability of intentional attitudes like belief to gain traction with the world in an unmediated way, but without the classical Given. The *belief itself* "that P" is warranted by the perceptual state; it is not the belief *about* the perceptual state which warrants the belief "that P." To deny this, McDowell thinks, amounts to denying that there is any case in which a perceptual state excludes the possibility of falsehood. But this denial, in turn, involves an incoherent understanding of fallibility—one that is "pervasive in epistemology."[31] "It is typical," he writes, "for discussions of the epistemology of perceptual knowledge to begin with the assumption . . . that experience itself cannot provide better than inconclusive warrant for belief."[32] This assumption is underwritten by another: that what it means to say that perception is a fallible capacity is equivalent to saying that we can never be certain that falsehood is avoided, or, in McDowell's way of speaking, that we can never be certain that features of "the objective environment [actually are] perceptually present to one's self-consciously rational awareness."[33] A capacity cannot *be* fallible without *also being able* to do what it is a capacity to do: to make the objective environment perceptually present to one, at least occasionally, in a non-defective way. It is only with this corrected conception of fallibility, McDowell thinks, that we can make sense of how reason is integrated with animality. After all, "if we see capacities that belong to reason as operative in our form of responsiveness, mediated by the senses, to features of our environment," then we will have no difficulty seeing the sort of perception of which linguistically initiated human beings are capable as operations of rationality, and, therefore, as a capacity for knowledge, even if, more generically speaking, perception can also be non-rational.[34] To translate into Whiteheadian terms, we will only avoid the bifurcation of nature and its concomitant theory of psychic additions and secondary qualities, if perception is seen as a mode of concrete, potentially rational relation to the environment. Burge's blindspot amounts to an inability to think beyond the dualism of mind and world, such that experience could be a rational capacity.

MCDOWELL'S CRITIQUE OF THE "INTERIORIZATION" OF REASON

The blind spot of which McDowell accuses Burge is the same one he accuses Brandom of a few years prior. But before we can understand why Brandom invites this charge, we need to understand the piece which initiated their conversation in the first place: McDowell's 1995 article "Knowledge and the Internal."[35] It is here that I take McDowell to most clearly diagnose the "epistemological syndrome" incapacitating analytic philosophy from de-problematizing intentionality. His central claim is this: "Perception could not yield us standings in the space of reasons at all without some indebtedness to the world."[36] It was precisely the nature of this indebtedness that I am trying to work out of his account, both in order to demonstrate McDowell's (historically unappreciated) likemindedness with Whitehead when it comes to epistemological concerns, but also, eventually, the insufficiency of McDowell's efforts to explain how indebtedness is possible.

In this 1995 work, McDowell characterizes his epistemological concern in terms of a problematic "interiorization of the space of reasons."[37] We interiorize the space of reason, on his understanding, when we subscribe to a picture of "the objective world as set over against a 'conceptual scheme' that has withdrawn into a kind of self-sufficiency."[38] This is the same critique he made of Rorty in "Towards Rehabilitating Objectivity" (2000), which I covered in chapter 3. Scheme-content dualism is, per Davidson's original argument, the third and last dogma of classical empiricism. The question McDowell thinks we are left with is how to rehabilitate experience without the relinquished dogmas. Describing this dualism in ways that clearly render standard readings of Plato at fault, he writes, "The dualism yields a picture in which the realm of matter, which is, in so far as it impinges on us, the Given, confronts the realm of forms, which is the realm of thought, the realm in which subjectivity has its being."[39] McDowell's contemporary conversations partners—at least the one's he seriously considers—do not maintain the "full-fledged" version of this dualism. They do not, that is to say, explicitly insist upon the ontological gap between subject and object, inner and outer. To do so runs immediately into performative contradiction—something we saw Whitehead demonstrate in chapter 1. For McDowell, fully fledged dualism tries to conceive of what "we want to think of as the space of concepts, the realm of thought, in a way that alienates it so radically from the merely material that we . . . undermine our right to think of it as the realm of thought at all." In uprooting the space of concepts from the objective world, in short, McDowell argues we cease to be able to justify moves within that space as involving content.[40] This concern with content recalls the importance for McDowell of reinterpreting Kant's Transcendental Aesthetic to allow for the formed-ness of intuitions.

Interlocutors such as Brandom are not so easily disputed; their version of this dualism, McDowell might say, is underwritten by half-measures. What McDowell is contesting in this 1995 article are these "hybrid" epistemologies: ones that "aim to set off the inner from the outer, but in a way that stops short that disastrous extinguishing of content."[41] The problem with so-called hybrid epistemologies is that they try to account for the contentful provisions of the world to reason by way of "appearances." Appearances serve the role as "starting-points" or entry moves into the space of reasons by the way in which we can draw inferences from them. Similar to his 2005 critique of Burge's externalist allowance—that one could *be* justified without *being able* to justify one's beliefs—McDowell's critique of the hybrid account is that it is fundamentally unstable insofar as it externalizes truth and internalizes justification (e.g., reliability).[42] Here, to "externalize" means to make it depend on something "outside" the space of reasons, and so on something like "the thing-in-itself" to which we can never have direct awareness, and to "internalize" justification means to make it entirely dependent on the coherence of something like a conceptual scheme. To separate these is fatal to any theory of knowledge, in any robust sense of the term.

In a comment with which Whitehead would wildly agree, McDowell expands on the implications he finds in hybrid accounts: they end up denying that "reality is prior, in the order of understanding, to appearance."[43] Even more striking is the similarity of what McDowell goes on to say with the comments Whitehead offered Russell in his handwritten correspondence from 1911 regarding how to argue with a skeptic: "The considerations I have offered suggest a way to respond to skepticism about, for instance, perceptual knowledge; the thing to do is not to answer the skeptic's challenges, but to diagnose their seeming urgency as deriving from a misguided interiorization of reason."[44] Whitehead critiques Russell for entirely failing to repute Kant's idealism insofar as Russell got caught up in the duplicity of speaking about "physical space" as "real" space, as opposed to "apparent space," in such a way that at once denied and assumed access to "things-in-themselves." The key, for Whitehead, was to refuse to play the game of opposed appearance and reality in the first place. Likewise, for McDowell, the key is to realize in advance of engaging the skeptic that their first premises are hopeless; in this case, the premise we saw in Burge that a perceptual state cannot, under any circumstances, exclude the possibility of falsehood and thereby provide one indefeasible warrant for claiming to know "that P."

Again like Whitehead, McDowell demonstrates how this approach works in conversation with Hume's *Enquiry*. "Consider," writes McDowell, "a characteristic Humean formulation of the predicament that is supposed to invite inductive skepticism: 'It may, therefore, be a subject worthy of curiosity, to enquire what is the nature of that evidence, which assures us of any . . . matter of fact, beyond the present testimony of our senses . . . ' [David Hume, *An Enquiry Concerning Human Understanding,* §4]. Taking it seriously that what is in question is the testimony of our senses, we must think in terms of something content-involving—something in which, say, colors figure as apparent properties of objects."[45] And yet, McDowell argues, there could never be a case in which one receives testimony from one's senses without having taken any inductive steps. For an experience of color to count for a subject as a testimony of the senses, the subject must already know something significant about experiences of color—say, something about how colors appear differently at dusk than they do at noonday, and thus about standard versus nonstandard viewing conditions. McDowell's point is that, for a subject to have an experience serve as testimony of the senses, she must already know something about the relationship between the world and her cognitive access to it.[46] In short, *"There is no making sense of perceptual appearances—the testimony of one's senses—without making sense of the possibility that the objective world can be immediately present to the senses."*[47]

This is precisely the point Whitehead made about the structural necessity of Kant's "suppressed premises" that "intuitions are never blind,"[48] or the point he made about the empirical backwardness of Locke and Hume's sensationalist doctrine. It is also the point he made about the consequent operation of Locke's suppressed principle, according to which some sort of perception of "particular existents" must be possible, with similarities to what he viewed as Hume's mingling with a suppressed objectivist principle.[49] Recall from chapter 4 that Whitehead finds Kant's problematic notion of "noumena" to be a direct consequence of spatializing mind—just as McDowell is here critiquing skepticism as a direct consequence of internalizing the space of reasons. There is not much new here that McDowell is contributing. Rather, he simply demonstrates ever more clearly the intuitional ignorance of Whitehead's salience. If only Hume would have thought through "the idea that [his] subject already has the testimony of the senses," McDowell thinks, he would have realized that his problem with induction was based entirely upon an unempirical "interiorizing epistemology for perception."[50] We might rephrase thus: if only Hume had recognized his own suppressed objectivist principle, he would not have let nature bifurcate ontologically before he could even worry about it epistemologically. So says Whitehead, of course.

BRANDOM'S SOCIAL-INFERENTIALIST REPLY

In a response of the same year to McDowell's 1995 article, Brandom says that he also wants to free us from a problematic picture of the space of reasons.[51] But whereas McDowell construes the problem as an internalizing of the space, Brandom thinks that the real problem is an even prior *individualizing* of it by ignoring "its essentially *social* articulation."[52] To see this, Brandom insists that we "keep our eyes on the actual practices of giving and asking for reasons, the practices that give a point to the abstract notion of a space of reasons."[53] What McDowell calls "standing in the space of reasons" is, for Brandom, an entirely social status to be understood in terms of *"commitments* and *entitlements* that are practically acknowledged by those engaging in such practices."[54] On these terms, the (social) process of assessing one's "standing" in the metaphoric space as a "knower"—that is, as committed to justified true beliefs—consists of three practices: (1) attributing a commitment (and so fulfilling the belief condition); (2) attributing an entitlement (and so fulfilling the justification condition); and (3) undertaking a commitment (and so fulfilling the truth condition by *taking*-true). Belief, on this account, is, therefore, construed as a status conferred upon one who is recognized as making (or having made) a propositionally contentful commitment. Justification, meanwhile, is construed as a status conferred upon one who is recognized as being entitled (i.e., as being able to give reasons for that prior commitment). Truth, here, has nothing to do with attributing some status to the first commitment (the belief); rather, the truth condition is entirely met, on an inferentialist model, by the practice of taking-true, which is to say, not by attributing a status to another's commitment, but by *undertaking* one oneself. This undertaking amounts to an endorsement of the first commitment.[55]

I have taken time to explain Brandom's account of "standing in the space of reasons" in terms of these actual practices because it is instructive to see what he thinks truth must become in order to avoid what he calls "metaphysical" theories of truth. Brandom insists that truth-taking exhausts what it means to say that another *knows* that P. The mistake he attributes to "metaphysical theories" of truth is their assimilation of steps 1 and 3; that is, they assimilate "what I am doing when I take *your belief* to be true to what I am doing when I take *you* to believe it."[56] When these steps are assimilated, truth becomes a "property" rather than an action—it becomes something that supposedly does not rely upon social practices or the distinction between social perspectives.[57] This is how we "individualize" the space of reasons, according to Brandom.

If Brandom were to stop here, he would appear guilty of something closer to McDowell's "full-fledged" dualism. To be fair, at times it appears as if McDowell *is* accusing Brandom of this, for instance, when he calls his inferentialism "transcendental sociologism" (see my chapter 2, ftn. 26; see also my chapter 3). If Brandom had stopped with his account of truth qua truth-taking, this might be accurate. But he would also be guilty, per McDowell's warning, of having extinguished content altogether. In this case, he would have to deny the possibility of anything remotely like non-inferential knowledge by means of perception. This is where we can spot in Brandom's account the half-measures characteristic of McDowell's "hybrid" epistemologies. Brandom thinks we (he) have (has) to concede one point to the externalist: that a subject can *be* justified without *being able* to justify herself.[58]

Of course, this will be exactly Burge's claim ten years later. And McDowell's response is the same: that Brandom's argument "depends on taking me to hold that there cannot be justification for a belief sufficient to exclude the possibility that the belief is false."[59] In short, Brandom's externalist appeal is predicated upon the assumption that perception can never yield knowledge. This assumption commits Brandom to a duplicitous (hybrid) account of "truth" (reminiscent of what I tried to show in chapter 2): on the one hand, he takes truth to be nothing other than the undertaking of a commitment, and on the other, truth is "just what the tradition always took it to be: saying of what is that it is."[60] On first glance, these might seem to be the same move: namely, that truth is primarily a *saying*. But a closer look reveals the hybridity: it is a saying of *what is*. It is this duplicity that enables Brandom to make sense of situations in which one can *be* justified without *being able* to justify one's belief; he only maintains this because he thinks it is equivalent to saying that one can be entitled without inheriting "that entitlement from *other* commitments inferentially related to it as reasons."[61] According to McDowell, Brandom is only able to equate these two situations because he holds an insufficient conception of justification to begin with—insufficient because internalized. It is because Brandom makes precisely the mistake McDowell had warned against in his 1995 article that he is forced to concede to the externalist's claim. Thus, Brandom is forced to concede, in the case of perception, that, on the one hand, truth *really is* an external element to the space of reasons, while on the other, justification is entirely *internal*—which is why he denies that perception can ever yield sufficient warrant to exclude the possibility of its falsehood (and so produce *knowledge*). At best, Brandom admits that perception can lead one to hold a true belief, but never a justified true belief—can never make one a knower.

Guilty of hybridity, Brandom's epistemology of perception is, therefore, internally unstable: if pressed to is logical conclusion, it will never be able to explain how reason has "the resources it would need in order to evaluate the *reliability* of belief-forming policies or habits."[62] Once again, we witness the disastrousness of driving an ontological wedge between entitlement and truth, here achieved by denying that justification can be given by experience (e.g., by means of the formed-ness of intuition). McDowell concludes: "What I object to is interiorizing *entitlements*, in the sense of refusing to let the connivance of the world enter into constituting them." He goes on, "Applied to the entitlements that perceptual, for instance visual, experience affords, the interiorizing move restricts them to appearances. . . . I argue that it is not satisfactory to leave entitlements thus interiorized but add that what the putative knower takes to be so is in fact so, conceiving this as an extra condition over and above an interiorized entitlement."[63] It would seem that Brandom is in danger of holding something like the very "metaphysical" conception of truth the latter sought to avoid; that is, of conceiving truth as a property of a commitment that corresponds to an external condition. But in trying to maintain this externality without committing himself to a Given, Brandom simultaneously wants to say that the most perception can give us are inconclusive warrants for belief; that is, in effect, appearances.

Brandom's primary aim in his response to McDowell in 1995 was to correct what he viewed as the latter's neglect of the centrality of social practice in creating the metaphorical space of reasons. The irony, McDowell thinks, is that it is Brandom who ends up with a picture of subjects individually incapable of achieving standings in the space of reasons, "who somehow nevertheless keep one another under surveillance."[64] This ambivalence will beset any account of knowledge that does not allow for the world to exercise more than causal constraints upon our thinking. The question now is: does McDowell submit his own thinking to the full implication of this critique? Is he, in short, able to fully account for the connivance of the world?

THE METAPHYSICS OF CONNIVANCE

I'd like to return to the relationship between what McDowell has been calling reason and animality. To be sure, he sees nothing to bridge here. What he does see, however, are degrees of integration. On the spectrum of sentience to sapience, non-rational perception is ontologically prior to rational perception. McDowell rejects Brandom's accusation that he has forgotten the social nature of knowledge; insofar as what it takes to count as a rational perceiver is the acquisition of language, McDowell could not imagine denying the sociality of rationality. And yet, in order to avoid Brandom's problematic account of incapable individuals somehow keeping tabs on one another, McDowell thinks we need to admit the way in which language acquisition actualizes conceptual capacities that *transform the individual's ability to experience*. "[A]s I see things," he writes, "the [conceptual] capacities transform their possessor into an individual who can achieve standings in the space of entitlements *by her own efforts*."[65] Recalling the title of his Marquette lecture, perception becomes, in the hand of a language-user, an *individual* capacity for knowledge.

I see no immediate issue with McDowell's account of the difference language makes to experience, as far as it goes—but it doesn't go far enough. It doesn't, for instance, involve anywhere near sophisticated or detailed enough account for how world and society conspire to produce individuals who might graduate from non-rational perceivers to rational perceivers. In large part, McDowell's failure to do so is due to his resistance to metaphysics and the resultant perpetuation of Kant's mentalization of experience. As long as McDowell continues to predicate his notion of experience upon consciousness, he will never be able to account in sufficient detail for the connivance of the world that he himself insists we need in any non-self-defeating account of knowledge. My purpose in the previous chapter was to show how Whitehead does offer such detail, and, as I addressed in this chapter, he does so in order to remedy the inconsistencies he found in Locke and Hume—the *very same* mistakes McDowell identifies almost a century later.

The philosophy of organism was designed to avoid these mistakes. At the beginning of *Process and Reality,* in the very first paragraph in which Whitehead introduces his Categoreal Scheme, he writes: "Philosophical thought has made for itself difficulties by dealing exclusively in very abstract notions, such as those of mere awareness, mere private sensation, mere emotion, mere purpose, mere appearance, mere causation. These are the ghosts of the old 'faculties,' banished from psychology, but still haunting metaphysics. There can be no 'mere' togetherness of such abstractions. The result is that philosophical discussion is enmeshed in the fallacy of 'misplaced concreteness'."[66] At the same time, and for the same reason, it was designed to expound a conception of experience that was in no way dependent upon reason, consciousness, or even animality in the common sense of the word. He writes: "in the cosmological scheme here outlined one implicit assumption of the philosophical tradition is repudiated. The assumption is that the basic elements of experience are to be described in terms of one, or all, of the three ingredients, consciousness, thought, sense-perception. . . . According to the philosophy of organism these three components are unessential in experience, either physical or mental."[67] All three ingredients are important to notice here, but especially, given our considerations of McDowell, the third.

In the previous chapter, I exposited Whitehead's language of prehension. What the notion of prehension—along with others, like "actual entity"—does for Whitehead is serve as a single term for that which modern philosophy used two terms. A prehension is a concrete form of relation; it is the most basic unit by which experience is possible, regardless of whether it is conventionally construed as "physical" or "mental." The reason, then, that experience in no way depends upon consciousness, thought, or sense-perception is because *they* depend upon (and indeed are themselves complexes of) ontologically prior modes of prehension. I used the term sense *re*ception to indicate an earlier mode of *per*ception which involved more "directness"—that is, more complete conformation to the subject's immediate past.[68] This distinction is meant to communicate something which McDowell asserts but fails to explain, namely, the real possibility of a subject's having some feature of her environment *there* for her, perceptually *present* to her. He thinks this is achieved by a rehabilitated notion of intuition, but, so far as I can see, as long as intuitions continue to be conceived as dependent upon consciousness, and as long as consciousness is conceived mentalistically, intuition will never be able to explain the possibility of this presence. The aesthetics of experience outlined in the previous chapter begins from ontological togetherness, and this is consistent with Whitehead's understanding of the task of a philosopher is to explain the more abstract in terms of the more concrete, rather than vice versa.[69]

In pursuing this task, Whitehead took himself to be developing with more systematic coherence upon William James's thought. It is instructive, therefore, to consider some statements of James's that bear upon the present concerns. James writes in a September 1904 essay provocatively titled "Does 'Consciousness' Exist?": "In its pure state, or when isolated, there is no self-splitting of [experience] into consciousness and what the consciousness is 'of' (i.e., content). Its subjectivity and objectivity are functional attributes solely, realized only when the experience is 'taken', i.e. talked-of, twice, considered along with its two differing contexts retrospectively, by a new retrospective experience, of which the whole past complication now forms the fresh content."[70] Experience, in other words, lacks the "inner duplicity" implied by a distinction between the subject perceiving and the content perceived.[71] It is worth noticing that *this* sort of duplicity is one of which even McDowell is still guilty, even while he admonishes "hybrid" epistemologies as being disastrously duplicitous *precisely because* they "extinguish content."

To be clear, I am by no means accusing McDowell of scheme-content dualism. I have no interest in going in circles. What I am trying to do is to show how the very efforts of thinkers like Davidson, Sellars (on some readings), and McDowell to get *beyond* scheme-content dualism are themselves hampered by tacit metaphysical assumptions which made dualism tempting in the first place. In so doing, I am following McDowell's own prescription for how to deal with the threat of skepticism, which is to say, I am diagnosing his seeming urgency as deriving from a misguided understanding of the basic components of subjecthood. Moreover, so long as McDowell remains unwilling or unable to relinquish a Kantian (however, "rehabilitated") framework of experience—and the modernist dismissal of metaphysics that comes along with it—he will never recognize the full extent of what needs rehabilitation.

In his Foreword to Isabelle Stenger's *Thinking with Whitehead: A Free and Wild Creation of Concepts* (2011), Bruno Latour makes the following observation: "Among his many misfortunes, Whitehead had the very bad one [particularly in America] of provoking too much interest among theologians and too little among epistemologists." I would amend this statement by saying that Whitehead provoked too little interest among *both* groups, but especially the latter.[72] Latour continues,

[Whitehead] also suffers from the terrible stigma of having indulged in metaphysics, something one is no longer supposed to do after the edicts of [Wittgenstein], even though those who think that metaphysics is passé know usually much less science than Whitehead and swallow—without an ounce of criticism—hook, line, and sinker the entirety of metaphysical beliefs about nature that one can easily derive by lumping together the least-common-denominator views of geneticists and so-called cognitive scientists.[73]

There are plenty of reasons to doubt that the edicts of the later Wittgenstein *were* as such.[74] Nevertheless, it is clear that McDowell takes them to be so.[75] And yet, if McDowell's aim is to reconceive experience in order to make sense of how empirical content is so much as possible, but in a way that avoids the interminable oscillation between Givenness and coherentism, it will not be enough to insist on seeing experience as itself conceptual—not, that is, if we continue to think of the conceptual as something unique to linguistically initiated human subjects. Continuing to do so remains complicit in a problematic (i.e., Kantian) order of explanation, whereby we begin with subjectivity in order to redeem objectivity. This is precisely backwards.

If McDowell is equally committed to avoiding "baldly naturalist" accounts of mind and world as idealistic ones, then he would do well to take Whitehead's advice: "The point . . . is that a philosophy of nature as organic [e.g., non-bifurcated] must start at the opposite end to that requisite for a materialistic philosophy." He continues,

The materialistic starting point is from independently existing substances, matter and mind. The matter suffers modifications of its external relations of locomotion, and the mind suffers modifications of its contemplated objects. There are, in this materialistic theory, two sorts of independent substances . . . . The organic starting point is from the analysis of process as the realization of events disposed in an interlocked community. The event is the unit of things real.[76]

In order to rehabilitate empiricism so as to make sense of what is "given" in experience without the threat of skepticism (without reinstating a bifurcation of nature), Whitehead is insisting that we must invert the modernist order of explanation. Recruiting Stengers, Latour comments, "Against the tradition inaugurated by Locke and Descartes, then pushed to the limits by Kant, until it was terminated by William James, Whitehead offers another role for the object of study to play: 'The object [for Whitehead] is neither the judge of our production nor the product of our judgments' (93)."[77] Latour continues, "This new distribution of the former functions of subject and object is what Whitehead calls actual occasions. In his hands, the two arch-modernist concepts of subject and object, instead of designating spatial domains of the world, have become temporal markers: past (object) and present (subject)."[78] The implications are striking: there is no conceivable way, if we rely on Whitehead's categoreal scheme, to "internalize" or "individualize" the space of reasons; in fact, there is never even the temptation to invoke the spatial metaphor, insofar as it relies upon a scientistic, Newtonian conception of absolute space which Whitehead deemed highly abstract.[79] Whitehead rejected from the outset the very modernist terms of expression that would engender the urgency McDowell exhibits to reclaim the connivance of the world.

DEMYSTIFYING ONTOLOGICAL THRESHOLDS

Perhaps the most obvious limitation for McDowell is his failure to challenge Sellars on his equation of language-acquisition with rational self-consciousness. Reason and animality, on this model, are only integrated for human beings initiated into the natural languages of human societies. There does not seem to be any indication in McDowell's work of gradations of rational development. The language of "initiation" is cryptic at best, and McDowell allows it to carry too much conceptual freight without doing the work to explore all that he takes for granted by doing so. Linguistic initiation is McDowell's conceptual bridge between animality and reason; between the capacity for non-rational perception and rational perception; between conscious ways of knowing and self-conscious ways of knowing.

McDowell refuses to challenge Sellars on this point because he refuses to challenge Kant on it. He identifies a precedent for Sellars's equation of language acquisition with rational self-consciousness in the first *Critique*. To be sure, he doesn't take Sellars or Kant to be explicit about their use of "knowledge" being restrictive, such that we observe them using "knowledge" to refer to non-rational or non-language-involving instances, that is, "animal" knowing. But he does think "we miss anything Sellars has reason to insist on if we take him to conceive his topic as a species of a genus, which, for all he cares, can be recognized as being instantiated also in the lives of at least some non-human animals, and, we might add, in the lives of human children in whom the potential for rationality has not yet been brought into first actuality." As McDowell reads him, Sellars "is not making a pronouncement about how we may properly use the word 'know' and its cognates. He is noting that his topic is knowledge as an act of reason in a sense that he connects with language and self-consciousness." His definition, therefore, "need not be prejudicial to a more liberal application of epistemic concepts, for purposes other than his."[80] Likewise, when Kant sets out his task as answering the question, "What can I know?" (A804–5/B832–3), McDowell takes him to exemplify the self-conscious rational subject asking, in the first person, about the parameters of the space of reasons. And insofar as he is asking the question of himself, Kant at least implicitly, on McDowell's reading, links this self-conscious rationality with being a language-user.[81]

The language of species and genus allows McDowell to avoid charges of human exceptionalism. However, insofar as it leaves us wondering about just how the threshold between non-rational and rational ways of knowing gets crossed—ontologically, historically, or developmentally speaking—McDowell's account of second nature remains liable to the charge of being merely assertionary. This is why I have insisted upon Whitehead's aesthetics of experience, because it is the result of doing the real work of establishing the necessary ontological continuity.

In the previous chapter, I focused mainly on how Whitehead's aesthetics of perception and judgment obviates any in-principle worry about their objective purport. The actual entity is Whitehead's solution to the ontological dualism of modernism's subject-object split. It is the ontological togetherness of actual entities, of which subjectivity and objectivity are reconceived as temporal markers, that demystifies intentional relations. What I only suggested at the end of that chapter, however, was how Whitehead's metaphysics of experience relates to his metaphysics of symbolism, in general, and his metaphysics of language, in particular. In this chapter, therefore, my aim was to demonstrate how McDowell's attempted rehabilitation of experience beyond the modernist dualism fails, unlike Whitehead's, to do the ontological legwork necessary to succeed.

As a result, I argued, McDowell stops short of recognizing the ways in which he is perpetuating a problematic metaphysics of subjectivity, insofar as (1) it is predicated upon consciousness and (2) it bifurcates itself into rational and non-rational species by means of the ingredient of language which (3) renders a picture of language as the ontological origination of conceptual capacities that (4) assumes that concepts are the sole possession of conscious thoughts—this last assumption being precisely the premises with which I showed Whitehead to take issue in the previous chapter. As a result of remaining committed to (1)–(4), McDowell further perpetuates the idea that intuitions qua subjective "havings" of a world require consciousness, such that the ontological threshold for what it means to be a subject *at all* depends upon an under-scrutinized notion of mentality. As a further consequence, then, McDowell (5) promotes a picture of "first" nature (qua non-rational) as devoid of meanings (conceived as exclusively linguistic), which plays right into the modernist paradigm.

Whereas I have already argued how Whitehead avoids (1)–(4) in the previous chapter, it is my task in the next chapter to illustrate how he also avoids (5). Whitehead's metaphysics of symbolism is not a latecomer; it underwrites his entire aesthetics of experience such that, when we come to human linguistic practices, there is no temptation to allow nature to bifurcate along classical lines.

The truth is that McDowell has *already* allowed nature to bifurcate when he treats reason and experience as two distinct phenomena, the former operating in the medium of language and the latter operating at some more basic level of intuition. What underwrites *this* bifurcation is a prior one between mind and body. In all his work to avoid bifurcating mind and world, McDowell pays shockingly little attention to the one lingering between mind and body. The overwhelming privilege that McDowell (indeed, the entirety of the literature surrounding analytic philosophy of mind) gives to visual examples of perception further suggests to me his discomfort with examples that blur the boundary between experience and reason, body and mind, first nature and second nature.[82] But discomfort can be instructive; it can show us the weakest points of our thinking. In McDowell's case, it shows us the emptiness of concepts, like "consciousness," which are supposed to hold the line around which so many of his other distinctions congregate.

Whitehead is keenly aware of the danger posed to our thinking by unsupervised abstractions. In place of allowing "consciousness" to do the work of an entity, the way he saw Berkeley's "mind" as functioning, Whitehead substitutes "a process of prehensive unification."[83] Using "prehension" to heal the subject/object dichotomy, Whitehead follows James in denying that "consciousness" adds anything to our understanding of thoughts. Rather, "consciousness 'stands for' a 'function', a function that thoughts 'perform' and which is called 'knowing'."[84] In James's word, "Consciousness connotes a kind of external relation, and does not denote a special stuff or way of being. The peculiarity of our experiences, that they not only are, but are known, which their 'conscious' quality is invoked to explain, is better explained by their relations—these relations themselves being experiences—to one another."[85] According to James, we needn't add any new type of metaphysical entity to our account of experience in order to understanding how those experiences get reported. Thus, he continues, "Were I now to go on to treat of the knowing of perceptual by conceptual experiences, it would again prove to be an affair of external relations. One experience would be the knower, the other the reality known, and I could perfectly well define, without the notion of 'consciousness', what the knowing actually and practically amounts to."[86] In other words, if we are to avoid nature bifurcating, we are going to have to figure out a way to explain the ability to *know* that something is the case without adding anything to our outstanding account of how things can *be* the case.

For Whitehead, the key to doing this is to account for the sorts of activities we call rational by means of the same organic function that accounts for non-rational ones. Among other things, this means that we cannot rely upon a prior understanding of human subjectivity, qua McDowell's rational self-consciousness, for instance, to explain the efficacy of language and the styles of thought made possible by it. It will have to be the other way around; we will need to explain human subjectivity in terms of the efficacy of the sign.[87] In the next chapter, I will show how Whitehead does just that through his aesthetics of symbolism. For Whitehead, the aesthetics of symbolism, by which he accounts for the organic efficacy of the sign in the most elemental of events constituting the creative passage of nature, is ultimately explanatory of the process by which language and generic modes of thought are possible.

NOTES

1. Sec. 3, para. 3.
2. Whitehead, *Process and Reality*, 113.
3. Ibid.
4. Ibid.
5. Ibid.
6. McDowell, *Having a World in View*, 99.
7. Ibid., 100.
8. Sellars, *Science and Metaphysics*, 4; McDowell, *Having a World in View*, 98.
9. McDowell, *Having a World in View*, 98.
10. Ibid., 99.
11. Kant, *Critique of Pure Reason*, B160–161n. Original emphasis.
12. McDowell, *Mind and World*, xx.
13. Ibid.
14. Marquette University Press published the lecture under the same title later that year as a book, to which all subsequent page numbers refer.
15. Wilfrid Sellars, *Empiricism and the Philosophy of Mind* (Cambridge and London: Harvard University Press, 1997), 76.
16. McDowell, *Perception as a Capacity for Knowledge* (Marquette University Press, 2011), 11.
17. Ibid., 10.
18. Ibid., 14.
19. Ibid., 10.
20. Ibid., 14–15.
21. Ibid., 13.
22. Tyler Burge, "Perceptual Entitlement," *Philosophy and Phenomenological Research*, ed. Ernest Sosa vol. 67, no. 3 (2003): 503–548, esp. 504.
23. Ibid., 505.
24. McDowell, *Perception as a Capacity for Knowledge*, 30.
25. Ibid., 30–31.
26. Ibid., 31.
27. Ibid.
28. Ibid., 33. Emphasis mine.

29. Ibid. First two emphases are mine.
30. Ibid., 30.
31. Ibid., 36.
32. Ibid.
33. Ibid., 37.
34. Ibid., 57.
35. John McDowell, "Knowledge and the Internal," *Philosophy and Phenomenological Research*, vol. 55, no. 4 (Dec. 1995): 877–893).
36. Ibid., 878.
37. Ibid., 888.
38. Ibid.
39. Ibid., 889.
40. Ibid.
41. Ibid.
42. Ibid.
43. Ibid., 890.
44. Ibid.
45. Ibid., 891.
46. Ibid.
47. Ibid. Emphases mine.
48. Whitehead, *Process and Reality,* 139. See my chapter 4, page 6.
49. See my chapter 4, pp. 13–15.
50. Ibid.
51. Robert Brandom, "Knowledge and the Social Articulation of the Space of Reasons," *Philosophy and Phenomenological Research,* vol. 55, no. 4 (Dec. 1995): 895–908, esp. 895.
52. Ibid.
53. Ibid., 899.
54. Ibid., 902.
55. Ibid., 903.
56. Ibid, 903 fn. 4. Emphases mine.
57. Ibid.
58. Ibid., 904.
59. John McDowell, "Knowledge and the Internal Revisited," *Philosophy and Phenomenological Research,* vol. 64, no. 1 (Jan. 2002): 97–105, esp. 97.
60. Ibid., 903 fn. 4.
61. Brandom, Knowledge and the Social Articulation, 904.
62. McDowell, Knowledge and the Internal Revisited, 883.
63. Ibid., 101.
64. Ibid., 105.
65. Ibid.
66. Whitehead, *Process and Reality,* 18.
67. Ibid., 36.
68. See, for instance, my chap. 4, p. 31.
69. Whitehead, *Process and Reality,* 20.

70. William James, "Does 'Consciousness' Exist?," *The Journal of Philosophy, Psychology, and Scientific Methods,* vol. 1, no. 18 (Sept. 1904): 477–491, esp. 485.

71. Ibid., 480.

72. Thanks to an anonymous peer reviewer for bringing my attention to the non-necessity of insisting that Whitehead has had too much influence among theologians because he hasn't had enough among epistemologists.

73. Bruno Latour, "What Is Given in Experience?," Foreword to Isabelle Stengers, *Thinking with Whitehead: A Free and Wild Creation of Concepts,* trans. Michael Chase (Harvard University Press, 2011).

74. See, for instance, George Lucas's "Whitehead and Wittgenstein: The Critique of Enlightenment and the Question Concerning Metaphysics," in *Process and Analysis: Whitehead, Hartshorne, and the Analytic Tradition,* ed. George W. Shields (SUNY, 2003), 67–93.

75. John McDowell, "Wittgenstein's 'Quietism'," *Common Knowledge* 15:3 (Duke UP, 2009), 365–372. He writes, "Therapeutic philosophy is designed to spare us the travails of positive philosophy." (372).

76. Whitehead, *Science and the Modern World* (The Free Press, 1925/1953), 152.

77. Latour, 2; citing Stengers, 93.

78. Ibid., 8.

79. I will say much more on this point in the next chapter, specifically in section 3.

80. McDowell, 2011, 14–15.

81. Ibid., 16.

82. It is interesting to note, on this point, what Whitehead says about the exemption of the experience of the "pushiness" of the body from the realm of secondary qualities in eighteenth and nineteenth century materialist accounts of perception. See, for example, Whitehead, *Concept of Nature,* 43.

83. Whitehead, *Science and the Modern World,* 69.

84. Stengers, *Thinking with Whitehead,* 149.

85. James, "Does 'Consciousness' Exist?," 486.

86. Ibid.

87. Stengers, "A Constructivist Reading of Process and Reality," *Theory, Culture, and Society,* vol. 25, No. 4 (2008): 91–110, esp. 102.

Chapter 6

Symbolism and Language

INTRODUCTION

The challenge of this chapter is to maintain an appreciation of the self-reflexive nature of talking about language, while resisting the traditional modes of thought that leave one mystified by this reflexivity. I concluded the previous chapter with an indication as to how Whitehead allows us to maintain this balance, namely, by never asking the explanandum (e.g., rational self-consciousness) to be the ontological guarantor of the explanans (e.g., language). To do so is to beg the question of the (in this case, human) subject in a way that ultimately sustains some form of the bifurcation. In McDowell's case, it was in the form of a divide between experience and reason, with the concomitant divide between nature-as-factful and nature-as-meaningful. To avoid these erroneous implications, we need an about-face; we need an account of the possibility of linguistic practices and generic modes of thought by way of an ontology of symbolic efficacy. This chapter details how Whitehead provides it.

To recall some conceptual groundwork, in chapter 4 I explored the ways in which Whitehead's aesthetic, event-based ontology enables ways of "taking account" of things that avoid the bifurcation of nature. I exposited both the distinction and continuity between receptive and perceptive modes of this taking account, including how preconceptual ways of taking account not only precede but remain caught-up in conceptual ones. Vital to this inversion of the classical empiricist theory of perception and judgment, with its treatment of the cognitivity of sense-data (Whitehead's "presentational immediacy") as primitive and relations of efficient causality (Whitehead's "causal efficacy") as a derived from analysis, is the rejection of its implicit doctrine of simple occurrence or simple location. Taking events rather than substances as the final units of analysis effects such a rejection, and with it, the spatialization of thought and of the conceptual that precipitates from it—with the attendant "problem" of mind and world.

On the basis of real ontological togetherness, Whitehead is able to reconceptualize the traditional metaphysical quandary of how individuality and community relate—how, we might say, they are in community with one another at the same time that they are individuated. The mechanisms of community are not antithetical to those of individuality for Whitehead; they are co-constitutive. The forces that bind, that unite, are, at an ontological level, not external but internal—not coercive but purposive. But so are the forces that dissolve and disunite. This point has substantive implications for discussion about the efficacy of cultural and political forms of community, but the focus of this chapter will be more basic. I will examine the mechanisms of community and individuality, of uniqueness and collectivity, in terms of what Whitehead calls relations of "symbolic reference." This examination will serve the broader purpose of the book by suggesting how symbolism in general and language in particular fit within the aesthetic ontology that I have employed to vindicate intentionality. It will serve the further purpose of extending my analysis of individual intention to one of collective intention, thereby opening the project up to pressing questions about the social vocation of reason.

"Reference" is not an epistemological term for Whitehead; it is an aesthetic one. A relationship is referential when one experience elicits another not geographically approximate. It is because of this definition that Whitehead wonders why "we say that the word 'tree'—spoken or written—is a symbol to us for trees," as disquotationalists maintain. On his account, both the word "tree" and trees "enter into our experience on equal terms," such that we could just as well say that trees are a symbol for the word "tree."[1] Referentiality is the mode in which symbol and meaning are "together." And this togetherness of symbols and meaning is parasitic upon the real togetherness of durations—a togetherness not afforded by substance metaphysics. To illustrate this fact, I will discuss Whitehead's fixation on the ambiguity of the language of conjunction: "and," "with," "together," and so on. Analysis of their ambiguity exposes the inadequacy of classical conceptions of time as point-like seriality or space as "occupied by" things.

It is upon such classical conceptions, for instance, that understandings of "sense-data" have failed to address the skeptic's worries. According to Whitehead, sense-data are intrinsically relational and can "with equal truth be described as our sensations or as the qualities of the actual things which we perceive."[2] They have a double reference—this double reference is the basis of the "whole physiological theory of perception," even while it is one explicitly denied by classical empiricists. In other words, there must be a "partial community of structure"³ for sensation to be possible. Sense-data, properly understood, represent this partial community: I taste the acidity of the coffee, I taste it *with* my tongue. The bitterness of the coffee is not only *given*, it is given *by*.

On Whitehead's analysis, Hume tacitly assumes the necessity of this double reference: "[Hume] writes: 'If it be perceived by the eyes, it must be a colour; if by the ears, a sound; if by the palate, a taste; and so of the other senses'. Thus in asserting the lack of perception of causality, he implicitly presupposes it. For what is the meaning of '*by*' in '*by* the eyes', '*by* the ears', '*by* the palate'? His argument presupposes that sense-data, functioning in presentational immediacy, are 'given' by reason of 'eyes', 'ears', 'palates' functioning in causal efficacy. Otherwise, his argument is involved in a vicious regress."⁴ Even while Hume tacitly assumes these two modes, presentational immediacy and causal efficacy, Whitehead thinks, he explicitly maintains only the former, taking presentational immediacy or the experience of the givenness of sense-data as the primitive phenomenon, and, therefore, treats causal efficacy as the product of inference or reasoning. This is an "inversion of the evidence" on Whitehead's account.⁵

Whitehead argues that the trouble we have with understanding this "taking account" in the form of causal efficacy depends upon the assumption that time is "merely the generic notion of pure succession."⁶ To understand symbolism likewise requires us to recognize the untenable nature of the idea of simple location, insofar as the fallacies are analogous. Symbolic reference depends upon the quantum of durations, messily overlapping in multiple dimensions, not upon durationless "points" that in principle have no internal relations to their predecessors. Whitehead's concern with this topic preceded his explicitly philosophical works by a decade or more, while he was still writing in the capacity of an applied mathematician. An initial discussion of these works, and the interactions with contemporary interlocutors that frame them, will assist our understanding of his theory of symbolism.

MEANING AND PHYSICAL EXPLANATION

On June 1, 1916, Whitehead published a paper from the 37th session of the Aristotelian Society entitled "Space, Time, and Relativity."⁷ This was the same issue in which Nunn's "Sense-data and Physical Objects" appeared, which I discussed in chapter 1. The paper, some explanatory notes of which Whitehead had delivered to the Society on January 3 of that same year, was intended to provide an interface for the various working theories of space-time in contemporary scholarship across metaphysics, experimental psychology, and mathematical physics. His concern was to characterize the relation between "mathematical" and "physical" (or phenomenological) concepts of time and space—a distinction often lost by "common sense" assumptions about them.

Whitehead begins by examining the idea of "an infinite unchangeable space."[8] This is the "Absolute Theory of Space" that conceives of "the points of space as self-subsistent entities which have the indefinable relation of being occupied by the ultimate stuff (matter, I will call it) which is there."[9] He continues, "Thus, to say that the sun is *there* (wherever it is) is to affirm the relation of occupation between the set of positive and negative electrons which we call the sun and a certain set of points, the points having an existence essentially independent of the sun."[10] It is not difficult to see the compatibility between the basic tenets of substance metaphysics and the Newtonian conception of "empty space." This idea of space, as "a certain set of points" existing independently of the objects "in" space whose distance "between" one another we measure by varying units, is not the space of direct observation, even if we have come to talk of space in this way so routinely that we have come to "see" it in that way. But Whitehead is apt to point out that we never encounter such an absolute space except by imaginative reconstruction for the purposes of mathematical physics.

The common idea of space as an infinite and unchangeable extension of definite points had, however, been recently challenged by Albert Einstein's Theory of Special Relativity. The Relative Theory of Space holds that our concept of space is nothing other than a concept of the "relations between things" such that "there is no such entity as a self-subsistent point." A "point" is nothing more than a name for "some peculiarity of the relations between the matter which is, in common language, said to be in space."[11] Whitehead is not certain that his contemporary mathematicians had yet fully realized the challenge that such a theory posed to their assumption of the nature of a "point," which hitherto had served as "the ultimate starting ground of their reasoning."[12] I suspect that by the phrase "ultimate starting ground" Whitehead is referring to the opening lines of Euclid's *Elements,* the 13-book mathematical treatise from 4th century Alexandria that established the logical development of the principles of plane geometry. The first line of the treatise reads: "That which has position but not magnitude is called a point."[13] This is the fundamental idea upon which the principles of Euclidean geometry were to be built; a point is that which cannot be defined in terms of dimensional attributes. It is pure position, pure location. A point is particular, unique, and unchanging. This last descriptor, the point as "unchanging," is perhaps the most significant for my purposes here. To deny change is to define the essence of a point in completely atemporal terms; of course, this is precisely what we commonly think of "space" as, namely, *not* time. As Whitehead writes years later in *Modes of Thought* (1938), "the extension of space is the ghost of transition."[14] The fundamental notion of mathematical space, Whitehead argues, therefore, depends upon the idea of disconnection; that is, upon the definition of a point as that which has no parts.

This conception of points as the fundamental things of which "space" is composed has a temporal correlate, namely, "instants" of time. These notions are pervasive in our everyday ways of speaking, and yet, Whitehead points out, they are not phenomenologically correct. "We live in durations, and not in points," he writes, and it takes little reflection to realize that "points in space" and "instants of time" are not notions deriving from the "direct deliverance of experience."[15] They are, in short, deductions.

It is important to note, however, that Whitehead is not so much as dismissing these notions wholesale as putting them into proper context. Whereas it may be true that "no one lives in 'an infinite given whole', but in a set of fragmentary experiences," it is also true that we need to account for why the ideas of "points in space" and "instants of time" are the "necessary outcome of these fragments by a process of logical building up."[16] In other words, even once we have recognized the distinction between mathematical space-time and what Whitehead calls "physical" space-time, we still need to account for the fact that those notions arise by way of deductive reasoning, and that they are the ones upon which our conceptions of a "common world" depend.

These early considerations by Whitehead of the notions of space and time demonstrate his concern with maintaining a close watch on generality. I stressed in chapter 4 the importance to Whitehead of explaining the more abstract in terms of the more concrete. Even in his early thinking, we can see his conviction that our conceptions of the "real" world ought to do justice to our "apparent" world, and not the other way around. Giving a clear voice to the "directness" of experience, and untangling it from the notions we have learned to import in the analytical aftermath, is one of the main objectives of this 1916 work. What we do not see in this article is a worry about how conceptual schemes can infiltrate this directness in and of itself, and, therefore, the worry about language structuring our perceptions of the world. In short, Whitehead maintains a clear distinction between linguistic and non-linguistic ways of being in touch with the world, and the sense in which we feel more than we know. These metaphysical intuitions became more systematic in his later years, but it is helpful for my purposes to explore further how their early articulations were wrapped up with the theory of time and space. It is helpful insofar as an appreciation of his later account of symbolism in general, and language in particular, as non-problematic ways of "having" a world in view depends upon a prior scrutiny of problematic conceptions of time and space—namely, the conceptions of "points" and "instants" qua expressions of the fundamental disconnectivity of reality.

In 1919, Whitehead led a symposium on "Time, Space, and Material" for the proceedings of the Aristotelian Society that expanded upon his 1916 theme. In his introductory paper to the symposium, Whitehead introduces his critique of the "mathematical" concept of time that had permeated the "general scientific" thought, such that time in the form of disconnected "instants" was regarded as "expressive of the ultimate structure of time."[17] His critique of the "traditional" concepts of space and time would be published shortly after the symposium as *An Enquiry into the Principles of Natural Knowledge* (Cambridge, UK: Cambridge University Press, 1919). His *Enquiry* begins with a chapter on "Meaning" and its opening line asks, "What is a physical explanation?" The fact that Whitehead begins his discourse on meaning with a question about the nature of a physical explanation indicates that he is not starting with any hard distinctions between conceptuality and physicality. What he seems to indicate, rather, is that the semantic is a species of the aesthetic.

Whitehead is not explicitly talking about meaning in a semantic sense in this opening question. Instead, he is asking about what counts as an explanation for the physical sciences. Later, in 1927, when Whitehead gives the Barbour-Page Lectures at the University of Virginia, his topic is precisely symbolism and symbolic expression, including but not singularly linguistic expression. Even when the semantic is on his radar, then, a first order explanation of meaning is aesthetic. He is committed to what I will call the physicality of meaning.

Explanation and meaning are conceptually bound up in one another for Whitehead, insofar he understands meaning in terms of effect, and explanation in terms of determining cause. To ask about what counts as a physical explanation is another way of asking about the "ultimate facts" for science. Something is explained, on this account, when we have appealed to an ultimate fact. What count as ultimate facts thereby determine the end of explanation. We say that we have explained the phenomena of conduction, for instance, when we appeal to the excitability of atoms according to the laws of thermodynamics. We can appeal thermodynamic equations to indicate extensive quantities that correspond to physical properties, and thereby allow us to solve for variables unknown by variables known. We explain physical phenomena in terms of extensive quantities—that is, in terms of space and time.

But this is precisely why Whitehead is asking about physical explanations. It seemed to him, in 1919, odd that if he were to ask a scientist what the data of his or her work were, the answer would inevitably be some variation of "the observed universe." And yet, if what the scientist was really in search of were physical explanations—explanations couched in terms of measurable time and measurable space—the data of science are not products of direct observation but are deductive notions of time, space, and the material that is said to be "in" them. What he calls the "orthodox" answer to the question "What is a physical explanation?" would without exception "be couched in terms of Time (flowing equably in measurable lapses) and of Space (timeless, void of activity, Euclidean), and of Material in space (such as matter, ether, or electricity)."[18] But if the "data" of science are deductive notions and not observed entities, why does there seem to be such consensus—popular and scientific—that we *live* in "instants" of time and "points" of space? And what is the consequence of mapping the data of science so uncritically onto our experiences—in short, of *explaining* phenomenological temporality and spatiality in terms of mathematical time and space? Of specific concern for Whitehead on this occasion is the fact that mathematical time and space, according to the "orthodox" view, are notions premised upon a metaphysics of discreteness and discontinuity.

The consequence, then, is that phenomenological temporality and spatiality—of lived experience qua durational, continuous, and deeply interrelated—is commonly understood as explainable in terms of a fundamental lack of relation. The ultimate facts being unrelated in principle, meaning qua effect will always seem mystical. We need to scrutinize the assumption that extension means disconnection, Whitehead argues, before we can understand why "events" must replace "things" as the ultimate facts. Whitehead's case for the necessity of this scrutiny is not heteronomous; it is the product of immanent critique. Science cannot makes sense—cannot provide *physical* explanations—of change, duration, velocity, motion, acceleration, and other related notions until it has scrutinized its assumptions about time and space. We live in durations, not instants of time and points in space. Until it is recognized that the latter are deductive notions and not the products of direct observation, we will continue to explain continuity in terms of discontinuity. The consequences of so doing include, among other things, problematic accounts of mind and world, conceptual and physical, past and future, actuality and possibility, efficacy and purpose. What all these have in common is a need for concrete explanation, but so long as our conceptions of explanation depend upon misplaced concreteness with respect to "instants" of time and "points" in space, our explanations of the former will be found wanting. I suspect, then, that the reason that Whitehead began his chapter on meaning with the question about what counts as a physical explanation is because meaning or significance is nothing if not the contiguity of the past with the future—and this is a contiguity that is felt more than it is known.

"ABSOLUTE TIME" AND "ABSOLUTE SPACE"

Meaning will always remain mysterious so long as what counts as explanation is predicated upon discrete units of extension that render this contiguity problematic at the quantum level. So long as the principle governing our account of explanation is that extension expresses disconnection, moreover, there will continue to be inconsistencies in our accounts of "matter" or "material" (or whatever we take to be extended). On the one hand, Whitehead argues, "This principle issues in the assumptions that causal action between entities separated in time or in space is impossible and that extension in space and unity of being are inconsistent."[19] On the other hand, he argues, "This governing principle has to be limited in respect to extension in time. This concession introduces the many perplexities centering around the notion of change which is derived from the comparison of various states of self-identical material at different times."[20] What we are left with is a picture of an ultimate fact as being "a distribution of material throughout all spaces at a durationless instant of time," where each additional ultimate fact would be *another* such timeless distribution in temporal succession. But then, what are we to make of change? We can make nothing of change if temporal extension is not itself ingredient in ultimate facts. In different language, we cannot account for velocity, acceleration, momentum, or kinetic energy *at all* without temporal extension—without, that is, "some reference to the past and the future."[21] It was on this basis that Einstein's general relativity theory was, or ought to have been, particularly devastating to the fundamental assumption of science that its "facts" are to be found in durationless instants of time. This is because, among other things, his theory proved that the gravitational field is not *distributed throughout* space; the gravitational field *is that space* itself. The earth's orbit is not caused by some invisible force acting at a distance to "attract" it; the earth continually falls toward the sun because the sun's mass bends space around it so that the earth circles the sun as a marble in a funnel.

Our grammar presents some difficulty here, for the sun doesn't really "bend" space; the mathematical equations developed by Bernhard Riemann demonstrate that the properties of a curved space are *equivalent* to the energy of matter. After all, Einstein's $E = mc^2$ demonstrates that mass and energy are the same physical entity. What this means is that "space" is the relation between two things, not what they are "in." But it is not only space that bends, but time too. So these "things" are events with no absolute space or absolute time; space and time are relative according to what an event is in reference *to*. It was in 1919 that Einstein's prediction that the sun causes light to deviate in its course was confirmed—the same year Whitehead published his *Enquiry*.[22]

Whitehead suspected that change could not be accounted for on the traditional view of space and time, and Einstein's reconsideration of Newton's notion of "absolute space" in order to account for the force of gravity without action at a distance expresses similar suspicion. For Whitehead, the problem was with what counts as "points of contact" in causal relations. To account for change on the assumption of serially ordered distributions of matter in space—in short, "substances" as ultimate facts—causal relations must be described in terms of "the transmission of stress across the bounding surface of contiguous materials."[23] But if the contiguous materials are essentially disconnected, what "contact" could mean is unclear. The orthodox view, therefore, forces us into an infinite spatial regress—the "infinitesimals" whose possibility I said Whitehead rejected (see chapter 1). But there are no "infinitely small volumes"; only "smaller and smaller volumes." If this is the case, then we not only have to reject the idea of internal relations, but external ones, too.[24]

His point is, in effect, that in the process of trying to make sense of "stress" in light of ultimate facts as "continuous distribution of diverse (because extended) entities through space," we will be forced to define the nature of that unity "under stress" *in terms of that stress*—that is, in terms of the relation qua stressful. This is why we need a philosophy of organism, because the concept of an organism "cannot be expressed in terms of a material distribution at an instant."[25] Organisms are defined in terms of biological function, and "functioning takes time."[26] They are none other than a unity with spatiotemporal extension.

Biological phenomena are not different in kind from other sorts of physical phenomena for Whitehead. It is just that, at the level at which biological sciences operate, the necessity of bringing time back into definitions of ultimate facts becomes more apparent, or, rather, the inconsistencies of *not* doing so are more glaring. Whitehead, therefore, states that his "fundamental assumption" in the *Enquiry* is that "the ultimate facts of nature, in terms of which all physical and biological explanation must be expressed, are events connected by their spatio-temporal relations, and that these relations are in the main reducible to the property of events that they can contain (or extend over) other events which are parts of them."[27] That is, "space" and "time" are understood as the deductive notions we use to express the properties of events, and the properties of events are how events interrelate. "In other words," he continues, "in the place of emphasizing space and time in their capacity for disconnection, we shall build up an account of their complex essences as derivative from the ultimate ways in which those things, ultimate in science, are interconnected."[28] Demonstrating the *mathematical* origins and, therefore, the *mathematical* utility of the orthodox conceptions of space and time, while also demonstrating the problems with letting them replace physical or phenomenological ones, is the "constructive task" of his *Enquiry*.

The assumption that points are "ultimate given entities," while extremely useful for the "logical purposes of mathematicians" working on the "foundations of geometry" in the nineteenth century, is nevertheless "a metaphysical fairy tale."[29] In *The Concept of Nature* (1930), he writes, "Instantaneousness is a complex logical concept of a procedure in thought by which constructed logical entities are produced for the sake of the simple expression in thought of properties of nature. Instantaneousness is the concept of all nature at an instant, where an instant is conceived as deprived of all temporal extension."[30] He continues, "For example we conceive of the distribution of matter in space at an instant. This is a very useful concept in science especially in applied mathematics; but it is a very complex idea so far as concerns its connexions with the immediate facts of sense-awareness."[31] The theory of absolute space only works so long as we are still working with Euclidean geometry, within which we need to be able to define what a point is. Without a definition of points, we cannot account for the "space" between them. Euclid began his *Elements* by defining a point so that he could then define a straight line, and then a plane. Euclidean geometry, as plane-based geometry, therefore, requires the assumption of space as absolute and non-relative, because if it weren't, then the notion of measurability "between" points—in short, of geometry—would be nonsensical. The concept of absolute space, as the concept of "persistent ultimate material distributed among the persistent ultimate points in successive configurations at successive ultimate instants of time,"[32] is an intellectual construction.

The problem is that it hasn't been treated as such. Hume assumed that what we perceive are just such "durationless instants," and he was, therefore, led to conclude that we do not perceive connection, but disconnection. Whitehead isn't saying that points are not "real," only that they have been misconceived by the general scientific community, and that this misconception has been encouraged by the tacit assumptions of substance metaphysics that have permeated Western intellectual history. In any case, the consequence of relativity is that "spatial relations must now stretch across time."[33] It is precisely this point, that spatial relations do not exist in a temporal vacuum, which informed the account of perception and judgment presented in chapter 4. Accordingly, the ultimate units of perception are not points or instants, but durations; what we perceive, when we perceive, is the continuity of existence. Events are "those immediate deliverances of observation," the relations between and the characters of which we express in terms of concepts of space, time, and material. We will properly regard these concepts only if we can express them "as issuing from fundamental relations between events and from recognitions of the characters of events."[34] And insofar as meaning or significance is, as I said above, nothing if not the contiguity of the past with the future, it follows that significance is not detachable from experience in the way Hume assumed. In other words, perceptions are not "in the mind" and nature "outside the mind"—if one begins with experience and then tries to discover its significance, skepticism will be unavoidable.

We do not perceive discrete instants and then try to determine their significance for one another; we perceive the relatedness of things, which is to say, we perceive significance. "Certainly if we commence with a knowledge of things, and then look around for their relations," Whitehead quips, "we shall not find them."[35] In what sounds like a description of what will be termed "eternal objects" by the time he writes *Process and Reality*, Whitehead writes that the "so-called properties of things" are nothing other than "relatedness to other things unspecified."[36] Science operates with an "entirely incoherent philosophy of perception so far as it restricts itself to the ultimate datum of material in time and space, the spatio-temporal configuration of such material being the object of perception."[37] The data of science are not things in space in serial order—the theory of relativity exposed the limits of the absolute theory of time and space. What relativity theory means for our understanding of the ultimate data of science, which Whitehead was concerned to indicate, is that the percipient event is *of* and *within* nature, with the further implication that notions of "the common world" or "all of nature" are not only deductive, but shot through with notions of "absolute time" and "absolute space" that are equally deductive.

As encountered in the *Enquiry,* Whitehead's concern to maintain a careful watch on abstraction, so as to not commit the fallacy of misplaced concreteness, challenged the prevailing understanding of what counts as "physical explanation," according to which meaning could have no part. Redefining the ultimate data of science and, therefore, the terms by which we express physical explanations, as durations that are in principle spatiotemporally extended, writes meaning back into the very nature of experience. Meaning is no longer mystical, supervening, or merely "conceptual" in the classical sense; it is the basis of efficacy. With the foregoing critique of orthodox views of time and space, and its implications for our understandings of the data of science, the nature of physical explanation, and the reality of meaning, we are in a position to better appreciate the nature of symbolic reference.

EXTENSIONALITY

In *Symbolism,* Whitehead defines symbolic reference as the "organic functioning whereby there is transition from the symbol to the meaning."[38] As discussed in the previous section, "meanings" are the direct deliverances of perception insofar as each event expresses, in aesthetic terms, the significance of prior events. This "priority" is not an absolute character but a relative one—it is best understood in terms of filial, rather than universal, order. Meaning is not separate from experience; it is of the very nature of experience qua perceptive event.

As I discussed in chapter 4, Whitehead makes distinctions in his later work between different "modes" of experience. In this 1927 work, he details precisely three. The first two modes of experience will be familiar by now to the reader; they are the "perceptive modes" of presentational immediacy and causal efficacy. The third he calls experience in the mode of "conceptual analysis." It is important to remember that these "modes" are never "pure" in experience. In *Process and Reality*, he writes, "When human experience is in question, 'perception' almost always means 'perception in the mixed mode of symbolic reference.'"[39] The modes of perception compound, and when they do, they become caught up in feedback loops, augmenting the intensity and clarity of, but also the possibility of error in, experience. This is what Whitehead means when, as I mention later on, he writes that synthesis and analysis require each other.

Perceptive experiences "introduce into human experience components which are again analyzable into actual things of the actual world and into abstract attributes, qualities, and relations, which express how those other actual things contribute themselves as components to our experience." He continues, "These abstractions express how other actualities are component objects for us."[40] It is an important point for Whitehead that symbolic reference is not the product of conceptual analysis, even while it is "greatly promoted by it."[41] Before an organism can be capable of experience in the mode of conceptual analysis, it must already be capable not only of perceptive experience in the mode of causal efficacy and presentational immediacy, but also of complex syntheses of the two modes into a single experience. This synthetic activity is symbolic reference. When symbolic reference occurs, there is a relation between the more abstract and the more concrete—between, that is, a symbol and a meaning. The hearing of the word "tree" is concrete, and the consequent abstract recollection of what trees look like follows. Likewise, the perception of a tree—the roughness of its trunk or the bristling of its leaves—may effect the recollection of the word "tree." Aural events of speech and visual events of writing are equally immediate experiences as the touching of the bark or the listening to the wind through the branches. What makes something a symbol and something a meaning is the role each plays in the relation under consideration. The more complex and derivative the relations of symbolic reference, the less the syntheses rely upon geographical proximity.

When signs become communal, they can be inherited or taught. With ready-made and explicit relations of symbolic reference, it becomes possible to experience things as tokens of a type, and, therefore, to work with classes of abstraction or genera. Genera, both despite being and precisely because they are highly abstract, promote a standardization or normativization of symbolic reference. Moreover, qua explicit, they make possible a new mode of experience in the mode of conceptual analysis, whereby experience is increasingly unconstrained by immediacy and particularity. With language, we can refer to broader durations—we can even conceive of the *broadest* duration or the least broad duration, formulating conceptions of infinitely large or infinitely small spatiotemporal extensions. The former enables us to speak of universal laws, and the latter, of the quantum of explanation.

And yet, such conceptions are abstractions, because there is no atomic structure of durations. As he writes in 1930, "the perfect definition of a duration, so as to mark out its individuality and distinguish it from highly analogous durations over which it is passing, or which are passing over it, is an arbitrary postulate of thought."[42] In *Process and Reality,* he defines a duration as "a locus of actual occasions, such that (α) any two members of the locus are contemporaries, and (β) that any actual occasion, not belonging to the duration is in the causal past or causal future of some members of the duration."[43] The key word in the foregoing is *some.* A duration is held together by the fact that its constituent occasions share a time-system with at least one other occasion, but not all. In other words, durations are polythetic, not monothetic. The polythetic constitution is sufficient to count as a "unison of becoming" or a "concrescent unison."[44] This means that, within a duration, some events could constitute one occasion's past, while the same event could constitute another occasion's future, and still this would count as the present duration. Presence is specious.

Whitehead was keenly aware of the entanglement between the conceptual and the perceptual, and, therefore, of the ways in which our language influences our perception. "[M]uch of our perception," he writes, "is due to the enhanced subtlety arising from a concurrent conceptual analysis."[45] Indeed, it was because of this concurrence that Whitehead observed no strict line between "physical" and "mental" phenomena, and acknowledged that it was purely by convention that he preferred to reserve the term "mental" for experiential activities involving "concepts in addition to percepts."[46] But because he emphasized concurrence and not an overhaul of the conceptual, he did not draw coherentist conclusions from this entanglement. Rather, he emphasized the "miracles of sensitiveness" that it occasions.[47] Entanglement does not mean that language is a "filter" of perception—there is a mutual qualification.

What Whitehead was concerned to emphasize was that, just as much as conceptual analysis enhances perception, by contributing an exactness of attention precisely by way of generality (such that sense-data can be tokens of types), it contributes, in *equal measure* to the expression of experience, the critiquability of those expressions. "Symbolic expression first preserves society by adding emotion to instinct," he writes, "and secondly it affords a foothold for reason by its delineation of the particular instinct which it expresses."[48] By adding "emotion," Whitehead means that symbols, when conventionalized, function to elicit shared meanings that serve to bind societies together. But these emotions, as symbolically conditioned actions, can become reflexive, effecting uncritical loyalties and prejudices. This happens,

Whitehead argues, when "the response of action to symbol . . . [becomes] so direct as to cut out any effective reference to the ultimate thing symbolized." The result is an "elimination of meaning," and such action or reaction to symbols without meaning he terms reflex action.[49] Prejudice is, no doubt, one of the strongest forces for binding groups together. But this elimination of meaning is the result of a failure to express the instincts to which emotion has been added by symbol. The second function of symbol—a function which I do not understand as *additive* but *co-constitutive*—is occasioning immanent critique. More can and should be said on the contributions Whitehead can make to understandings of the social vocation of reason, but that is beyond the scope of the present chapter.

For my purposes here—namely, the articulation of Whitehead's philosophy of language—the relevance of the foregoing is primarily the point about conceptual analysis as a promoter of symbolic reference, and, therefore, of greater sensitivities in both detail and expanse (including the amended accounts of time and space central to the aesthetics of these sensitivities). Whitehead's rejection of notions of "absolute time" and "absolute space" is helpful for getting a grip on his accounts of these various modes of experience, and the syntheses between them by means of symbolic reference. This is because there is a directly proportional relation between the complexity of an organism's mode of experience and its freedom from the immediacy of its local environment. Causal efficacy is disclosure of the immediate past and presentational immediacy is disclosure of the contemporary actual world.

"Contemporary" here means actualities of overlapping durations or of the same time-systems. To speak of the "contemporary external world" or "contemporary organisms" is, according to the abstractive nature of presentational immediacy (relation by way of the dual reference of sense-data), to speak in terms of spatial relations alone—where "space" is defined, à la Leibniz, as "the order of co-existences."[50] In *Concept of Nature*, Whitehead uses the language of "families" to describe different time systems. He writes, "The measurableness of time is derivative from the properties of durations. So also is the serial character of time. We shall find that there are in nature competing serial time-systems derived from different families of durations."[51] Describing time-systems by appealing to analogies with generational or filial orders is still part of quantum physics's best practices. As one contemporary physicist describes, order established by filiation is called "partial" order, in distinction from "universal order": "A partial order establishes a relation of *before* and *after* between certain elements, but not between any of them. Human beings form a 'partially ordered' set (not a 'completely ordered' set) through filiation. Filiation establishes an order (*before* the descendants, *after* the forebears), but not between everyone."[52] He continues, "Special relativity is the discovery that the temporal structure of the universe is like the one established by filiation: it defines an order between the events of the universe that is *partial*, not *complete*. The expanded present is the set of events that are neither past nor future: it exists, just as there are human beings who are neither our descendants nor our forebears."[53] And further, "Every event has its past, its future, and a part of the universe that is neither past nor future, just as everyone has forbears, descendants, and others who are neither forbears nor descendants."[54] I'll venture an example: Man A has two sons, Man B and Man C. Man C has a daughter, Woman A. Man B and Woman A have a son, Man D. With whom does Woman A share a filial "generation"? Is it with Man B, because they together created a descendant? This would mean that Woman A would be of the same generation as he father, Man C, since brothers (Man B and Man C) share a filial generation. But then Man B and Woman A would constitute a generation not identical to the generation constituted by Man B and Man C, which would mean that Man B was of multiple generations. Just as Woman A has no fixed generation affiliation, a duration has no "true" contemporaries. Contemporaneity is relative all the way down.

This view of contemporaneity is at odds with that of Newton, who, in *Philosophiae Naturalis Principia Mathematica,* defines "true" time not as experienced temporality, but that which is indicated in his equations of motion as t.[55] Contra Newton, Whitehead rejects the idea of and "absolute clock" that can be mathematically represented by a constant. In his 1916 paper, Whitehead had insisted that no single space-time concept can be "right" and that "even estimates of order" depend on the observer's standpoint.[56] The simultaneity of events might hold for one partial order, but not another—there is no universal order of durations by which to measure absolute simultaneity.

It was just this sort of resistance to non-relative variables that distinguished his philosophy of mathematics from that of Russell. As Bas van Fraassen notes in *An Introduction to the Philosophy of Time and Space* (1970), "Russell had attempted a thorough logical analysis of the foundations of (classical) physics in his *Principles of Mathematics* (1903). His view on time and space as developed there is basically Newtonian."[57] Russell's views on time and space became more sympathetic to the relational theories of that time in his subsequent work *Our Knowledge of the External World* (1914). Van Fraassen attributes this change to Whitehead's influence, but I think it is more likely because of the influence of the Vienna Circle and its members' consideration of Einstein.[58] But, perhaps to van Fraassen's point, it is noteworthy that Rudolph Carnap references Whitehead's relational theory of space-time in the course of expositing his own in *Abriss der Logistik: Mit Besonderer Berücksichtigung der Relationstheorie und Ihrer Anwendungen* (1929).[59] Later, in *Modes of Thought,* Whitehead would write of how the point-theory of space goes hand-in-hand with a notion of numerosity predicated upon the same assumptions of fundamental disconnection. Such a view regards "[e]ach individual thing as devoid of numerosity, whereas a static group is characterized by number. In this way process seems to be absent from our treatments of arithmetic." He continues, "Thus mathematics has been conceived as test case, which is the citadel for a false metaphysics."[60] But it is only when individuality is regarded in terms of disconnection that this false metaphysics can persist. Mathematics, properly regarded, is "simply the greatest example of a science of abstract forms."[61] When the arithmetical notions such as "addition," "multiplication," and "serial form" are understood as forms of process and, therefore continuity, the individuals ("numbers") can only be understood as characters of that process.[62] It is noteworthy that Whitehead takes this understanding of arithmetic to be a lesson of Plato's doctrine of "life and motion."[63]

The compositional nature of reality, indicated by Whitehead's notion of the actual occasion, involves in principle the evaluation of precedent actual occasions with which the subject is affiliated. There can be no *exact* contemporaries except by way of abstraction, because there are no "points" at which durations are delimited from the continual passage. When Whitehead says that there can be no relation to contemporary events, I take him to mean "in theory." In reality, what is *now* and *here* is, for Whitehead, simply what *presents* "immediately"—it is what we call the "present," and it is specious. Accordingly, he writes, "Thus the disclosure of a contemporary world by presentational immediacy is bound up with the disclosure of the solidarity of actual things by reason of their participation in an impartial system of spatial extension."[64] "Impartial" is a technical term here. For something to be aesthetically partial is to be evaluative or emphatic of what has just preceded it, such that a "partial" system would by definition entail temporal relations. So when Whitehead says that the present discloses an *impartial* system of spatial extension, he is bordering on redundancy—and likely for the reader's sake. Because durations, not substances, are the final realities, consideration of events purely in terms of spatial extension is possible only by contrivance. If space is the "order of co-existences," but contemporaneity is relative, then space-qua-impartial-system is too. "Contemporaries" cannot evaluate or be partial to one another, precisely because there can be no *change* in a purely spatial system. In Euclidean geometry, there can only be scalar descriptions. Change requires that there be *rates* of change, but rates require time.

In reality, however, there is no one order or even level of duration. Experience in the mode of presentational immediacy is itself only possible because the overwhelming majority of durations constituting an organism interrelate in immeasurable ways that never rise to the level of conscious experience. Part of the contemporary world disclosed to the perceiver is her own body, different aspects to which she can direct her attention, and others that can command it. Our manner of speaking is misleading: this grammar implies that her "attention" is somehow at a remove from her body. "Attention" is but another mode of feeling. When we attend to something, we say we are "present" to it. This feeling of presence—Whitehead avoids the phrase *ap*phrension because of the mentalistic connotations—is an *appearance* in an innocuous sense. It is our conception of the "real" world that should do justice to our "apparent" world for Whitehead, and not the other way around.

It is wrong to assert some version of the idea "things-in-themselves cause sensation or appearance," because the sensation or appearance is the thing-for-us. And the ways in which something is *for* others is the thing. This is what Whitehead means when he says, "Synthesis and analysis require each other."[65] An account of perception that does not face the fate of solipsism must be able to explain how two things can be actually (ontologically) together in a sense *derivative from* the sense in which each thing is actual.[66] Recall that Whitehead defines the "present" in *Concept of Nature* as "the vivid fringe of memory tinged with anticipation."[67] The rejection of the doctrine of simple occurrence entails that there is no thing "in between" memory and anticipation, past and future. There is just passage. It is thus that he writes, "The fact that our consciousness is confined to an analysis of experience in the present is no difficulty" because perception of the contemporary world is only "one factor" contributing to the datum of the present moment of experience.[68] The key point is that, for Whitehead, the datum for conscious thought is symbolic reference between perception in the mode of causal efficacy and presentational immediacy. Moreover, *this very consciousness*—the aesthetics of consciousness, if you will—is a mode of symbolic reference between perceptive experience and experience in the mode of conceptual analysis. Consciousness of the present is synthesis and analysis in dialogical interrelation.

Symbolism is not something of which one can get "outside," as if it were a space or a realm. It is "no mere idle fancy or corrupt degeneration" writes Whitehead, "it is inherent in the very texture of human life."[69] By identifying the work that the doctrine of simple occurrence (and its variant of simple location) does to mystify symbolism, Whitehead accounts for the concrete relations of symbolic reference in a way that has no room for worry about the reality of intentional objects or the success of the mind's relation to them. Whitehead has shown us that this is the wrong sort of picture to have.

ERROR IN PERCEPTION AND JUDGMENT

In the previous chapter, I discussed the numerous occasions on which McDowell argued that success must be possible in principle in order to make sense of error in perception. We have an incoherent conception of fallibility, he argued, if we think that falsehood can never be avoided. Reality, he declared in a related point, is prior in the order of understanding to appearance. Like Whitehead, McDowell is concerned to avoid any conception of appearance according to which it can only ever be "mere." However, I have been alleging throughout this project that McDowell fails to do the conceptual legwork to achieve this—to achieve, that is, a conception of experience in fully non-modernist terms. In consequence, McDowell not only fails to account for how success is the rule, but also fails, and for the same reasons, to adequately account for the nature of error. By contrast, Whitehead does both, and in ways that meet many of the requirements McDowell says we must—and that includes avoiding the incoherent understanding of fallibility he (McDowell, 2011) sees plaguing contemporary epistemology.

Whitehead understands that symbolic reference must, in general, be veridical if it is to be a fundamental mode of experience by which life advances upon the spectrum of sentience to sapience. If it were not, such life forms would not long survive; "Successful high-grade organisms are only possible, on the condition that their symbolic functionings are usually justified so far as important issues are concerned."[70] If the relations of symbolic reference constitutive of a sense perception are not on the whole correct, an organism will not succeed in its efforts to meet its basic needs.

A particularly elegant example of the necessity of successful attunement to one's environment by means of symbolic reference is a starling murmuration. A defensive tacit, a murmuration of starlings displays just how intricately calibrated each bird is to the others. A flock of thousands adjusts its speed and direction at what strikes the perceiver as exactly the same moment, in a way usually indicative of a single entity. The correlation between their signal processing is so strong that attempts to measure it struggle on account of its approximation of simultaneity. Some recent analyses of starling behavior have had to do so by recourse to mathematical equations of "critical transitions" used to describe avalanches and transitions between states of nature (a liquid to a gas, for instance) rather than what might traditionally have been described as strictly biological phenomena. These equations help us to understand how systems can be so readily poised as to incite large-scale pattern changes—in short, how systems can be "poised at criticality." Thierry Mora of the Lewis-Sigler Institute for Integrative Genomic and William Bialek of the Princeton Center for Theoretical Science have suggested that the same principle of criticality exhibited in starling murmurations explains such processes as how genes can determine the function of a cell, or how neurons form systems that issue in thoughts.[71] Whitehead's account of the organic function of symbolic reference demonstrates an effort sympathetic

Symbolism and Language

with these contemporary scientific efforts to make sense of the aesthetics of self-organizing systems at both the microscopic and macroscopic levels.

It is not too much of a stretch to say that, for Whitehead, symbolism is what makes life possible. But Whitehead does not hold that it is for survival power that symbolism persists, or that life continues to develop more complex and recursive forms of it. Not only does he deny to humans the origination of symbolism; he denies it to life in general. Symbolic reference is the structure of experience by which sentience is at all possible—and sapience as a special degree of sentience. It is a strange fact that the creatures whose very existence depends upon symbolic reference for their vital processes would come to regard it with suspicion.

And yet, this is just as it should be for Whitehead. He understands life not as the pursuit of greater survival power, but as a "bid for freedom." Life is "a bid for a certain independence of individuality with self-interests and activities not to be construed purely in terms of environmental obligations."[72] What symbolic reference makes possible—or what it exemplifies by way of the creative advance—is freedom from brute conformation and repetition. It is the structure by which physical relations incite mental ones, or causal relations incite rational ones. This incitation is possible precisely because of the real togetherness between the actual occasions—or, rather, the lack of "betweenness" at all, insofar as the perception is the event constituted by this togetherness. This occasion of togetherness is the "double reference" of sense-data mentioned earlier. Whitehead writes, "there are no bare sensations which are first experienced and then 'projected' into our feet as their feelings, or onto the opposite wall as its colour."[73] To assert such a doctrine is to fail to perceive what is right before us all along, namely, what Whitehead refers to in *Process and Reality* as the "witness of the body."[74] We feel *with* our feet and we see *with* our eyes. Failure to take care with our words, or to attend to the implicit work of our grammar, can obscure grand incompatibilities in what we say.

Whitehead points out this carelessness on Hume's part when he asserts, "If it be perceived by the eyes, it must be a colour."[75] It is not the working definition of "perception" or of "color" that stirs Whitehead, recall, but the inattention with which Hume uses the words "by" and "must." What these words imply is the very witness and directness of perception explicitly denied while implicitly affirmed.

This witness is not bidirectional. A perception qua instance of symbolic reference is the product of the efficacy of the symbol-meaning event. What this means is that the directionality of attention and intention are fully compatible with ontological togetherness between knower and known—the directionality is not of some universal reaching some particular, but of the confluence of functions issuing in the symbol-meaning event. Reference is unidirectional relationship, whereby the incipient is the symbol and the percipient is the meaning, and the roles of "symbol" and "meaning" may be switched on a different occasion.

This occasion, however, is what it is because of this particular relation. The occasion of symbolic reference is just that: one occasion. He writes in *Process and Reality,* "In the transition to a higher phase of experience, there is a concrescence [coalescence] in which prehensions in the two modes are brought into a unity of feeling: this concrescent unity [becoming or actual occasion] arises from a congruity of their subjective forms [percepts] in virtue of the identity relation ['common ground'] between the two prehensions [i.e., experience in the mode of causal efficacy and experience in the mode of presentational immediacy]."[76] The symbolic occasion, while singular or atomic, is a unity that holds things together, not apart. There are not two different "instants," one "symbolizing" and one "symbolized." There is only the unified event of symbolic reference, grown out of the "natural potentiality" inherent to even the most geologic instances of causal efficacy.[77] By eliminating the fallacy of simple occurrence, Whitehead avoids postulating an infinite temporal regress of symbolism or an interminable chain of signification. The regress is eliminated precisely because symbolic reference must finally originate from a "common ground" between the two modes of experience involved: that provided by the double-reference of sense-data, and that provided by the "locality" or the shared space-time system.[78] All chains of symbolic reference must finally trace back to percepts in the mode of direct recognition, free of symbolic reference. Whitehead's realism thereby ensures that there is a real element of correlation or correspondence that must be in place for such relations to obtain.

Symbolism is, at its most fundamental level of exhibition in the cosmos, the relational structure creative of novel experiences with no discernible upper limit. At the ontological level (or "cosmological" in Whitehead's words), the symbolic event exhibits two different modalities of space-time, neither of which involves the brute seriality of "instants" or "points." On the one hand, the symbolic event qua instance of becoming is non-extended—it is something entirely new. It is the one that becomes of the many. On the other hand, the symbolic event is nothing but the continuous passage of nature. In *Process and Reality*, Whitehead explains, "The actual occasions are the creatures which become, and they constitute a continuously extensive world. In other words, extensiveness becomes, but 'becoming' is not itself extensive."[79] "But," he continues, "atomism does not exclude complexity and universal relativity. Each atom is a system of all things."[80] Creatures are the creations of continuity, but they themselves are atomic. We can think of events by way of the analogy to photons: depending on how you look at them, they can be both particles and waves.

And there is the key: *depending on how you look.* Of course, in the photon analogy, "looking" is really another metaphor for measurement. But the principle is the same, because *both* ocular perception *and* mathematics are examples of symbolic reference at varying degrees of fundamentality. Whitehead writes, "Symbolism from sense-perception to physical bodies is the most natural and widespread of all symbolic modes."[81] But there is also symbolism of the Cathedrals of Medieval Europe. Language and mathematics exemplify more "fundamental" types of symbolism than the latter, but less than the former.[82]

When Whitehead picked up the topic for his Barbour-Page Lectures, he did so out of a need to account for how error is possible, given the doctrine of direct experience. Why should we be able to err in ways that are not possible for less complex modes of existence? The way of taking account of one's environment in terms of symbolic reference introduces, at once, greater capacity for sensitivity and subtlety, and greater capacity for error. Error here is understood in terms of nonconformity, resulting from symbolic reference, between perception in the mode of causal efficacy (physical relations) and presentational immediacy (sense-data as ways of relating that are internally related only to the percipient).[83] Because the relation between two modes of perception is the relation between symbol and meaning, error is a product of symbolic reference even before conceptual analysis comes into play.

Error in itself is not a negative phenomenon for Whitehead. To the contrary, it is a source of creativity and progress. In the language of *Science and the Modern World,* error is when "the actual includes what (in one sense) is not-being as a positive factor in its own achievement."[84] It is the confrontation of fact with alternatives.[85] Symbolic reference is distinguished from the more elementary modes of perception by the added element of "originative freedom."[86] Whitehead explains in *Process and Reality,* "Accordingly, while the two pure perceptive modes are incapable of error, symbolic reference introduces this possibility." He continues, "Thus, in general human perception is subject to error, because, in respect to those components most clearly in consciousness, it is interpretative. In fact, error is the mark of the higher organisms, and is the schoolmaster by whose agency there is upward evolution. For example, the evolutionary use of intelligence is that it enables the individual to profit by error without being slaughtered by it."[87] The educational metaphor is fitting for Whitehead, who was a critic of educational systems that required rote memorization of systems of facts, producing "minds in grooves." The capacity to err, and the capacity to realize when and why one has erred, is critical to intelligence. This is no mere cliché about there being no bad questions; it is a fundamental cosmological principle that novelty requires the sort of freedom that brings the possibility of error.

In light of the foregoing, we can return to the topic of chapter 4 to see how the aesthetics of perception and judgment are intimately involved in this play of novelty and error by way of symbolic reference. There, I said that, if our goal is to make sense of the sorts of experience like conscious awareness, no account based solely on efficient causation or all-determining laws of nature will be complete. Such schemes have no room for confusion or error. Consciousness awareness, I said, is neither perception without interpretation (purely physical), nor perception of the absolutely indeterminate (purely conceptual). Recall that propositions, as potential matters of fact, are the sorts of entities that Whitehead says must be the object of prehension for there to be a possibility of being "correct" or "incorrect" in perception and judgment. Truth and falsehood are always "grounded" upon a "reason" (that is, by way of actual entities). This "reason" is the "common ground" linking symbols and meanings in the single event of symbolic reference. Whitehead's "propositions" stand for the unity of this common ground with the possibility of a degree of deviation from fact.

In order to account for the possibility of being wrong, Whitehead thinks we must first account for the possibility of entertaining possibility. Without a proposition, understood as a potential matter of fact—not as the object of a sentence but as "a full Whiteheadian sociological field"[88]—Whitehead could not account for the possibility of deviation from the facts, which amounts to the possibility of accounting for originality. A proposition is a real potentiality or conditioned indetermination felt by a subject. It is the object of perception or judgment that involves in its nature the sheer givenness required for that perception or judgment to be true or false. In the language of chapter 4, the predicative pattern of the proposition is *that* which is true or false of the logical subjects. The diversity of origination of the logical subjects and the predicative pattern, to recall, was directly related to the degree of "imaginative freedom" involved in the propositional feeling, which serves to distinguish, in no absolute way, conscious perceptions from intuitive judgments. Conscious perceptions are "perceptive feelings" maintaining a maximal degree of directness to the facts, whereas intuitive judgments (the evolutionary frontier of all judgments) are "imaginative feelings" involving a greater degree of indirectness or non-conformation to the facts (immediate past). Thus, whereas in perception there are sense-data and locality preserving the shared world by which symbolic reference is grounded, intuitive judgments occur by way of relations of symbolic reference between modes of experience in greater contrast to one another.

I described in chapter 4 that an intuitive judgment, on Whitehead's account, involves two separate physical feelings in its composition, the indicative and the predicative, whereas conscious perceptions involve only one. We should not think of the oneness of "one" or the twoness of "two" here in terms of discrete points or instances, but in terms of unity and diversity of locality. "Locality," as introduced in this chapter, implies a common space-time system. This means, in effect, that in perception the logical subject and the predicate of a proposition are derivative of the same space-time system, or duration.

Whitehead's use of numerical and geometric linguistic symbols to describe the emergence of freedom and error within modes of concrete relation is an instance of itself. That is, he is exemplifying symbolism by way of itself, demonstrating the dialectic of synthesis and analysis. Language, while not the most fundamental example of symbolism, is nevertheless a particularly penetrating exemplification of it. In language, written or spoken, the recursivity of symbolic expression is peculiarly available to us at a conscious level. In the proceeding section, I argue that this availability is tied up with Whitehead's metaphysical analysis of publicity.

ONTOLOGICAL PRIVACY AND ONTOLOGICAL PUBLICITY

In this section, I discuss Whitehead's understanding of the relationship between ontological privacy and ontological publicity. I contend that a sufficient grasp of the reciprocal nature of privacy and publicity is a prerequisite to an adequate account of the relationship between thought and language. The problematic conceptions of this relationship owe, I take Whitehead to show, to the prior assumption, challenged above, that extensionality means disconnection.

The term "public" is relational. At a metaphysical level, what counts as "public" as opposed to "private" events is relative in a way analogous to "individual" and "society" or "atomicity" and "continuity." For Whitehead, a human person is composed of personally ordered societies of actual occasions. Like the Latin *persona,* "personal" order means for Whitehead something like the capacity to sustain a character. Human individuals are metaphysical societies. Each actual occasion is itself a non-temporal unity, but it is this unity by way of becoming. Becoming, as noted above, is itself non-extended for Whitehead, even is extensionality itself *becomes* by way of it. There is atomicity because there is continuity, and there is continuity because there is atomicity. Neither is reducible to the other.

In his account of perception, Whitehead has maintained this logic. Experience in the mode of presentation immediacy is at one and the same time "public fact" and "private experience." The difference between the public and the private character has to do with whether or not we describe it in terms of significance. On the one hand, presentational immediacy is "barren"; we can describe it solely in terms of its particularity. We can provide, for instance, the definite mathematical relations sufficient to locate it. On the other hand, however, it would thereby exhibit "that complex of systematic mathematical relations" participative in *all* events of the current cosmic epoch.[89] A single experience discloses the "systematic relations which dominate the environment," while "the environment is dominated by these relationships by reason of the experiences of the individual occasions constituting the societies."[90] It is only because individual experiences do so disclose the "systematic relations" of the environment that scientific accuracy is possible, or what Whitehead calls the "intellectual comprehension of the physical universe."[91]

It is precisely due to this last point that Whitehead takes issue with what he calls "the modern doctrine" of "private psychological fields."[92] The notion is the "logical result" of Hume's theory of perception. The "impressions of sensation" collect to form private experiences or qualia, where "private" does not mean phenomenological privacy but an ontological one. For Hume, the impressions of sensation disclose nothing of public fact. For Whitehead, this is only half of the story. Without the other half, he thinks, Hume would not be able to make sense of the possibility of measurement. Whitehead writes, "Measurement depends upon counting and upon permanence. The question is, what is counted, and what is permanent?"[93] *What* we measure are observations, and we measure by means of a relative permanence of instrument. He gives the example of the original yard-stick as having only an "approximation to straightness" and measurements against it being approximate themselves:

> Minute variations of physical conditions will make the rod vary slightly, also sense-perception is never absolutely exact. But unless there be a meaning to "exactitude," the notion of a "slight variation" and of a "slight defect from exactitude" are nonsense. Apart from such a meaning the two occasions of the rod's existence are incomparable, except by another experiment depending upon the same principles. There can only be a finite number of such experiments; so ultimately we are reduced to these direct judgments.
>
> However far the testing of instruments and the corrections for changes of physical factors, such as temperature, are carried, there is always a final dependence upon direct intuitions that relevant circumstances are unchanged. Instruments are used from minute to minute, from hour to hour, and from day to day, with the sole guarantee of antecedent tests and of the *appearance* of invariability of relevant circumstances.
>
> This "appearance" is always a perception in the mode of presentational immediacy. If such perceptions be in any sense "private" in contradistinction to a correlative meaning for the term "public," then the perceptions, on which scientific measurement depends, merely throw light upon the private psychology of the particular observer, and have no "public" import.[94]

Appearances, observations, or collections of the single experiencer are what form the "groundwork of common experience" which science and philosophy alike exist to elucidate. Again, it is the *apparent* world to which our accounts of reality ought to do justice, and not the other way around.

The sense in which Whitehead can say that the perceptive mode of presentational immediacy is "barren" (the half of the story that Hume tells) is that in which they are considered "apart from symbolic transference."[95] In practice, the experiencing subject is never purely receptive. Subjects always maintain the "triple character" of "recipient, patient, and agent" for Whitehead, as must be the case for an account that emphasizes the vectorial character of relations.[96] "But none of these operations can be segregated from nature into the subjective privacy of a mind." He continues, "Mental and physical operations are incurably intertwined; and both issue into publicity, and are derived from publicity. The vector character of prehension is fundamental."[97] Only in analysis can experience in the mode of presentational immediacy be considered apart from the subject forms it involves—"elements emotional, appreciative, purposive."[98] The subjective form of an experience in the mode of presentational immediacy is its *meaning*, the effect of the symbolic transference involved in the perception. The simplicity of Hume's "impressions" is not originative of experience; simplicity is derivative of complexity, and accuracy is derivative of vagueness. By means of symbolic reference, Whitehead argues, an organism "suppresses the mere multiplicities of things, and designs its own contrasts."[99] To analytically tease out the symbol from the meaning in the perceptive event—an event in which symbol and meaning are Janus-faced—is, therefore, to tell only half the story. It is to reduce a contrast to only one of its elements, that is, to the element disclosing the contemporary world devoid of meaning. It is, therefore to tell the part of the story that has no public import, the part that tells us nothing of the cosmos patient of experiences of an "apparent" world.

The full story of presentational immediacy must involve those organisms for which the "presented durations" are important data in their self-preservation and self-realization. Symbolic transference involving presentational immediacy is the means by which the past is "lifted into the present" such that "[t]he delicate activities of self-preservation" become possible by "the transference of the vague message of the past onto the more precisely discriminated regions of the presented duration."[100] Symbolic transference is the means by which private experience gives way to public fact, and public fact gives way to private experience, such that information is possible.

Symbolic reference exemplifies the augmentative character of experience, that later phases grow out of earlier ones, and then act back upon them in original and generative ways. Symbolic reference is how Whitehead understands the ways in which the modes of experience grow recursively.

Whitehead writes that presentational immediacy is an "outgrowth" of the "complex datum" supplied by causal efficacy, meaning that presentational immediacy expresses the very same datum as that expressed in the mode of causal efficacy, but it does so "under different proportions of relevance."[101] When Whitehead speaks of "phases" of experience, such that presentational immediacy is "later," I take him to mean this not in a temporal but rather an analytical sense. The later phases are cosmologically unsustainable unless the earlier ones are already presupposed in any genetic account of an event. Experiences are never purely in any "mode" designated by analysis. The function of the distinction for Whitehead is primarily to indicate the increasing degree of origination involved in "later" modes of experience. By "origination" Whitehead means "integrative" or evaluative—even "interpretive." In fact, when there are sufficiently distinct modes of experience for there to be yet a third mode by means of symbolic reference, Whitehead says, we have the "interpretive element in human experience."[102] Language is a unique example of the ways in which human experience can be all but overwhelmed by the interpretive element, insofar as language, for Whitehead, refers "almost exclusively" to interpretations of sense-data: "we say that 'we see the *stone*' where *stone* is an interpretation of *stone-image*" and "we say that 'we see the *stone-image* with our eyes'."[103] "The stone," "the stone-image," and the witness of "our eyes" are all interpretations, but they are not for that reason wrong; the point is that linguistic expression deals with interpretations because it functions symbolically. Symbolism is interpretive in principle; it is the business of effecting meanings.

Whitehead prefers to use the example of language over other types of symbolic expression because, as demonstrated by its use here, its conventionality renders its constitutive elements more evident compared to other sorts of symbolic expression. In his discussion of symbolism, Whitehead deals mostly with two levels: the microscopic level of sensory perception, and the macroscopic level of natural languages. He often switches back and forth between these two levels of exemplification without notice, and it can be difficult to know when he is speaking about the non-extended occasion of becoming or the binding forces of national symbols. And yet, the fluidity of these switches is due to the analogy between them. There is a continuity of structure between the simplest causal feelings, the complex integrative feelings of conscious perception, and the inheritable symbolic systems by which social purposes are sustained. Language becomes possible somewhere between the second and the third of these phases, acting back upon the second to make possible the third. What is inadmissible on this account is any view that regards words as "primarily the vehicle of thought."[104]

What we hear are sounds and what we see are marks (even while sounds and marks are also interpretive, though in a less refined sense). The hearing of the sound is an experience of presentational immediacy. In order for the perception of spoken sounds or written marks to count as hearing or seeing *words*, on Whitehead's account, the hearing of the word or the seeing of the mark must elicit meanings in the form of relevant past events. But the elicitation of memory is always interpretive because the sounds and the marks are never identical—they are always unique events that bear some relevance to one another in terms of pitch, intonation, accent, rhythm, intensity, and so on. "Thus," Whitehead writes, "a word is a species of sounds, with specific identity and individual difference." This "specific" identity is its species-identity, in the technical sense of the word, which is polythetic and not monothetic in composition. The exact composition will be different for each percipient because of his or her unique history, but by way of enculturation, the species identity still obtains. The hearing of a sound, for instance, elicits the "contrasts and identities of other percepta" in the same mode of presentational immediacy. If this is the percipient's first time hearing the sound, there will not be many relevant occasions to elicit—the meaning will not be well-defined. But if there is a history of events with this specific identity, then the meaning of the sound will be more defined.

Language depends on the specific, recognizable, functional identity of sounds and marks. This identity is, in the case of natural languages, established by instances of use for collaborative purposes. For the individual percipient, the identity is identi*fied* by the qualitative pattern of emotion it elicits—what Whitehead calls the subjective form. This subjective form is that which is perceived "in its capacity for being a private sensation."[105] We can analyze the subjective form of hearing a musical note, for instance, in terms of the musical qualities it exhibits. This analysis—of its timbre, key, overtones, and so on—relies upon the recognizability of tonal (or atonal) qualities. In Whitehead's language, the analysis of a musical note "reveals an abstract qualitative pattern" constitutive of it. Just as a single word is not one definite sound, a musical note is a complex event of fundamental tones and overtones that each have its own resonance. The experience of "hearing an A in the key of C" involves a synthesis of these qualities in perception. This synthetic experience is experience in the mode of presentational immediacy, which depends on the relation to the sound-event by feeling abstractive, qualitative pattern. To perceive in the mode of causal efficacy is to be so overwhelmed by detail as to be buried by vagueness. There can be no attention in this mode. Presentational immediacy, however, attends by way of abstraction. Being able to identify the note as "A in the key of C" is an interpretation of presentational immediacy by way of symbolic reference.

Whitehead's view contests the hypostatization of linguistic expression. The hearing of a word or the seeing of a mark is not different in kind from the hearing of any other sound or the seeing of any other object. What is different, however, is the element of arbitrariness of the sounds and marks we call words. In the first chapter of *Process and Reality,* Whitehead echoes John Stuart Mill, who wrote, "scientific investigation among the Greek schools of speculation and their followers in the Middle Ages, was little more than a mere sifting and analyzing of the notions attached to common language. They thought that by determining the meaning of words they could become acquainted with fact."[106] What Whitehead adds to this sentiment is a rejection of the idea that verbal expression can adequately express a proposition. To the contrary, language, on Whitehead's account, is thoroughly indeterminate as to its meaning. This indeterminacy of expression owes to the fact that linguistic symbols persist through convention. In this way, languages sustain systematic presuppositions about the world that are not easily challenged.[107] And yet language is a "triumph" of human ingenuity, whereby mankind "has fabricated its manageable connections with the world into a means of expression."[108] Language is the "systematization of expression"—or "the civilization of expression."[109]

It is easy to focus on the conventionality of linguistic expression, and to overlook the notion of expression itself. But Whitehead's account of symbolic reference starts with expression; it provides an aesthetic description of how symbolism works, and how the structure of expressivity is fundamental not only to consciousness but to perception in its simplest forms. It is written into the very compositionality of actuality. Of all the ways that human beings could have evolved to communicate, the reason Whitehead speculates that we refined the voice-produced sound is because it comes from the depths of bodily existence. Sound resonates through bodies and has the power to "excite the intimacies of bodily existence."[110] "The voice-produced sound," he writes, "is a natural symbol for the deep experiences of organic existence."[111] Whitehead defines a body as a "primary field" of expression. When we are profoundly grieved, our bodies express this in various ways. We may lash out, or wail, or become catatonic. One woman's guttural expressions of grief can stir those around her to the core. The voice-produced sound, Whitehead argues, produces a sense of "reality" that is largely responsible for "the effectiveness of symbolism."[112] Language is one mode of human expression; by means of conventional sounds and marks, we are able to express, to make explicit or public, what our body may have already communicated in a less-defined manner.

The expressive and interpretive function of language is, however, only part of the story. The other part of the story is the way in which language enables new ways of experiencing—something we have seen McDowell, in his conversation with Brandom, argue in order to defend the possibility of rational modes of perception. And yet, I've argued that McDowell relies upon a problematic order of explanation, whereby subjectivity produces symbolism and thinkers produce thoughts. In this way, I've also argued, McDowell is perpetuating a version of the bifurcation. Whitehead is clear to distance himself from the taproot of this way of thinking: "Descartes in his own philosophy conceives the thinker as creating the occasional thought. The philosophy of organism inverts this order and conceives the thought as a constituent operation in the creation of the occasional thinker. The thinker is the final end whereby there is the thought. In this inversion we have the final contrast between a philosophy of substance and a philosophy of organism."[113] In the same vein, he writes, "It is said that 'men are rational'. This is palpably false: they are only intermittently rational—merely liable to rationality."[114] In no sense, then, can we say that language is the essence of thought for Whitehead.

It is nevertheless true for him that "apart from language, the retention of thought, the easy recall of thought, the interweaving of thought into higher complexity, the communication of thought, are all gravely limited."[115] It is in this way that language and civilization co-create one another by ever-expanding the limits of their earlier forms. Language augments its possibilities of thought by liberating it from "complete bondage to the immediacies of mood and circumstance."[116] Just as, at microscopic levels, symbolic reference is the means by which the past is "lifted into the present"[117] insofar as it is the synthesis of the disclosure of the past in the mode of causal efficacy and the disclosure of the contemporaneous world in presentational immediacy, the more complex forms or higher syntheses of symbolic reference in the form of spoken or written language expand the breadth of durations informing the "presents" of which we can be mindful.

The difficulty of contemporary discussion of the relationship between thought and language (or experience and language), have much to do with the treatment of either as having an essence wholly distinct from their defining functions. In a way, the difficulty owes to the "spatializing" of thought and of language alike. There is no such thing as "pure thought" or "pure language" on Whitehead's account. We struggle to avoid such spatialization with our ways of speaking, however. We say that language "expresses" thought, but this is not quite right. There is no thought *without* expression; "Thought is the outcome of its own concurrent activities; and having thus arrived upon the scene, it modifies and adapts them."[118] These "concurrent activities" are emotional, physical, bodily activities that predate and remain caught up in our own modes of thought. Once we have rejected the picture of "points" of space and "instants" of time, we can no longer entertain a picture of thought and language as discrete happenings.

Whitehead provides an apt metaphor for depicting the non-discrete interrelation of thought and language qua physico-mental phenomena:

> A thought is a tremendous mode of excitement. Like a stone thrown into a pond it disturbs the whole surface of our being. But this image is inadequate. For we should conceive the ripples as effective in the creation of the plunge of a stone into the water. The ripples release the thought, and the thought augments and distorts the ripples. In order to understand the essence of thought we must study its relation to the ripples amid which it emerges.[119]

By insisting upon the efficacy of the ripples in the plunging of the stone, Whitehead reminds us of the complexity of trying to draw definitive lines between mental and physical, linguistic and non-linguistic, cognitive and non-cognitive events. Indeed, when we think about the function of language in self-communication or so-called internal dialogue, we are no longer referring to the language of sound or of sight. Whitehead finds the phenomena of self-conversation to be striking examples of the "ripples" and the "stone" augmenting one another. What this metaphor communicates is the distinctive way in which language renders the past in the present. This "distinctness" is, according to Whitehead, "borrowed from the well-defined sensa" of the past, present by way of linguistic expression. "In this way," he writes, "an articulated memory is the gift of language, considered as an expression from oneself in the past to oneself in the present."[120] Moreover, the past experiences constituent of one's articulated memory can be imaginatively recombined, reinterpreted, and narrated by way of communication with another.

Let me provide a bit of an extended example that I hope will be helpful in clarifying the confluence Whitehead describes. In psychoanalysis, the neglect experienced in one's childhood may be treated by a process called "transmuting internalization," whereby a therapist seeks to create in the patient internal structures mimicking those undeveloped by the empathic failures or misattunement of the patient's childhood caregiver. The therapist seeks to establish a presence in the patient's psyche that serves whatever function was ill-fulfilled by the initial caregiver(s), such that they can re-parent the patient. The neglectful caregiver is "present" in the patient's psyche in the form of psychological structures, or enduring psychological functions, that manifest in terms of various psychopathologies. A patient whose childhood attempts at self-expression or communication were repeatedly ignored or punished was never able to internalize healthy social responses to those attempts. The therapist, by helping to create new psychological structures that mimic what the parent or caregiver should have instilled, can enable someone with borderline or narcissistic personality disorder to develop more skillful forms of self-communication. The therapist's relationship to the patient serves as the object of "transmuting internalizations" that gradually establish a new caregiver presence in the psyche. This process of transmuting internalization, between therapist and patient, exemplifies the complex ways in which an articulated memory enables one (or another) to have access to one's past in efficacious ways.

Language is a highly complex mode of synthetic experience by way of symbolic reference, and these linguistic experiences are never "pure." On this account, in fact, as instances of symbolic reference, linguistic events are in principle experiences in a "mixed" mode. *That* which is synthesized in a symbolic experience can involve events localized to the body or events in the wider environment, including other people. The modes of thought involved in what we typically call "internal discourse" are possible in just that sort of way because of a history of linguistic development that both societally and personally predates the phenomena under consideration. Conventionalized communication is created from the ground-up. Communicative acts are conventionalized by individuals-in-community, and that conventionalization is reciprocally related to the socialization of new generations of language-users. As Whitehead is concerned to explain the more abstract in terms of the more concrete, he makes some efforts to indicate how the transcendent characteristics of language themselves evolved. I should note that I mean "transcendent" here not in terms of vertical transcendence, but in terms of the horizontal transcendence of being able to creatively refer to non-immediate or non-local objects or events.

The capacity to refer to more abstract (because non-local) objects is an achievement of increasingly generic ways of speaking. Whitehead explains, "Language arose with a dominating reference to an immediate situation. Whether it was signal or expression, above all things it was *this* reaction to *that* situation in *this* environment." He continues, "In the origin of language the particularity of the immediate present was an outstanding element in the meaning conveyed.... What language primarily conveyed was the direction of attention to these birds, here, now, amid these surroundings."[121] Before language can enable us to speak in general, it enables us to locate attention to the particular. From "green" meaning merely a particular percept of this patch of moss on this tree at this moment, we can come to think "green" in terms of the shared qualities of diverse events. Thus, "We have to understand language as conveying the identities upon which knowledge is based, and as presupposing the particularity of reference to the environment which is the essence of existence."[122] These "identities" are those indicated by our conceptual categories—the types of which there are tokens, or the genera of which there are species. The reality of these identities are what Whitehead is talking about when he says that the "genus *bird* remained in the background of undiscerned meaning" when language was still in its earliest stages and could only be used to direct joint attention.[123] Yet when we begin to speak in terms of genera, this presupposed background entails all the particular birds, or better, all the particular bird-perceiving occasions. Abstract thought, with the creative freedom it introduces, presupposes the particularities of reference to a concrete environment that Whitehead demands of all actuality in the form of his Ontological Principle.

CROSSING THE RUBICON

In this chapter, I have examined Whitehead's aesthetics of symbolism, with a specific focus on language. A primary concern of mine has been to elucidate the concrete process by which generic modes of thought are possible. I have also drawn some preliminary conclusions as to the implications of a Whiteheadian approach to meaning for our understanding of the relationship between thought and language. Most importantly for the current project is the implication this approach has for helping us account, in a way that McDowell cannot, for how human beings pass the ontological threshold between non-rational and rational modes of experience—how, to use Whitehead's turn of phrase, with humanity "[t]he Rubicon has been crossed"[124]—without recourse, incidentally or otherwise, to obscurantist notions like consciousness.

In so doing, Whitehead's aesthetics of symbolism in general, and language in particular, curtails the analytic problem of mind and world by emptying the terms of its expression. The crossing of the ontological Rubicon cannot serve as the explanation of what it requires, namely, the ability to entertain possibility as such. For Whitehead, propositions must first be conceived as metaphysical entities in order to make any sense as linguistic ones. "Here," observes Stengers, "is the metaphysical requirement imposed by the Rubicon we crossed: language must require, indeed presuppose, the feeling of those tales that may be told; it must not create them."[125] This is why Whitehead introduces propositions as metaphysics entities. Without the real availability of possibility, a subject could never achieve the freedom from factiveness necessary to generate generic modes of thought by way of the conventionalization of symbolic expression.

By means of the aesthetics of symbolic efficacy, Whitehead accounts for the possibility of rational self-conscious human thinkers without reintroducing the bifurcation. This is just what McDowell aims but struggles to achieve on account of his indebtedness to Kant. Reason and animality remain for McDowell indebted to a bifurcation of first and second nature which breaks over the introduction of meanings into the world. He is, therefore, left to worry about vindicating the contentfulness of intuition in order for his theory of knowledge to count as such. By contrast, Whitehead has shown us how meaning has been there all along, such that the nature of human beings is different from other forms of animality only in degree, while still being able to account for how the magnificent "extent of the degree makes all the difference."[126] Linguistically sophisticated animals are indeed capable of staggeringly complex forms of experience, including the sorts we might call rational. But if there is any sense in which we can legitimately still speak of the distinction of thinker and content, it is only in the sense that the latter produces the former and never the other way around.

NOTES

1. Whitehead, *Symbolism: Its Meaning and Effect* (Fordham University Press, 1985 [1927]), 11–12.
2. Ibid., 21–22.
3. Ibid., 53.
4. Ibid., 51.
5. Ibid., 52.
6. Whitehead, *Process and Reality*, 40.
7. Whitehead, "Space, Time, and Relativity," in *Proceedings of the Aristotelian Society*, New Series, Vol. 16 (1915–1916), 104–129.
8. Ibid., 105.
9. Ibid., 106.
10. Ibid.
11. Ibid.
12. Ibid., 106–107.
13. Euclid, *Elements*, Book 1 "Fundamentals of Plane Geometry Involving Straight-lines," trans. H. M. Taylor (Cambridge University Press, 1893), 2.
14. Whitehead, *Modes of Thought* (Free Press, 1968 [1938]), 96.
15. Whitehead, "Space, Time, and Relativity," 107–108.
16. Ibid. 120.
17. Whitehead, "Time, Space, and Material: Are They, and If so in What Sense, he Ultimate Data of Science?" in *Proceedings of the Aristotelian Society, Supplementary Volume*, Vol. 2, (Problems of Science and Philosophy, 1919), 44–108.
18. Whitehead, *An Enquiry into the Principles of Natural Knowledge* (Cambridge, UK: Cambridge University Press, 1919), 1.
19. Ibid.
20. Ibid.
21. Ibid., 2.
22. This account of the implications of Einstein's equations is assisted in large measure by the work of physicist Carlo Rovelli. See his *Seven Brief Lessons on Physics* (New York: Riverhead Books, 2016) and *The Order of Time* (New York: Riverhead Books, 2018).
23. Whitehead, *An Enquiry*, 2.
24. Ibid., 2–3.
25. Ibid., 3.

26. Ibid.
27. Ibid., 4.
28. Ibid.
29. Ibid., 5–6.
30. Whitehead, *Concept of Nature*, 56–57.
31. Ibid.
32. Whitehead, *An Enquiry*, 5–6.
33. Ibid., 6.
34. Ibid., 8.
35. Ibid., 12.
36. Ibid.
37. Ibid., 14–15.
38. Whitehead, *Symbolism*, 8.
39. Whitehead, *Process and Reality*, 168.
40. Whitehead, *Symbolism*, 17.
41. Ibid., 19.
42. Whitehead, *Concept of Nature*, 59.
43. Whitehead, *Process and Reality*, 320.
44. Ibid.
45. Whitehead, *Symbolism*, 20.
46. Ibid., 20.
47. Ibid., 87.
48. Ibid., 69–70.
49. Ibid., 73.
50. A. E. Taylor notes that both he and Whitehead credit Leibniz for first articulating this understanding of "space." Taylor, *A Commentary on Plato's Timaeus*, 350.
51. Whitehead, *Concept of Nature* (1930), 55.
52. Carlo Rovelli, *The Order of Time* (New York: Riverhead Books, 2018), 47.
53. Ibid., 48.
54. Ibid., 50.
55. Isaac Newton, *Philosophiae Naturalis Principia Mathematica*, Book I, def. VIII, scholium (1846).
56. Whitehead, *Space, Time, and Relativity*, 118.
57. Bas C. van Fraassen, *An Introduction to the Philosophy of Time and Space* (New York: Random House Publishing, 1970), 171.
58. Van Fraassen notes that, along with Whitehead and Einstein's theories of relativity, there was also that of Alfred A. Robb.
59. Van Fraassen, *An Introduction*, 172.
60. Whitehead, *Modes of Thought*, 96–97.
61. Whitehead, *The Function of Reason* (Princeton, NJ: Princeton University Press, 1929), 74.
62. Whitehead, *Modes of Thought*, 97.
63. Ibid.
64. Whitehead, *Symbolism,* 23.
65. Ibid., 26.

66. I am at this point in a similar situation to that which Whitehead expresses part way into his lectures on symbolism; namely, that it is impossible to fully argue for an account of the direct experience of the external world without getting too far afield. Whitehead suggests that his reader read George Santayana's *Scepticism and Animal Faith* (1923) for "conclusive proof of the futile 'solipsism of the present moment' . . . which results from the denial of this assumption" (Ibid., 28–29); Santayana writes, "Scepticism may thus be carried to the point of denying change and memory, and the reality of all facts. Such a skeptical dogma would certainly be false, because this dogma itself would have to be entertained, and that event would be a fact and an existence: and the sceptic in framing that dogma discourses, vacillates, and lives in the act of contrasting one assertion with another—all of which is to exist with a vengeance." He continues, "For the wayward sceptic, who regards it as no truer than any other view, it also has some utility: it accustoms him to discard the dogma which an introspective critic might be tempted to think self-evident, namely, that he himself lives and thinks. That he does so is true; but to establish that truth he must appeal to animal faith. If he is too proud for that, and simply stares at the datum, the last thing he will see is himself." [George Santayana, *Scepticism and Animal Faith: Introduction to a System of Philosophy* (New York: Charles Scribner's Sons, 1924), 40–41].

67. Whitehead, *Concept of Nature* (1920), 73.

68. Whitehead, *Symbolism*, 46–47.

69. Ibid., 61–62.

70. Ibid., 6.

71. Thierry Mora and William Bialek, "Are Biological Systems Poised at Criticality?" in *Journal of Statistical Physics* 144:268–302 (2011).

72. Ibid., 65.

73. Ibid., 14.

74. Whitehead, *Process and Reality*, 64 and 81.

75. Whitehead quoting Hume in *Symbolism*, 51.

76. Whitehead, *Process and Reality*, 168.

77. Whitehead, *Symbolism*, 50, 53.

78. Ibid., 49.

79. Whitehead, *Process and Reality*, 35.

80. Ibid., 36. "Atoms" here means atomic events, not the units of particle physics.

81. Whitehead, *Symbolism*, 4.

82. Ibid., 2.

83. Whitehead, *Symbolism*, 19.

84. Whitehead, *Science and the Modern World*, 176.

85. Ibid., 177.

86. Whitehead, *Process and Reality*, 168.

87. Ibid.

88. Isabelle Stengers, "Whitehead's Account of the Sixth Day," in *Configurations*, vol. 13, no. 1 (Winter 2005: 35–55), 52.

89. Whitehead, *Process and Reality*, 327.

90. Ibid.

91. Ibid.

92. Ibid., 326.
93. Ibid., 327.
94. Ibid., 329.
95. Ibid., 326.
96. Ibid., 316.
97. Ibid., 317.
98. Ibid., 327.
99. Ibid., 317.
100. Ibid., 178.
101. Ibid., 173.
102. Ibid., 173.
103. Ibid., 173.
104. Ibid., 182.
105. Ibid., 234.
106. Whitehead, *Process and Reality*, 12; He cites Mill's *Logic,* Book 5, chapter 3.
107. Whitehead, *Process and Reality*, 13.
108. Whitehead, *Modes of Thought* (1938)*,* 31.
109. Ibid., 34.
110. Whitehead, *Modes of Thought,* 32.
111. Ibid.
112. Ibid.
113. Whitehead, *Process and Reality,* 151.
114. Ibid.*,* 79.
115. Whitehead, *Modes of Thought*, 35.
116. Ibid.
117. Whitehead, *Process and Reality,* 178.
118. Whitehead, *Modes of Thought*, 36.
119. Ibid.
120. Ibid., 33.
121. Ibid., 38.
122. Ibid., 39.
123. Ibid., 38.
124. Ibid., 27.
125. Isabelle Stengers, "Whitehead's Account of the Sixth Day" in *Configurations,* Volume 13, Number 1, Winter 2005, pp. 35–55: 51.
126. Whitehead, *Modes of Thought*, 27.

Conclusion

This is not a call to conversion. Whitehead is not asking us to believe him, not if that means taking his description to provide a picture that better "fits" reality. What Whitehead does instead is demonstrate what Stengers calls "the (pragmatic) art, or craft of forging efficacious propositions" so as to resist "the lure of serving truth against illusions."[1] He is not giving us a theory of reality, not if theory means something contrasted with practice. Whitehead is very much *doing* something in writing philosophy, and he expects his reader to be no less active a participant in the experience of that writing. The reader is asked to entertain the possibility that the categories with which we have been asking ultimate questions are not themselves ultimate. He challenges us to educate our attention, to take care to notice the abstractions that dominant our modes of thought, including the ones that have convinced us that abstractions (like appearances and artifice) are somehow second-class citizens of reality.

We cannot think without abstractions, but we cannot think skillfully without keeping careful watch upon them.[2] But, as I ventured to demonstrate by means of his aesthetics of symbolism, thinking itself is never wholly abstract for Whitehead. The assumption that it is, observes Michael Halewood, "characterizes the specific and constraining mode of thought which lingers throughout modernity."[3] It is, rather, an "abstractive activity" that is by cosmological necessity "always a located activity."[4] It is located primarily in our very bodies, our most immediate environment and primary field of experience. The importance of a proposition for the one who entertains it is primarily to be understood in terms of the intense feeling it evokes of alternative possibilities.

The value of Whitehead's conceptual construction therefore lies in the efficacy, when entertained, of the expressive propositions he formulates by way of it. One of the tales he tells is about this efficacy itself, about the reality of our ideas and our words, as well as the efficacy of the tales *they* tell about what was, is, will be, could have been, might, or may never be the case. In the first sense, this telling is by means of linguistic expression; in the second sense, this telling is by means of cosmological implication. It has been the running theme of this project to demonstrate how the latter sense is, by necessity, ontologically prior to the former sense. This is why Whitehead insists, "The interest in logic, dominating over-intellectualized philosophers, has obscured the main function of propositions in the nature of things. They are not primarily for belief, but for feeling at the physical level of unconsciousness. They constitute a source for the origination of feeling which is not tied down to mere datum."[5]

When Whitehead writes in the "Final Interpretation" of his essay in cosmology, "Philosophy may not neglect the multifariousness of the world—the fairies dance, and Christ is nailed to the cross,"[6] he is not thereby asserting the truth of these propositions. He is rather insisting that we account for their possibility as well as their efficacy as entertained by subjects. Whether or not the tales these propositions tell are true is of secondary importance, cosmologically speaking, to the interest they evoke.

Whitehead, therefore, is not primarily in the business of distinguishing truth from falsehood. His primary business is in educating our attention so that we can take notice of what is presupposed by our valuation of one over the other. Even when it succeeds in doing so, however, his philosophy never loses its status of "an experimental adventure."[7] Again, this adventure is as much empirical and pragmatic as theoretical. It is not interested in trading one conceptual scheme for another, but in playing a different game entirely.

This is not to say that Whitehead has no interest in truth, but his interest in it derives solely from its efficaciousness.[8] But this efficaciousness is not due to some property inherent to the propositions themselves; "its own truth, or its own falsity, is no business of a proposition." Rather, the question of truth or falsity "concerns only a subject entertaining a propositional feeling with that proposition for its datum."[9] This is not to say that truth is relativistic, even if it is relational; it is to say that there are no such things as matters of facts that are not also matters of concern.[10]

The efficacy of thinking with Whitehead is itself not a matter of belief, but of concern. It is a matter of paying attention to implications, complications, and explications of our ways of speaking and thinking; of paying attention, that is, to what is both entailed and precipitated by the abstractions shaping our lives. Whitehead's contention with modern thought had nothing to do with postmodernist accusations of the arrogance of realism or the hopelessness of critique; for Whitehead, empiricism wasn't empirical *enough*, critical thought wasn't critical *enough*. Modern philosophers repeatedly failed to interrogate the assumptions enabling their own critiques.[11] I have argued that the same can be said of the Pittsburgh School.

In the style of Whitehead, I have sought to develop the most promising insights within this tradition while identifying the assumptions that prohibit them from being coherently worked out. Whether or not what I have achieved here is true is less important than the experience of self-disclosure my writing has evoked in the reader. My aim has been therapeutic: to de-problematize intentionality for contemporary analytic philosophy by transforming the conceptual framework of its plausibility. In Whitehead's own work, such transformation is achieved not by narrowing our attention; at one point in *Process and Reality,* Whitehead names "narrowness in the selection of evidence" as the "chief danger" to philosophical thought.[12] This is how we run the risk of not being empirical or critical enough. Rather, Whitehead achieves such transformation by expanding our appreciative awareness, by inducing "a broadening of feeling due to the emergence of some deep metaphysical intuition, unverbalized and yet momentous in its coördination of values."[13] If, in some measure, I have made the problem of intentionality less palpable for the reader by transforming the context in which it appears as such, then I will have done so by way of this "broadening of feeling"—by way of what Whitehead calls, in the same breath, *peace*.

NOTES

1. Isabelle Stengers, "Experimenting with Refrains: Subjectivity and the Challenge of Escaping Modern Dualism," *Subjectivity*, 22 (2008): 38–59, esp. 40. She writes later: "If I love Whitehead, it is precisely because of the efficacy of his seemingly arcane concepts, as I experienced them, in breaking the powerful spell [of modernist categories], taking as hostage our very experience" (53).

2. Whitehead, *Science and the Modern World,* 59: "You cannot think with abstractions; accordingly, it is of the utmost importance to be vigilant in critically revising your *modes* of abstraction. It is here that philosophy finds its niche as essential to the healthy progress of society."

3. Michael Halewood, *A.N. Whitehead and Social Theory: Tracing a Culture of Thought* (Anthem Press, 2011), 6.

4. Ibid.

5. Whitehead, *Process and Reality*, 186.

6. Ibid., 338.

7. Ibid., 9.

8. "After all has been said and done," he writes in *Adventures of Ideas*, "yet the truth-relation remains the simple, direct mode of realising Harmony. Other ways are indirect, and indirectness is at the mercy of the environment. There is a blunt force about Truth, which in the subjective form of its prehension is akin to cleanliness—namely, the removal of dirt, which is unwanted relevance. The sense of directness

which it carries with it, sustains the upstanding individualities so necessary for the beauty of a complex. Falsehood is corrosive" (266). See also: 266–68, 270, 281–83, 292–93.

9. Ibid., 258.

10. Bruno Latour, "What Is the Style of Matters of Concern?" in *The Lure of Whitehead,* eds. Nicholas Gaskill and A.J. Nocek (University of Minnesota Press, 2014: 92–126), 115.

11. Halewood (2011, 18–19) makes a similar point.

12. Whitehead, *Process and Reality*, 337.

13. Whitehead, *Adventures of Ideas,* 285.

Epilogue
Reclaiming Whitehead's Theology

INTRODUCTION

In my exposition of Whitehead's aesthetic ontology for the purposes of demystifying the sense in which our thinkings and sayings can be "about" the world—in de-problematizing intentionality—I have minimized recourse to his explicit uses of "God." I have done this so as to avoid a hijacking of the reader's mind by the very metaphysical picture from which Whitehead intends to emancipate us. I have picked—or delayed—my battles.

My focus on Whitehead's epistemology, rather than on his theology, has been a conscious attempt to correct the undue emphasis that American interpreters of Whitehead have put on the latter at the expense of the former. The mistake, however, has not only been one of emphasis. Indeed, in the process of enlisting Whitehead for the purposes of liberalizing theology, these interpreters have in some senses domesticated him.

If my delayed consideration of Whitehead's God-talk strikes the reader as irresponsible, it is likely because a classical presumption about the role "God" ought to play in a cosmology lingers still. On the contrary, if the reader wishes I had said "good riddance" to Whitehead's theology, it is likely because of the same. What Whitehead names "God" goes by many other names, of which "God" provides an interpretation. Whitehead's God-function is introduced to solve a technical problem, not a religious one—not, at least, insofar as the latter stands for some doxastic need. Naming that function "God" is entirely the result of Whitehead's appraisal of the human history of the concept and his conceptual appropriation of it on the basis of that history.

Whitehead, it is safe to say, does not "have" a theology. What he has is a metaphysics that radically revises Aristotle's "Unmoved Mover" by means of his broad-scale elimination of the bifurcation of nature. He has, in addition, a reinterpretation of the concept of God in relation to the radicality of those revisions, so as to amplify its friction with its historical precedents. But he does not "theologize" except insofar as he experiments with concepts traditionally posed as antithetical to "the world" in order momentarily to hold apart, for the purposes of analysis, the characteristics of the cosmic passage. In fact, of all the preceding authorities to which one might appeal if one were interested in "doing theology," few would, as Whitehead does, appeal to David Hume. But this is just what Whitehead does. More specifically, Whitehead thinks Hume admits of precisely the God-function Whitehead advocates, only to dismiss it (wrongly) as anomalous. Before we can appreciate this relationship, however, more needs to be said about this God-function itself, and this requires a more detailed analysis of the cosmological problem which Whitehead's theory of concrescence seeks to address.

THE COSMOLOGICAL PROBLEM

When Whitehead calls something a "problem," he is speaking not as a moralist but as a mathematician. A mathematician encounters a problem when she is faced with a question that cannot be answered, or a situation that cannot be resolved, with information at her immediate disposal. Inherent to problems in this sense, however, is their solvability in principle. The solution may require revision of the terms, a calculating procedure, or both. But its solution is imminent, contingent upon the foregoing operations of thought. For the metaphysician, these operations involve the reformation of general notions,[1] so as to exhibit how the abstractive procedures necessary for analysis (e.g., scientific) collude with actuality.[2]

At its simplest, the problem he calls "cosmological"[3] is twofold: "actuality with permanence, requiring fluency as its completion; and actuality with fluency, requiring permanence as its completion."[4] This dual problem is one and the same, insofar as its unity construes the nature of creative advance, with its dual requirement of order and novelty, mutually implicated. In its more complicated form, it is the problem of accounting for how novel occasions achieve independent unity amid a multiplicity of inheritance. Whitehead explains, "The problem dominating the concrescence is the actualization of the quantum *in solido*."[5] In other words, the problem is of accounting for the fundamental relevance of singularity and multiplicity.

In the description just quoted, the quantum is the actual entity—the novel event—and the concrescence is its becoming. Insofar as this becoming is the origination of a novel occasion, the concrescence itself is non-temporal; it is not divisible into earlier and later acts of becoming.[6] However, what becomes (i.e., the event) is constitutive of temporal extensiveness by reason of its relation to past and future events as subject and superject.[7] This distinction is important so as not to confuse concrescence with temporal succession. After all, what needs explication is the achievement of subjectivity, which is a mode of existence of the quantum of explanation, that which must be non-divisible in principle: the actual entity. A subject, for Whitehead, is a self-regulating process of realization. This self-regulation functions by means of what Whitehead calls "subjective unity": "The actuality," he writes, "is the totality of prehensions with subjective unity in process of concrescence into concrete unity."[8] Subjective unity is attained by means of a subjective aim that guides the concrescent actuality's objective inheritance. This aim is the subject's ideal of itself, its purpose, which informs the *how* of its becoming, which motivates *this* taking of the givenness of the past rather than any other form of taking.

Here, I am with liberty using "taking" instead of "prehending" for simplicity. The cost of this substitution, however, is that it fails to conceptually guarantee the implication of internal relatedness of which Whitehead is so protective, hence his many neologisms. We can correct this omission by applying Whitehead's "principle of process": "That how an actual entity becomes constitutes what that actual entity is; so that the two descriptions of an actual entity [its 'being' and its 'becoming'] are not independent."[9] The principle of process synthesizes his ontological principle[10] (that actualities are the only reasons), with its implication of ontological atomicity or "extreme monism,"[11] with his principle of relativity[12] (that it belongs to the nature of "being" that it is a potential for every "becoming"), with its implication of extreme ontological porosity or "undifferentiated endurance."[13] Thus, *how* a subject "takes" (the objective data of its immediate past) constitutes *what* the subject "is." The question that remains for Whitehead concerns what directs *this* taking rather than *that* taking; in other words, it concerns how a subject (qua process of novel actuality) determines its own particularity.

To answer this question requires Whitehead to account for the nature and origin of a subjective aim. Ultimately, by reason of the ontological principle, a subjective aim can only be derived from an actuality (can only be the result of prehending an actual entity), but qua purposive, it cannot be derived from a past actuality. It is the prehension of unrealized possibility, not realized fact. But it is the prehension not of all possibility, but possibility *for itself*; they are, to recall chapter 4, "real potentials" or what is realizable for that subject. Thus, the object of a subjective aim is part of the category of existence or existential type of *propositions*. "The 'subjective aim'," writes Whitehead, "which controls the becoming of a subject, is that subject feeling a proposition with the subjective form of purpose to realize it in that process of self-creation."[14] The primary ontological function of propositions, according to Whitehead, is as lures for prehension. Propositions, as potential matters of fact, can be felt in a variety of ways, but primarily in terms of aversion or adversion (also per chapter 4), or more simply, in terms of affirmation or negation. What I have not yet addressed (what I did not address in chapter 4 or elsewhere) was a crucial element for propositions: exactly how they are relevant to subjects, which is to say, how potentiality inheres in actuality in such a way that it can function as lure rather than obligation, and thus differently than objective data of the past.

These elements (the efficient and the purposive) are two different characters of a single actual entity.[15] In their turn, final and efficient causes have both been overstressed; the former in the Christian middle ages and the latter in the modern scientific period.[16] Whitehead's test of a sound metaphysics is that it exhibits efficient and final causation in proper proportion;[17] failing to do so would render any account of the creative advance deficient insofar as it would obscure either the ground of obligation represented by established fact or the internal principle of unrest that constitutes the progressive element of the universe. According to Whitehead's account, "efficient causation expresses the transition from actual entity to actual entity; and final causation expresses the internal process whereby the actual entity becomes itself."[18] The fundamental cosmological problem is not how to reconcile change and permanence; it is accounting for the fact that change requires permanence for its fulfillment, and permanence requires change for its own, as well.[19] Subject and object are not two things, but two sides of this problem; subjectivity characterized by unrest and objectivity characterized by finality, neither being possible without the factoring of the other, and ultimately indistinguishable by any form of measurement.

But we have not yet accounted for how a potential matter of fact becomes an actual one; how the proposition that is aimed at comes to be realized so as to become a fact—a ground of obligation—for subjects in its relative future. Whitehead's refusal to let nature bifurcate requires him to account for the availability of the propositions to the subject, which will be felt as its purpose, and thus supply the *how* that will determine the subject's *what*.[20] To have a purpose is to entertain a possibility concerning a particular situation. How it is possible to do so must be complicit not only at the level of finite thinking, but all the way down, to the quantum of explanation in and of itself. To be able to entertain possibility in this way requires some form of ontological access to unrealized potentialities. But all ontological access must obtain by means of relations between actualities; "everything is positively somewhere in actuality, and in potency everywhere."[21] It seems, then, that there is no way around the conclusion that there must be some actuality unique from all others insofar as its subject aim involves the *complete* valuation of all possibilities, such that by prehending it, the concrescing subject can entertain potential matters of fact about/as itself.

This actuality must be unlike all others in being unconditioned by any finite decision which would characterize it as temporally extended; it is the one infinite actuality by which possibility attains "real relevance to the creative advance."[22] It is not "boundless, abstracted possibility," but relevant possibility.[23] To be real requires agency, but the only agents are actual entities. Thus, potentialities can only be existent for subjects insofar as those subjects prehend some actual entity—the only of its kind, in principle—whose identity is constituted in reverse from all others; that is, by entertaining all predicates at once, without any conditioning by a past.

WHITEHEAD'S GOD

Whitehead calls this entity the "primordial created fact";[24] the "non-temporal act of all-inclusive unfettered valuation";[25] the "timeless source of all order";[26] the "primordial superject of creativity";[27] the "complete envisagement of eternal objects";[28] the "principle of concretion";[29] the "initial 'object of desire'";[30] and the "primordial unity of relevance of the many potential forms."[31] He also happens to call it "the primordial side of the nature of God."[32] When he does so, however, he admits to introducing a "note of interpretation."[33] The name "God" lacks "a certain ultimate directness of intuition" enjoyed by his aesthetic descriptions.[34]

In fact, very early on in his usage of the name in *Process and Reality*, Whitehead explains his choice to do so as directly related to how it has historically been used to describe that "timeless source of all order" whose relationship to humankind "acquires that 'subjective form' of refreshment and companionship."[35] This subjective form or feeling is on Whitehead's account that "at which religions aim."[36] While this construal of "religions" and their "aims" is utterly replete with problems, this is not the occasion on which to appeal to genealogical critique of his terms. If Whitehead did not consider "God" an interpretive leap, it might be such an occasion, but he clearly does not allow the name to do any conceptual work not already achieved by the other descriptors.

In any case, the name recurs, and the fact that it does has attracted readers with interests in liberalizing Christian theology rather than those interested in remedying modernist epistemology. More often than not, Whitehead's epistemology has been read as incidental to his theology, rather than the other way around. Reading him in this way requires a significant degree of motivated attention and amounts to a domestication of his thought. For instance, Whitehead never uses the term "theology" to describe what he is doing with his God-talk; the term only ever occurs as a description of what he is standing against (e.g., "Western theology"[37] or "contemporary theologians"[38]).

When speaking of Aristotle's "unmoved mover," he uses the word "God" and not *Theos*.[39] He likewise uses "God" when describing "the Semitic Jehova,"[40] as in the description "the Semitic theory of a wholly transcendent God creating out of nothing an accidental universe."[41] What Whitehead sees Greek and Semitic thought, as well as the incipient Christian traditions of thought, to have in common is their embodiment of "the notions of a static God condescending to the world, and of a world *either* thoroughly fluent, *or* accidently static, but finally fluent."[42] In other words, these traditions of God-talk have misconceived the God-function in the universe insofar as they have misconceived the nature of the cosmological problem as constituted by the relation between two diverse actualities, the static and the fluent, rather than by the contrast of fluency requiring permanence and permanence requiring fluency.

This misconception is underwritten by the ever-recurrent bifurcation of nature: "The vicious separation of the flux from the permanence leads to the concept of an entirely static God, with eminent reality, in relation to an entirely fluent world with deficient reality." The theological expression of the bifurcation is, on Whitehead's understanding, inevitably tied up with an epistemological one: "But if the opposites, static and fluent, have once been so explained as separately to characterize diverse actualities, the interplay between the thing which is static and the things which are fluent involves contradiction at every step in its explanation. Such philosophies must include the notion of 'illusion' as a fundamental principle—the notion of '*mere* appearance'."[43] The same conceptual opposites—God and World, subject and object, spirit and nature, mind and body—have structured classical theological and modernist epistemological discourses, but with different emphases. Privileging one side of the dichotomy over the other still imports the omitted term by defining the admitted one in terms of its omission—such is the amodernist critique Bruno Latour pursues in his work.

The elimination of the bifurcation requires a complete conceptual sweep. By demonstrating a revised form of God-talk in a way that is consonant with his reconception of the question which metaphysics seeks to answer, Whitehead is showing how the notion of God can be reimagined according to the fundamental principles of his philosophy of organism. His interest in saving the notion of God is directly related to its historical roles (at least the ones Whitehead observes) in naming some element in the universe after which human beings long. Precisely because his use is intended to stand in critical contrast to this history, however, it is demonstrative only; there is no metaphysical or epistemological necessity behind the name, only anthropological interest. To borrow from Catherine Keller, "that for which God is a nickname cares not whether you believe in God. Doesn't give a damn. Isn't in the damning business."[44]

Whitehead does not always succeed in this reimagining. He never provides any justification for his continued application of male pronouns, for one, even while this maleness fails to serve its classical purpose (i.e., as indicative of force over persuasion, order over chaos, ideality over materiality, transcendence over immanence).[45] But I have not yet said enough to make this obvious. I have only thus considered the "primordial side" of the nature of "God" understood as the counterpart to the givenness of established fact. This is the nature of the "primordial created fact" abstracted from its "commerce with 'particulars'" and thus not yet generative of propositional modes of existence. As such, "God" is completely "deficient in actuality," considered "in abstraction"[46] from the "World."[47] In Whitehead's conceptual apparatus, God-qua-primordial considered in abstraction is about as unstable a concept as relevance without relations. It is like considering the actual entity in terms of its subjective aim without an objective datum, a *how* without a *what*. It is just that, with the one primordial actuality, every *how* is relevant because there is not yet[48] any *what* to condition it.

The situation is the reverse for finite actualities, for whom, as subjects, the *what* is already given. As a reminder, primordiality is a non-temporal description; it has nothing whatsoever to do with being temporally *before* the concrescent subject; after all, "everything is positively somewhere in actuality, and in potency everywhere." Qua the actuality of potency, God-qua-primordial is not before but *with* every becoming, as mutual instruments of creativity. God and World share the exact same character, just in different order. God qua embryonic act conditioning all becoming is the one non-temporal creature; this is God-as-(Potential)-Superject, God-as-(Potential)-Object for the World, but without ever having achieved actuality, without having satisfied its (in principle unsatisfiable because unlimited) subjective aim, conceptual valuation of all possibility. Far from being the "pure actuality" of Aristotle's Unmoved Mover, the actuality of Whitehead's God is fully dependent upon finite actualities—just as finite actualities are dependent upon the infinite actuality for their conceptual origination.

Moreover, it is only because of finite historical processes that the fullness of possibility can be felt by finite subjects in an order of relevance. One the one hand, the primordial side of the nature of God "includes in its appetitive vision all possibilities of order, possibilities at once incompatible and unlimited with a fecundity beyond imagination." And yet, "Finite transience stages this welter of incompatibilities in their ordered relevance to the flux of epochs." Such that, on the other hand, "the process of finite history is essential for the ordering of the basic vision, otherwise mere confusion."[49] This description demonstrates Whitehead's "doctrine of mutual immanence": that either side of an antithesis can only be described in terms of factors common to both.[50]

Exhibiting this doctrine, Whitehead describes the second side of the nature of God. The way actualities become, the way the temporal order develops by realizing certain possibilities rather than others, changes the relevance of possibilities for future subjects. This change constitutes the "consequent" side of the nature of God, insofar as finite history serves to actualize what was qua God merely potential, and having actualized it, creates what can serve as instrument for God's becoming. Without the finite actualities to serve as the logical subjects of a proposition for God, God lacks God's own subjective aim and, therefore, subjective unity. It is because of the "World" that God can be a subject. As subject, what God becomes as object for future subjects amounts to an "ultimate, basic adjustment of the togetherness of eternal objects on which creative order depends"—amounts to, that is, the basis of relevance.[51]

ANTITHESES

The only reason developing this point matters is because what "God as subject" means is that *everything* matters. Ultimately, there are never any twos in Whitehead's cosmology: there is only the one and the many. "God and World" serve to express "the final metaphysical truth that appetitive vision and physical enjoyment have equal claim to priority in creation."[52] What is interesting in contemporary efforts to "de-theologize" Whitehead is how little scrutiny is given to his conceptual counterpart "the World." After all, Whitehead says that this term is just as much the introduction of an interpretation. "The World," the one that functions as the conceptual counterpart to "God," is not synonymous with "the universe"; it is that aspect of the universe which exhibits passage. It is the measurability of the universe. But immediately this description must be amended—or rather "amplified."

When Whitehead says that a statement of his "requires amplification," it means that the reverse of the statement is also true, but in stating the reverse, there is a shift in the meaning of the terms involved.[53] The shift of meaning converts the opposition into a "contrast."[54] A contrast is that category of existence constituting the unity of the opposed entities; a proposition is a type of contrast, holding together as it does actuality and possibility as a unit for feeling. "All the 'opposites' are elements in the nature of things, and are incorrigibly there";[55] they cannot finally be torn apart.[56] In the final interpretation of his cosmological scheme, it is just as true to say "the World is permanent and God is fluent," "the World is one and God many," "the World is immanent in God," "the World transcends God," and "the World creates God," as the reverse.[57]

The "final summary" can only be expressed in terms of "groups of antitheses"[58] attempting to elucidate the dynamic efforts of existence. In this sense,

Whitehead acknowledges an analog to the philosophy of organism in Hegel,[59] but whereas Hegel posits a "hierarchy in categories of *thought*," Whitehead posits a "hierarchy of categories of *feeling*."[60] But with this emendation, the analog holds fairly well:

> The universe is at once the multiplicity of *rēs verae* and the solidarity of *rēs verae*. The solidarity is itself the efficiency of the macroscopic *res vera*, embodying the principle of unbounded permanence acquiring novelty through flux. The multiplicity is composed of microscopic *rēs verae*, each embodying the principle of bounded flux acquiring "everlasting" permanence. On one side, the one becomes many; and on the other side, the many become one. But *what* becomes is always a *res vera*, and the concrescence of a *res vera* is the development of a subjective aim. This development is nothing else than the Hegelian development of an idea.[61]

It is just this aspect of the philosophy of organism, as analogous to and yet divergent from the Hegelian school, that Whitehead seeks to elaborate upon in his "final interpretation," in terms of the antithesis of God and World.

Whitehead's dialectic involves two kinds of fluency: concrescence and transition, extended and non-extended, subjectification and objectification.[62] The many become one and are increased by one; the third moment results in a positivity. The dialectic exhibits the ontological principle that everything is positively somewhere in actuality or everywhere in potency. Whitehead's antitheses issue into a new dimension of positivity—it turns an opposition into a contrast.[63] His is a Hegelian dialectic without its "(Christianizing) sublation."[64] By comparison, Hegel's dialectic involves a contradiction followed by its negation; the dialectic cancels the antithesis in a third moment, resulting in a determinate negation. To follow Whitehead's thinking, it is because Hegel restricts the efficacy of ideas to the categories of *thought* that the inevitable result is an "evolutionary monism" in which particularity is finally lost.[65]

To lose particularity, according to Whitehead, is to lose actuality, and to lose actuality is to lose all meaning, all value. He writes, "The value inherent in the Universe has an essential independence of any moment of time; and yet it loses its meaning apart from its necessary reference to the World of passing fact. Value refers to Fact, and Fact refers to Value."[66] Here "reference" is not linguistic but ontological.[67] He continues, "This statement is a direct contradiction to Plato and the theological tradition derived from him."[68] According to Whitehead, Hegel, like the tradition of Greek thought preceding him, categorically misconceived the nature of ideas and "their status in the Universe."[69] By treating "ideas" as independent existences, this tradition invited contradiction at every point in their efforts to explain their effectiveness: "The notion of a purely abstract self-enjoyment of values apart from any reference to effectiveness in action was the fundamental error prevalent in Greek philosophy, an error which was inherited by the hermits of the first Christian centuries, and which is not unknown in the modern world of learning."[70] Ideas are not independent existences; there are no such modes of existence. To the contrary: "An 'Idea' is the entity answering questions which enquire 'How?' Such questions seek the 'sort' of occurrence."[71]

Of course, by the time we are asking questions, we have already passed the Rubicon. The abstraction involved in the creation of any actuality proceeds to a second order of abstraction, constituting consciousness. "This procedure," acknowledges Whitehead, "is necessary for finite thought."[72] It abstracts "finite constituents of the actual thing" from that thing. Such abstraction "is the basis of science," which seeks measurability. But the task of philosophy is the reverse: to provide "the general notions by which to conceive the infinite variety of specific instances which rest unrealized in the womb of nature."[73] The concept of "God" is, for Whitehead, "the way in which we understand this incredible fact—that what cannot be, yet is."[74]

THE ONTOLOGICAL EFFICACY OF UNREALIZED POSSIBILITY

The notion of "God" interprets, for Whitehead, just this general characteristic of the Universe: the fact that that which is unrealized can be effective. This efficacy is appetitive, not coercive. Thus, he writes that God "is the lure for feeling, the eternal urge of desire. [God's] particular relevance to each creative act, as it arises from its own conditioned standpoint in the world, constitutes [God] the initial 'object of desire' establishing the initial phase of each subjective aim."[75] The similarity to Aristotle's description of the Unmoved Mover in his *Metaphysics* (Book XII, 1072a) is recognized. But, for Aristotle, the initial object of desire is the same as the primary object of thought—and "thinking is the starting point."[76] According to Whitehead, "Aristotle had not made the distinction between conceptual feelings and the intellectual feelings which alone involve consciousness. But if 'conceptual feeling', with its subjective form of valuation, be substituted for 'thought' . . . the agreement is exact."[77] *Mutatis mutandis,* both Aristotle and Whitehead can agree that the actual entity's process of completion is motivated by its conceptual prehension of God. This conceptual prehension is of a proposition of itself, with the subjective form of desire, appetition, lure, or purpose.

Propositions, we have seen, are primarily "lures for feeling" for the concrescent subject. But we can now add that propositions depend upon the relevance of unrealized ideals to serve as the ontological predicate. When

Whitehead thus speaks of God's "particular relevance" to each concrescent subject, he is speaking of the subject's ability to entertain a proposition about itself. (But, of course, it is just as true to say that the subject *is* this entertainment of the proposition.) The subjective form of this relevance of God is thus the subject's aim at an ideal of itself that, once "satisfied,"[78] results in a novel actual entity. When this aim is realized, it ceases to be a subject. Thus, he can say "no subject experiences twice" just as "[n]o thinker thinks twice"—this is his extension of "[t]he ancient doctrine that 'no one crosses the same river twice'" and is what "Locke ought to have meant by his doctrine of time as 'perpetual perishing'."[79]

The subject is the experience; it is the unity of the datum for a feeling "*as felt.*"[80] This is finally Whitehead's solution to the problem of accounting for how novel occasions achieve independent unity amid a multiplicity of inheritance, the problem of the "actualization of the quantum *in solido*" mentioned at the outset. "The quantum," he writes, "is that standpoint in the extensive continuum," this standpoint being the "conditioned standpoint" whose mode of existence is that of a contrast. It is a proposition felt as subjective aim, whose entertainment is only possible because of the one non-temporal actual entity whose conceptual prehension is unconditioned and whose physical prehension of established fact results in just the conditioned possibility or real potential that results in a propositional mode of existence.

In this sense, a subjective aim is a propositional feeling. In a different sense, it can be conceived as a pure conceptual feeling. This alternation of senses refers back to Whitehead's notion of "amplification": it is *both* true to say that the originary phase of concrescence is physical *and* that it is conceptual.[81] Becoming isn't, after all, temporal, even if what becomes contributes to the extensive continuum. There is, rather, a "bewildering variety of originative amplification."[82] Classical empiricism "overbalances" the physical originations, presupposes a subject that encounters a datum and reacts to it. The philosophy of organism rebalances these originary factors; it "presupposes a datum which is met with feelings, and progressively attains the unity of a subject."[83] There is mutual amplification.

It is precisely because of this overbalancing of physical origination that Hume dismisses the problem of the missing shade of blue as "so singular, that it is scarcely worth our observing."[84] But, despite this ultimate dismissal, Whitehead finds[85] in this example from Hume a recognition of what Hume himself describes as "one contradictory phenomenon, which may prove that it is not absolutely impossible for ideas to arise, independent of their correspondent impressions."[86] In Whitehead's terms, this is the possibility of ideas providing a "lure for feeling," which is, far from being "so singular" a phenomenon as to be dismissible, utterly pervasive in every instance of becoming. The "principle of relevant potentials, unrealized in the datum and yet constituent of an 'objective lure' by proximity to the datum" constitutes an exception for Hume but the rule for Whitehead, for whom "the concrescent process admits a selection from this 'objective lure' into subjective efficiency" which is the meaning of the "subjective 'ideal of itself'" which guides the process" of becoming.[87] In short, Whitehead's "God" is one name among many for that actuality which accounts for Hume's acknowledged contradiction to the maxim that all ideas (all "conceptual feelings" for Whitehead) derive from the givenness of the past. It is little more than this.

SAVING GOD

At the outset of his most recent book,[88] George Allan declares that we need to "cleanse the philosophy of organism of its secular deity."[89] According to Allan, Whitehead is forced to admit God into his system because he failed to abide by his own axiom in developing the doctrine of eternal objects. By conceiving possibilities as "essentially eternal and self-contained, having no essential relatedness to either the actual world or one another," writes Allan, Whitehead is forced to "bridge the metaphysical chasm" between the eternal and the temporal by way of the (for Allan, incoherent) idea of an "eternal actual entity."[90] Contrary to such understandings, I have attempted to render this idea, in fact, coherent. I have, by extension, attempted to obviate the need to de-theologize Whitehead's metaphysics.

Whitehead is clear that the apparent self-contradiction of his "final summary" depends entirely on the "neglect of the diverse categories of existence."[91] From the very outset of *Process and Reality*, he obliges us to enlarge our appreciation of the "endless number of categories of existence" incumbent upon his concept of a "contrast."[92] It is only "[f]or the practical purposes of 'human understanding'" that he restricts consideration to a "few basic types of existence" and lumps "the more derivative types together under the heading of 'contrasts'."[93] Because "God and World" constitutes a contrast, it makes no more sense to "cleanse the philosophy of organism" of "God" than it does to "cleanse" it of "the World." To suggest otherwise is to commit the fallacy of misplaced concreteness by abstracting the former term from the opposition in which it has any meaning whatsoever. To do so is to reify the contradiction by refusing the contrast.

All such moves end up suspecting Whitehead's "God" of intervening to solve the problem of possibility's independent existence, misconceived as such by the neglect of Whitehead's many "amplifications." They end up, this is to say, accusing Whitehead's "God" of being a metaphysical imposter invoked to save the system from collapse—which is, of course, *precisely* what Whitehead tells us all along "God" must not and, on my reading, does not do throughout *Process and Reality*. Rather than being their exception, Whitehead's concept "God" is the chief exemplification of his metaphysical principles—and this is just what he says it is.[94] It is what ensures the mutual immanence of things, not what offends it. The fact that it continues to perplex readers is an indication only that they have failed to educate their attention in the way that Whitehead says we must, on pain of perpetuating the modernist assumption that matters of fact are not always already matters of value.

NOTES

1. Whitehead, *Process and Reality*, 17.
2. Whitehead, "Mathematics and the Good" (1941), in *Essays in Science and Philosophy* (New York: Philosophical Library, 1947), 113.
3. Whitehead, *Process and Reality*, xiii, 341.
4. Ibid., 347.
5. Ibid., 283.
6. Ibid. 69.
7. Whitehead uses the term "superject" to describe the subjective form of one's being an object for future subjects (See, for example: Whitehead, *Process and Reality*, 29, 84, 222, 245). In its subjective form, a subject's capacity for objectification is akin to its "purpose." More will be said on this point in a moment.
8. Ibid., 235.
9. Ibid., 23.
10. Ibid., 24, 244.
11. Ibid., 148.
12. Ibid., 22.
13. Ibid., 77. Whitehead writes, "The baseless metaphysical doctrine of 'undifferentiated endurance' is a subordinate derivative from the misapprehension of the proper character of the extensive scheme."
14. Ibid., 25.
15. Whitehead explains, "Thus an actual entity has a threefold character: (i) it has the character 'given' for it by the past; (ii) it has the subjective character aimed at in its process of concrescence; (iii) it has the superjective character, which is the pragmatic value of its specific satisfaction qualifying the transcendent creativity." Ibid., 87.
16. Ibid., 84.
17. Ibid.
18. Ibid., 151.
19. I recognize that I am using "permanence" here to refer to established fact, but it should be noted that Whitehead typically uses this term to qualify forms of realization considered in abstraction of any particular mode of exemplification (i.e., eternal objects).
20. See, for example: Ibid., 257–58.

21. Ibid., 40.
22. Ibid., 31.
23. Ibid., 220.
24. Ibid., 31.
25. Ibid.
26. Ibid., 32.
27. Ibid.
28. Ibid., 44.
29. Ibid., 345.
30. Ibid., 344.
31. Ibid., 349.
32. Ibid., 345.
33. Ibid., 341.
34. Ibid.
35. Ibid., 32.
36. Ibid.
37. Ibid., 342.
38. Ibid., 47.
39. Ibid., 342.
40. Ibid., 94.
41. Ibid., 95.
42. Ibid., 347.
43. Ibid., 346–47.
44. Catherine Keller, *The Cloud of the Impossible: Negative Theology and Planetary Entanglement* (Columbia UP, 2015), 306.
45. In fact, when he speaks in 1932 of the primordial nature of God as that element of "the final fact" which involves "a fecundity beyond imagination," Whitehead is much closer to the *tehom* of the Hebrew Genesis associated with its embryonic imagery than to the male God of the Christian one who creates out of nothing (see: Catherine Keller, *Face of the Deep: A Theology of Becoming* (Routledge, 2003), 43–64; Mary-Jane Rubenstein, *Pantheologies: Gods, Worlds, Monsters [Columbia UP, 2018]*, 65).
46. Whitehead, *Process and* Reality, 34.
47. More will be said in a moment on this notion of "the World," as well.
48. Non-temporally speaking.
49. Whitehead, "Process and Reality" (1932), *Essays in Science and Philosophy*, 118.
50. Ibid., 118, 82.
51. Whitehead, *Process and Reality*, 32.
52. Ibid., 348.
53. See, for example: Ibid., 225.
54. Ibid., 24.
55. Ibid., 350.
56. Ibid., 348.
57. Ibid.

58. Ibid.
59. Although it is more proper to say "the Hegelian school," as Whitehead does.
60. Ibid., 166.
61. Ibid., 167.
62. Ibid., 210.
63. Ibid., 348.
64. I borrow this phrase from Rubenstein; see *Pantheologies*, 34.
65. Ibid.
66. Whitehead, "Immortality" (1941), *Essays in Science and Philosophy*, 79–80.
67. Ibid., 82.
68. Ibid., 80.
69. Ibid., 83.
70. Ibid., 82.
71. Ibid., 83.
72. Whitehead, "Mathematics and the Good" (1941), *Essays in Science and Philosophy*, 113.
73. Whitehead, *Process and Reality,* 17.
74. Ibid., 350.
75. Ibid., 344.
76. According to Whitehead's translation by W.D. Ross; ibid., 344.
77. Ibid.
78. See, for example: Ibid., 87.
79. Ibid., 29.
80. Ibid., 24.
81. Ibid., 225.
82. Ibid., 117.
83. Ibid., 155.
84. David Hume, *An Enquiry Concerning Human Understanding and Selections from A Treatise of Human Nature* (Chicago: Open Court Publishing, 1912), 19. In a slightly different rendering: Whitehead, *Process and Reality*, 87.
85. Whitehead, *Process and Reality*, 86.
86. Hume, *Enquiry,* 18.
87. Whitehead, *Process and Reality*, 87.
88. George Allan, *Whitehead's Radically Temporalist Metaphysics: Recovering the Seriousness of Time* (Lexington Press, 2020).
89. Ibid., 27.
90. Ibid., 25–26.
91. Whitehead, *Process and Reality*, 348.
92. Ibid., 24.
93. Ibid.
94. Ibid., 343.

Bibliography

Allan, George. *Whitehead's Radically Temporalist Metaphysics: Recovering the Seriousness of Time.* Lexington Press, 2020.

Brandom, Robert. "Kantian Lessons about Mind, Meaning, and Rationality." *Philosophical Topics* 34, no. 1 (2006): 1–20.

———. "Knowledge and the Social Articulation of the Space of Reasons," *Philosophy and Phenomenological Research,* vol. 55, no. 4 (Dec. 1995): 895–908.

———. *Making It Explicit.* Cambridge, MA: Harvard University Press, 1998.

———. "Vocabularies of Pragmatism: Synthesizing Naturalism and Historicism." In *Rorty and His Critics,* ed. Robert B. Brandom, Malden, MA: Blackwell Publishing, 2000.

Burge, Tyler. "Perceptual Entitlement," *Philosophy and Phenomenological Research,* vol. 67, no. 3 (2003): 503–548.

Caird, Edward. *The Critical Philosophy of Immanuel Kant.* 2 vols. London, UK: Macmillan Publishing, 1889.

Caputo, John D., *The Prayers and Tears of Jacques Derrida: Religion without Religion.* Bloomington, IN: Indiana University Press, 1997.

Davidson, Donald. "The Method of Truth in Metaphysics." In *Inquiries into Truth and Interpretation.* Oxford, UK: Clarendon Press, 2001.

———. "On the Very Idea of a Conceptual Scheme." *Proceedings and Addresses of the American Philosophical Association* 47 (1973–1974): 5–20.

———. "Radical Interpretation." In *Inquiries into Truth and Interpretation.* Oxford, UK: Oxford University Press, 2001.

Euclid. *Elements, Book 1: Fundamentals of Plane Geometry Involving Straight-lines.* Translated by H. M. Taylor. Cambridge, UK: Cambridge University Press, 1893.

Friedman, Michael. *Reconsidering Logical Positivism.* Cambridge, UK: Cambridge University Press, 1999.

Hacking, Ian. *The Emergence of Probability: A Philosophical Study of Early Ideas about Probability, Induction, and Statistical Inference.* Cambridge, UK: Cambridge University Press, 1975.

Halewood, Michael. *A.N. Whitehead and Social Theory: Tracing a Culture of Thought.* Anthem Press, 2011.

Hylton, Peter. *Russell, Idealism and the Emergence of Analytic Philosophy.* Oxford, UK: Oxford University Press, 1993.

James, William. "Does 'Consciousness' Exist?," *The Journal of Philosophy, Psychology, and Scientific Methods,* vol. 1, no. 18 (Sept. 1904): 477–491.

Kant, Immanuel. *The Critique of Pure Reason.* Translated and edited by Paul Guyer and Allen W. Wood. Cambridge, UK: Cambridge University Press, 1998.

Keller, Catherine. *Cloud of the Impossible: Negative Theology and Planetary Entanglement.* New York, NY: Columbia University Press, 2015.

———. *The Face of the Deep: A Theology of Becoming.* New York, NY: Routledge, 2003.

Latour, Bruno. "What Is Given in Experience?," Foreword to Isabelle Stengers, *Thinking with Whitehead: A Free and Wild Creation of Concepts.* Translated by Michael Chase, Harvard University Press, 2011.

———. "What Is the Style of Matters of Concern?" in *The Lure of Whitehead,* eds. Nicholas Gaskill and A. J. Nocek, 92–126. University of Minnesota Press, 2014.

Locke, John. *An Essay Concerning Human Understanding.* Edited by Kenneth Winkler. Indianapolis, IN: Hacket Publishing, 1996.

Lowe, Victor. *Alfred North Whitehead: The Man and His Work,* Vol. 1, 1861–1910. Baltimore and London: The Johns Hopkins University Press, 1985.

———. "Whitehead's 1911 Criticism of Russell's *The Problems of Philosophy.*" *The Journal of Bertrand Russell Studies* vol. 13 (Spring 1974): 3.

McDowell, John. "The Constitutive Ideal of Rationality." *Crítica: Revista Hispanoamericana de Filosofía* vol. 30, no. 88 (April 1998): 29–48.

———. *Having a World in View Essays on Kant, Hegel, and Sellars.* Cambridge, MA: Harvard University Press, 2013.

———. "Knowledge and the Internal," *Philosophy and Phenomenological Research,* vol. 55, no. 4 (Dec. 1995): 877–893.

———. "Knowledge and the Internal Revisited," *Philosophy and Phenomenological Research,* vol. 64, no. 1 (Jan. 2002): 97–105.

———. "Meaning and Intentionality in Wittgenstein's Later Philosophy." *Midwest Studies in Philosophy,* vol. XVII (1992): 40–52.

———. *Mind and World.* Cambridge, MA: Harvard University Press, 1994.

———. *Perception as a Capacity for Knowledge.* Marquette UP, 2011.

———. "Towards Rehabilitating Objectivity." In *Rorty and His Critics,* edited by Robert Brandom, 109–122. Malden, MA: Blackwell, 2000.

———. "Wittgensteinian 'Quietism'." *Common Knowledge* 15:3 (Duke UP, 2009): 365–372.

Mora, Thierry and William Bialek, "Are Biological Systems Poised at Criticality?" *Journal of Statistical Physics* 144 (2011): 268–302.

Nachtomy, Ohad. "Leibniz and Russell: The Number of all Numbers and the Set of all Sets." In *Leibniz and the English-Speaking World,* edited by Pauline Phemister and Stuart Brown, 207–218. The Netherlands: Springer, 2007.

Newton, Isaac. *Philosophiae Naturalis Principia Mathematica,* Book I, def. VIII, scholium. New York, NY: Geo P. Putnam, 1850.
Nunn, T. Percy. "Sense-data and Physical Objects." *Proceedings of the Aristotelian Society,* New Series 16 (1915–1916): 156–178.
———. "Scientific Objects and Common-Sense Things: The Presidential Address," *Proceedings of the Aristotelian Society,* New Series 24 (1923–24): 58–75.
Prichard, H. A. *Kant's Theory of Knowledge.* Oxford, UK: Clarendon Press, 1909.
Quine, W. V. "Whitehead and the Rise of Modern Logic." In *The Philosophy of Alfred North Whitehead,* edited by Paul Arthur Schilpp, 127–63. Evanston and Chicago, IL: Northwestern University Press, 1941.
———. "Two Dogmas of Empiricism." *The Philosophical Review* 60, no.1 (1951): 20–43.
Redding, Paul. *Analytic Philosophy and the Return of Hegelian Thought.* Cambridge, UK: Cambridge University Press, 2007.
Rorty, Richard. "Dewey between Hegel and Darwin." In *Rorty and Pragmatism: The Philosopher Responds to His Critics,* edited by Herman J. Saatkamp, Jr., 1–15. Nashville, TN: Nashville University Press, 1995.
———. "Pragmatism, Davidson, and Truth." In *Objectivity, Relativism, and Truth.* Cambridge, UK: Cambridge University Press, 1991.
———. "Response to McDowell." In *Rorty and His Critics,* edited by Robert Brandom, 123–128. Malden, MA: Blackwell Publishing, 2000.
———. "Solidarity or Objectivity?" In *Relativism: Interpretation and Confrontation,* edited by Michael Krausz. Notre Dame, IN: University of Notre Dame Press, 1989.
———. "Ten Years After." In *The Linguistic Turn: Essays in Philosophical Method with Two Retrospective Essays.* Chicago, IL and London, UK: University of Chicago Press, 1992.
———. "Twenty-Five Years Later." In *The Linguistic Turn: Essays in Philosophical Method with Two Retrospective Essays.* Chicago, IL: University of Chicago Press, 1992.
Rovelli. Carlo. *The Order of Time.* New York, NY: Riverhead Books, 2018.
Rubenstein, Mary Jane. *Pantheologies: Gods, World, Monsters.* New York, NY: Columbia University Press, 2018.
Russell, Bertrand. "Causal Laws." In *The Analysis of Mind,* ed. S. Harris. New York, NY: Macmillan Company, 1921.
———. *A Critical Exposition of the Philosophy of Leibniz.* London, UK and New York, NY: Routledge, [1900] 1992.
———. *The Problems of Philosophy.* Oxford, UK: Oxford University Press, [1912] 2001.
Santayana, George. *Scepticism and Animal Faith: Introduction to a System of Philosophy.* New York, NY: Charles Scribner's Sons, 1924.
Sellars, Wilfrid. *Science and Metaphysics: Variations on a Kantian Theme.* London, UK and New York, NY: Routledge and Kegan Paul, 1967.
Sherburne, Donald. "Whitehead, Categories, and the Completion of the Copernican Revolution." *The Monist* 66 (July 1983): 367–386.

Stadler, Friedrich. *The Vienna Circle and Logical Empiricism.* New York, Boston, Dordrecht, London, Moscow: Kluwer Academic Publishers, 2003.
Stout, Jeffrey. "Radical Interpretation and Pragmatism: Davidson, Rorty, and Brandom on Truth." In *Radical Interpretation in Religion,* edited by Nancy K. Frankenberry, 25–52. Cambridge, UK: Cambridge University Press, 2002.
Stengers, Isabelle. "A Constructivist Reading of *Process and Reality,*" *Theory, Culture, and Society,* vol. 25, no. 4 (2008): 91–110.
———. "Experimenting with Refrains: Subjectivity and the Challenge of Escaping Modern Dualism," *Subjectivity,* vol. 22 (2008): 38–59.
———. *Thinking with Whitehead: A Free and Wild Creation of Concepts.* Translated by Michael Chase. Cambridge, MA: Harvard University Press, 2011.
———. "Whitehead's Account of the Sixth Day," *Configurations,* vol. 13, no. 1 (Winter 2005): 35–55.
Taylor, A. E. *A Commentary on Plato's Timaeus.* Oxford: Clarendon Press, 1928.
———. *Plato: The Man and His Work.* New York, NY: Lincoln MacVeagh, 1927.
Van Fraassen, Bas C. *An Introduction to the Philosophy of Time and Space.* New York, NY: Random House Publishing, 1970.
Watson, Richard A. "Shadow History in Philosophy." *Journal of the History of Philosophy,* vol. 31 (1993): 95–109.
Whitehead, Alfred North. *A Treatise on Universal Algebra: With Applications.* Cambridge: Cambridge University Press, 1898.
———. *Adventures of Idea.* New York, NY: Free Press, 1967.
———. "Appeal to Sanity." In *Essays in Science and Philosophy.* New York, NY: Philosophical Library, 1947.
———. *Concept of Nature.* Cambridge, UK: Cambridge University Press, [1920] 1930.
———. *An Enquiry Concerning the Principles of Natural Knowledge.* Cambridge, UK: The University Press, 1919.
———. *The Function of Reason.* Princeton, NJ: Princeton University Press, 1929.
———. "Immortality." In *Essays in Science and Philosophy.* New York, NY: Philosophical Library, 1947.
———. Letter to Bertrand Russell. 26 August 1911. The Bertrand Russell Archives. McMaster University, Ontario, Canada.
———. "Mathematics and Liberal Education: An Address" (1912). In *Essays in Science and Philosophy.* New York, NY: Philosophical Library, 1947.
———. *Modes of Thought.* New York, NY: Free Press, [1938] 1968.
———. "The Philosophical Aspects of the Principle of Relativity." *Proceedings of the Aristotelian Society,* New Series 22 (1921–1922).
———. *The Principle of Relativity with Applications to Physical Science.* New York, NY: Cambridge University Press, 1922.
———. *Process and Reality.* Edited by David Ray Griffin and Donald W. Sherburne. New York, NY: Free Press, [1929] 1978.
———. *Religion in the Making.* Lowell Lectures. New York, NY: Fordham University Press, 1996.
———. *Science and the Modern World.* Lowell Lectures. New York, NY: Free Press, [1925] 1967.

———. "Space, Time, and Relativity." In *Proceedings of the Aristotelian Society*, New Series 16 (1915–1916): 104–129.

———. "The Study of the Past—Its Uses and Its Dangers." In *Essays in Science and Philosophy*. New York, NY: Philosophical Library, [1933] 1947.

———. *Symbolism: Its Meaning and Effects*. Barbour-Page Lectures, University of Virginia. New York, NY: Fordham University Press, [1927] 1985.

———. "Time, Space, and Material: Are They, and If so in What Sense, the Ultimate Data of Science?" *Proceedings of the Aristotelian Society, Supplementary Volume* 2 (1919): 44–108.

———. "Uniformity and Contingency: The Presidential Address." *Proceedings of the Aristotelian Society*. New Series 23 (1922–1923), 13.

Wittgenstein, Ludwig. *Tractatus Logico-Philosophicus*. Translated by C. K. Ogden. London, UK: Routledge and Kegan Paul, 1922.

———. *On Certainty*. 1969.

———. *Philosophical Investigations*. 1953.

Index

Abriss der Logistik (Carnap), 153
Absolute Idealism, 32, 33, 36, 38, 46n1
absolute space, 10, 13, 132, 142, 152;
  absolute time and, 145–149
Absolute Theory of Space, 142
absolute transcendence, 90
abstraction, significance of, 10, 37,
  63, 175, 176, 177n2; aesthetics of
  experience and, 80–81, 86, 88, 99,
  100, 105; connivance of world and,
  129, 134; consciousness and, 94–98;
  symbolism and language and, 149–
  51, 154, 165; Whitehead's theology
  and, 185, 188, 191n19
"The Academic or Sceptical
  Philosophy" (Hume), 6
acquaintance, notion of, 8, 10, 121, 166
"Action, Meaning, and Self"
  (McDowell), 42
actual entities, 7, 36, 37, 160, 185, 188–
  90, 191n15; aesthetics of experience
  and, 79–81, 83–89, 91–92, 94,
  96–99, 101–103, 105–108, 110n58,
  111n78; connivance of world and,
  129, 133; cosmological problem and,
  180–83; intentionality and, 65, 67;
  of nexus, 98; objective immortality
  of, 111n78; order and organism and,
  88–89; proposition and, 87, 101;
  togetherness of, 80. *See also* actual
  occasions
actuality, 11, 27n37, 37, 65, 132;
  abstraction and, 188; aesthetics of
  experience and, 78, 81–88, 92–95,
  100, 103, 105; appetition and, 85; as
  compositional, 84, 166; concrescent,
  181; cosmological problem and,
  180–83; as determinate, 85; God
  and, 184–86, 190; loss of, 187;
  relatedness of, 36; symbolism and
  language and, 145, 150, 152, 170;
  vacuous, 36, 79, 89, 94
actual occasions, 131, 154, 158, 161.
  See also actual entities
Adventures of Ideas (Whitehead), 177n8
adversion, 95, 96, 182
aesthetic ontology, 4, 67, 78, 94, 100,
  104, 108, 109, 140, 179
Allan, George, 190
amplification, notion of, 189, 190
analogy, significance of, 20, 37, 67, 95,
  97, 152, 158, 164
Analysis of Mind (Russell), 6
analytic and synthetic judgments,
  dualism of, 53
antitheses, 186–88
appearances, 6, 8, 14, 23, 42, 156, 163,
  184; connivance of world and, 125,

201

127–29; hybrid epistemologies and, 124; intentionality and, 59, 62, 63; outer, 19; sensation and, 155
apperception, 42–43
appetition, 37, 85, 86, 100, 185, 186, 188
Aristotelian innocence, 21, 118
Aristotelian Society, 5, 8, 23, 33
Aristotle, 5, 13, 19, 37, 39, 118, 179, 184, 185, 188; Kant and, 40; McDowell and, 44–45; misuse of, 8
aversion, 95, 96, 182
axiomatization, 40

"bald" naturalism, 21, 43, 45, 85, 131
belief, 12, 176; aesthetics of experience and, 77, 107–109; connivance of world and, 119–22, 124, 126–28; intentionality and, 49, 52–55, 57–61, 64; and objective truth, 52
Bialek, William, 156
body: as primary field of expression, 166; witness of, 157
Bradley, F. H., 32, 36, 82
Brandom, Robert, 2, 4, 10, 16, 21, 41, 47n26, 49, 50, 57, 67, 119, 121–23; on causal relations, 61; Hegel and, 37–38; McDowell on, 57, 58, 125–28; pragmatism and, 69; Rorty on, 58; social-inferentialist reply of, 125–28; on social practices, 59, 70
Burge, Tyler, 120–22, 127

Caird, Edward, 28n52
Carnap, Rudolph, 153
Cartesian dualism, 62, 65
Categories (Aristotle), 38
Category of Conceptual Valuation, 93, 98
causal efficacy, 66, 67; symbolism and language and, 141, 150, 152, 155, 158, 159, 164, 167
causality, 2, 3, 6, 18, 25, 79, 117, 141; efficient, 85, 86, 97, 139; intentionality and, 65, 70; space and, 7

causal relations, 58–59, 62, 79; as action at distance, 7; actual entities and, 85; classical empiricism and, 65; justification and, 52, 61, 77; non-normative, 61; points of contact in, 146; rationality and, 44, 45, 157; stress and, 147; thinking as capacity and, 72n48; truth-taking and, 68
causation, 24, 65, 129; efficient, 8, 85, 160; final, 8, 27n37, 85, 103, 182; justification and, 61–64
A Commentary on Plato's Timaeus (Taylor), 3
community, significance of, 140
The Concept of Nature (Whitehead), 7, 11, 33, 147, 152, 155
conceptual analysis, 150–52, 155, 159
conceptual capacities, significance of, 44, 45
conceptualist attitude, 18
conceptual reversion, 93, 107
conceptual space, 21, 78; absolute space and, 13; instantaneous present and, 12–13; materialist thinking and, 12; natural philosophy and metaphysics distinction and, 14; Whitehead and, 11–14
concrescence, 180–82, 185, 187–90, 191n15; aesthetics of experience and, 80, 84, 85, 91; proposition and, 188–89; symbolic language and, 151, 158
conformal relations, 103
connivance, metaphysics of, 128–32. *See also* intuition; perception
conscious awareness, 86, 160
consciousness, 11, 27n37, 188; abstraction and, 94–98; aesthetics of experience and, 77–78, 82, 84–89, 92, 93; connivance of world and, 113, 116, 130, 133–35; experience and, 104, 129; perceptions and intuitive judgments and, 104–108; Pittsburgh Neo-Hegelianism and, 31, 37, 42; symbolism and language and, 154, 155, 159–61, 164, 166, 170

contemporaneity, significance of, 2–5, 8, 11, 118, 123, 177, 183, 186; aesthetics of experience and, 88, 105; intentionality and, 49, 59, 61; Pittsburgh Neo-Hegelianism and, 31–33; symbolism and language and, 141, 142, 151–57, 163, 167
context principle, 39
correspondence theory, of truth, 69, 79, 107
cosmic epoch, 89–90, 110n58
cosmological problem, 180–83
The Critical Exposition of the Philosophy of Leibniz (Russell), 34
Critique (Kant), 14–19, 114, 132; Brandom on, 16; Prichard on, 15–19
Critique of Pure Reason (Kant), 38

Darwin, Charles, 63
Davidson, Donald, 4, 49, 50, 123; on descriptive use of "true", 68; linguistic turn and, 51–53; McDowell and, 54; objectivity and, 54, 56, 76; pragmatism and, 69; Rorty on, 69; on truth as perspicuous, 69; on truth-taking, 68
Descartes, René, 36, 43, 49–50, 101, 103, 167
descriptive and normative, distinction of, 55–56
determinate negation, significance of, 39
Dewey, John, 63, 72n48; on sentiency, 64
directness, 157, 183; conscious perception and, 160; of experience, 143; loss of, 93, 97, 98, 106; of prehension, 92; sense of, 177–78n8; sense perception and, 97; sense reception and, 129
discursive entries, 57, 58
discursive exits, 57, 58
disorder, significance of, 90
"Does 'Consciousness' Exist?" (James), 130

duration, 27n37, 80, 81; definition of, 51; as polythetic, 151; significance of, 150–51; symbolism and language and, 140, 141, 143, 145, 148–54, 161, 163, 167. *See also* time

Einstein, Albert, 7, 142, 146
Elements (Euclid), 142, 148
"Emergence of Analytic philosophy and a Controversy at the Aristotelian Society: 1900–1916" (Aristotelian Society), 33
emotion and symbols, 151–52
empiricism, 40, 42, 54, 59, 76, 82, 125, 176–77; classical, 50, 51, 65, 75, 123, 139, 140, 189; cognition and, 116; experience and, 38; givenness and, 16, 131; judgments and, 16; renouncing, 60
Empiricism and the Philosophy of Mind (Sellars), 119
empty space, 142
An Enquiry Concerning Human Understanding (Hume), 124
An Enquiry Concerning the Principles of Natural Knowledge (Whitehead), 13–14, 144, 146, 147, 149
epistemological skepticism, 21, 51
epistemology, 1–4, 14, 16, 18, 21, 156, 179, 183, 184; aesthetics of experience and, 80, 87, 88, 91–93, 99, 108; connivance of world and, 113–14, 118, 122, 123–27; hybrid, 123–24, 126, 130; intentionality and, 54–55, 62, 63; modern, 1, 3, 54, 92, 101–102; ontology as preceding, 78; of perception, 126–27; Pittsburgh Neo-Hegelianism and, 36, 39, 47n26; representationalist, 70
error, significance of, 159
Essay (Locke), 115
eternal objects, 9, 149, 183, 186, 190, 191n19; aesthetics of experience and, 79, 84–87, 93, 95, 100, 104, 107;

ingression of, 85, 115; significance of, 81. *See also* pure potentials
ethnocentrism and relativity, 54–55, 68
event-based ontology, 2, 80, 139
existence, modes of, 159, 185, 188
experience: modes of, 149–50, 152, 158, 160, 163, 164, 170. *See also* judgment
Experience and Nature (Dewey), 63
extensionality, 6–7, 11, 14, 22, 23, 35, 41, 69, 189, 190; aesthetics of experience and, 81, 85, 108, 109; symbolism and language and, 142, 143, 145–55, 161. *See also* time

fallacious views of logical method, 10
falsehood, 12, 176, 173n66, 178n8; aesthetics of experience and, 76, 82, 86, 87, 101–104, 107, 108; connivance of world and, 122, 124, 127; intentionality and, 51–54, 58; Neo-Hegelianism and, 36, 37, 47n22; symbolism and language and, 154, 156, 160, 167
filiation, 152–53
formal constitution, 79, 86
The Foundations of Arithmetic (Frege), 39
freedom, 75–78, 152, 161; abstract thought and, 170; aesthetic abstraction and, 86; conceptual capacities and, 44; conditioned, 95, 103; imaginative, 94, 106, 160; life and, 157; linguistic norms and, 61; metaphysics and, 70; originative, 159; particularity and, 70; physical inheritance and, 91; significance of, 94
Frege, Gottlob, 1, 35, 39
Friedman, Michael, 39–41, 48nn41, 43; on logical positivism, 40–41

genera, significance of, 150, 169–70
givenness, notion of: aesthetics of experience and, 75, 79, 81, 82, 85–86, 88, 92, 103, 107; connivance of world and, 119, 122, 123, 128; empiricism and, 16, 131; intentionality and, 50, 59, 60, 62–64; novel sensa and, 98–100; significance of, 10–11, 14, 17, 181, 185, 190, 191n15; subjectivity and, 123; symbolism and language and, 141, 147, 160
God, views on, 183–86

Hacking, Ian, 50
Halewood, Michael, 175
Hegel, G. W. F., 2, 21, 31, 63, 187; analytic philosophy's return to, 32–37; Redding and, 37–38, 47n30; rethinking of return to, 37–41
Heidegger, Martin, 62
Helmholtz, Hermann von, 40
Hilbert, David, 40
historicism, 40, 61, 68; scientism and, 63, 65
Hume, David, 3, 5–8, 36, 46, 66, 82, 83, 87, 92, 93, 106, 108, 109, 115, 124, 125, 141, 148, 157, 162, 180, 189–90
hybrid epistemologies, 123–24, 126, 130

imagination, meaning and significance of, 19, 94, 105–107, 185
imaginative feeling, 104, 106, 160
imaginative freedom, 94, 106, 160
Immortality' (Whitehead), 27n37
impressions of sensation, 36, 82, 93, 106, 162
indicative feeling, 105–107, 160
inferentialism, 38, 39; aesthetics of experience and, 75, 104, 108; connivance of world and, 114, 119, 121, 126, 127; intentionality and, 50, 57–58, 60
inferential judgments, 104, 108
infinite unchangeable space, idea of, 142
informal constitution, 79, 86
instantaneousness, 147–48

instantaneous present, 12–13
intentionality, 4, 11, 21, 25, 41, 49, 140, 155, 179; aesthetics of experience and, 83, 85, 102, 103; connivance of world and, 113, 122, 133; descriptive and normative and, 67–70; historical context, 1–3; justification and causation and, 61–64; linguistic turn and, 50–53; objectivity and, 54–57; panpsychism and, 64–67; problem of, 1–3, 31, 45, 49–50, 52, 54, 59, 61, 63, 67, 70, 108, 114, 118, 123, 177; social practices and semantic level and, 57–61
intentional relations, significance of, 83
An Introduction to the Philosophy of Time and Space (Fraassen), 153
intuition, 10, 19, 21, 69, 81, 177, 183; connivance of world and, 113–14, 129–30, 134; consciousness and, 78, 84; formed-ness of, 114–18, 123, 127; judgment and, 59, 75–77, 104–108, 117–18, 160; Kant on, 59, 75, 78, 84, 85, 114–18, 125; mentalization of, 78, 84, 85, 92, 114, 118; Pittsburgh Neo-Hegelianism and, 42, 44; rehabilitated notion of, 129–30; spatial, 40; symbolism and language and, 143, 170

James, William, 11, 63–64, 99, 130, 131, 134
judgment, 4, 15–19, 21, 25, 37, 41; connivance of world and, 113, 117, 118, 131, 133; consciousness and abstraction and, 94–98; givenness and novel sensa and, 98–100; intentionality and, 53, 54; intuition and, 59, 75–77, 104–108, 117–18, 160; ontological togetherness and, 78–81; order and organism and, 88–94; perceiving particulars and, 108–109; propositions and, 36, 81–88, 101–104; significance of, 75–78;

symbolism and language and, 139, 148, 155–61
justification, 6, 77, 185; causal relations and, 52, 61, 77; causation and, 61–64; connivance of world and, 119, 120, 124, 126, 127; inferentialism and, 58; intentionality and, 52, 55, 58, 60

Kant, Immanuel, 5, 8, 9, 38, 76, 77, 84, 113; *Critique* of, 14–19, 114, 132; intuition and, 59, 75, 78, 84, 85, 114–18, 125; McDowell on, 42–45, 132–33; Redding on, 39–40; Russell and, 22–25, 43; spatialization of thought of, 19–21
Kant's Theory of Knowledge (Prichard), 15, 19
"Kantian Lessons about Mind, Meaning, and Rationality" (Brandom), 16
Keller, Catherine, 184, 192n45
Klein, Felix, 40
knowledge and opinion, distinction between, 55
"Knowledge and the Internal" (McDowell), 123

language, 57–66, 79, 164–67, 176; actuality and, 105, 145, 150, 152, 170; as civilization of expression, 166; givenness and, 141, 147, 160; initiation and, 31, 52, 76, 77, 119, 121, 122, 131, 132; McDowell on, 121, 128, 132–35; mind and, 1–2; ontology and, 139, 155; rational animal and, 119; representationalism and, 53; Sellars on, 57; spoken, 88; truth and, 52, 54, 68, 69, 76; T-sentences and, 56. *See also* symbolism and language. *See also individual entries*
Latour, Bruno, 130, 184
Leibniz, Gottfried Wilhelm, 13, 83, 95, 100, 152, 172n50; Russell on, 34–35
Leibnizian monads, 111n86

Lie, Sophus, 40
linguistic turn, 50–54, 68, 108
Locke, John, 49–50, 65, 82–84, 87, 92, 93, 108, 114, 115, 125
logical positivism, 39–41; rejection of, 53
logical subjects, 37, 160, 161, 186; aesthetics of experience and, 82, 87, 101, 103–107
Lowe, Victor, 25, 26n17, 27n23, 33

materialist thinking, 12
McDowell, John, 2, 3, 4, 21–22, 41, 47n26, 49, 50, 64, 70, 113, 137n75, 155; on Brandom, 57, 58, 125–28; on Burge, 120; critique of interiorization of reason, 122–25; Hegel and, 37–38; on Kant, 42–45, 132–33; on meaning-relations, 59; metaphysics of connivance and, 128–32; ontological threshold demystification and, 132–35; on perception, 76 (and entitlement, 118–22); on propositions, 77; on Rorty, 54–56, 59, 123; Sellars and, 115–17, 132; on sense-datum theorists, 60; on Transcendental Aesthetic, 115
meaning: elimination of, 152; -involving, significance of, 57, 59; physical explanation and, 141–45, 149. *See also* symbolism and language
mentality, 37, 133; conceptual prehensions and, 86; intellectual, 96; of intuition, 78, 84; meaning of, 86; significance of, 27n37, 94
Metaphysics (Aristotle), 37, 188
metaphysics. *See individual entries*
Mill, John Stuart, 166
Milton, John, 13
Mind and World (McDowell), 21, 42, 56, 76, 117
Modes of Thought (Whitehead), 142, 153
Monadology, 95

Moore, G. E., 32, 33; Redding on, 39, 43
Mora, Thierry, 156
Myth of the Given, 39, 42, 43, 58, 76

Nasim, Omar W., 33
natural philosophy and metaphysics, comparison of, 14
nature, 34; bifurcation of, 8–10, 14, 17, 21, 31, 45, 70, 79, 82, 106, 118, 122, 134, 184; reason and, 56; uniformity of, 6, 7
negativity and metaphysics, 39
neo-Kantian logical positivists, 39–40
Newton, Isaac, 8, 10, 90
nexus, 100; actual entities and, 80, 87–89, 98; causal, 67; of proposition, 39; significance of, 80, 104; transmuted feeling of, 94, 95; truth and, 107
Nietzsche, Friedrich, 62
non-evolution of matter, 10
non-inferential knowledge, 119, 121
normativity/norm, 1–3, 21, 31, 38, 43, 46, 70; conceptual, 58, 77; and descriptive, 55–56, 67–70; for inquiry, 52, 69; intentionality and, 54–61; linguistic, 61, 65
noumena, 9, 15, 84, 102, 125
Nunn, T. Percy, 32, 141

objectification, 2, 37, 187, 191n7; aesthetics of experience and, 94, 96, 97, 100, 103. *See also* real togetherness
objective purport, 2, 101, 108, 113, 115–18, 131
objectivity: aesthetics of experience and, 76, 78, 84, 85, 87–89, 92, 95, 96, 111n78; connivance of world and, 122, 123, 125, 130, 131, 133; intentionality and, 50, 54–57, 62, 70; linguistic turn and, 51–52; Pittsburgh Neo-Hegelianism and, 38, 42–43; significance of, 2, 21, 22, 143, 181, 182, 185, 190; solidarity and, 60

objects and mind, 15–17
observational knowledge, 119
observational reports, 119
Ontological Principle, 7, 36, 79, 86, 109, 170
ontological thresholds, demystification of, 132–35
ontological togetherness, 36, 78–81, 101–103, 108, 115, 118, 130, 133, 140, 157
ontology, 2, 4, 7, 16–18, 21–23, 176, 181, 182, 187; aesthetic, 4, 67, 78, 94, 100, 104, 108, 109, 140, 179; aesthetics of experience and, 75, 86–88, 95, 97, 99; connivance of world and, 114, 123, 125, 127–29; efficacy, of unrealized possibility, 188–90; intentionality and, 62, 63, 70; Pittsburgh Neo-Hegelianism and, 31, 32, 35–41, 43, 47n26; as preceding epistemology, 78; privacy and publicity and, 161–70; symbolism and language and, 139, 155
ontotheology, 62
organism, philosophy of, 13, 36, 37, 80, 101, 114–15, 129, 147, 187
Our Knowledge of the External World (Russell), 153

panpsychism, 63, 64–67
Paradise Lost (Milton) (poem), 13
partial order, 152, 153
particularity, of togetherness, 100
perception, 125, 128, 137n82, 139; Brandom's epistemology of, 126–27; as capacity for knowledge, 119; conceptual analysis and, 151, 155; conscious, 86, 104–108; of contemporary world, 155; direct, 93; double reference and, 140; duration and, 148; error in, 120 (and judgment, 155–61); Hume on, 66; immediacy of, 12; language and, 143, 151; McDowell on, 76, 118–22; meanings and, 148, 149; modes of, 150; non-rational, 128, 132; of objects, 16–17; organism and, 91; prehension and, 65; rational, 128, 132; "sensationalist" doctrine of, 82; sense, 92, 97, 99, 101, 129; symbolic reference and, 150, 155, 156; time and, 20. *See also individual entries*
"Perception as a Capacity for Knowledge" (McDowell), 118
perceptual space, 13
perceptual states, significance of, 120–22, 124
personally ordered society, 88
Phaedo, 9
phenomenological temporality and spatiality, 145
Philosophiae Naturalis Principia Mathematica (Newton), 153
"The Philosophical Aspects of the Principle of Relativity" (Whitehead), 8
Philosophical Essays Concerning Human Understanding (Hume), 6
phronesis, notion of, 44
physical explanation and meaning, 141–45, 149
physical feeling, 86, 94, 95, 104–105, 107, 160; pure, 106
physicality, of meaning, 144
physical object, significance of, 23–24
physical space, 23–25, 124, 143
Pittsburgh School, 31
Plato, 5, 13, 21, 105; misunderstanding of, 8
Platonic positivism, 39
Platonism, 10, 21, 22, 33, 41, 64, 79; rampant, avoiding, 77; remnant, 38, 43
Poincaré, Henri, 40
points, significance of, 142–43, 148
post-analytic critique, Whiteheadian anticipations of, 21–25; physical objects and, 23–24
postmodernism, 62–63, 69, 70, 176

pragmatism, 98, 175, 176, 191n15; intentionality and, 50, 57, 60, 62–64, 68–70; relativity and, 54–55
predicative feeling, 101, 103, 105, 160
prehension, 66–67, 79–81, 106, 129, 163, 183; as activity, 85; conceptual, 86, 93, 95, 188, 189; concrescence and, 158, 182; consciousness and, 134; directness of, 92; intellectual, 104; judgment and, 101; negative, 97–98; of nexus, 95; nonconformal, 103; perception and, 65; physical, 86, 95, 97, 107, 189; propositional, 82, 87, 88, 104, 160, 181–82; temporality and, 83; truth and, 177n8
presentational immediacy, 66, 67; symbolism and language and, 141, 150, 152, 154, 155, 158, 159, 161–65, 167
Prichard, H. A., 15, 21, 22, 28n52; on spatialization of time, 20
primordiality, 183, 185, 192n45
Principia Mathematica (Whitehead and Russell), 7, 22, 23, 34, 41, 153
Principle of Process, 99
The Principle of Relativity with Applications to Physical Science (Whitehead), 7
The Problems (Russell), 22
The Problems of Philosophy, 15
Proceedings of the Aristotelian Society (Whitehead), 5, 8, 23, 36, 46
Process and Reality (Whitehead), 7, 8, 11, 20–21, 25, 36, 64, 65, 102, 129, 149–51, 157–59, 166, 177, 183, 190, 191
propositions, 10, 24, 64, 120, 126, 175–76, 186; actual entities and, 87, 101; aesthetics of experience and, 77–78, 80, 94, 99, 105–108; concrescence and, 188–89; facts and, 102–103, 160, 181–82; false, 37, 47n22, 82, 101, 102; feelings and, 82, 87, 101–104, 160, 176, 181, 188, 189; judgments and, 81–88;
101–104; as metaphysical entities, 170; negative, 102, 107; Pittsburgh Neo-Hegelianism and, 35, 36, 39; prehension and, 82, 87, 160, 181–82; significance of, 37, 39, 47n22, 77, 175; symbolism and language and, 161, 166; true, 37, 47n22, 82, 101, 102, 105, 108
protective memory, 25, 33
pure potentials, 37, 84–86. *See also* eternal objects

Quine, W. V., 34–36, 53

"Radical Interpretation" (Davidson), 52
rationality, 3, 5, 6; aesthetics of experience and, 76, 79, 109; connivance of world and, 117–22, 128, 132–35; intentionality and, 52, 55, 58, 59, 69, 70; normativity and, 56; Pittsburgh Neo-Hegelianism and, 31–32, 35, 36, 44–46; as subdivision of aesthetics, 88; symbolism and language and, 157, 167, 170, 171
realism, 5, 36, 37, 116, 158, 176; intentionality and, 53, 55, 58, 62, 69, 70; of Nunn, 32, 33; of Plato, 8, 11, 21
Reality-as-it-appears to us, 33, 35
Reality-as-it-is, 33, 35, 53
real togetherness, 4, 114, 115, 118; aesthetics of experience and, 80, 82–84, 92, 101, 106. *See also* objectification
reason and nature, dualism of, 56
Redding, Paul, 10, 39–41; on absolute, 47n30; Hegel and, 37–38, 47n30; on Kant, 43; on Moore, 39; on Russell, 39, 43–44
reflex action, 152
Reichenbach, Hans, 48n43
relatedness, significance of, 36–37, 114, 148–49, 181, 190; aesthetics of experience and, 81, 93–97, 109, 111n86

"The Relation of Sense-data to Physics" (Russell), 32
Relative Theory of Space, 142
relativity, 7–8, 20, 26n10, 98, 111n101, 181; conceptual space and, 11; ethnocentrism and, 54–55, 68; intentionality and, 63, 65, 68, 69; Nunn on, 32–33; Pittsburgh Neo-Hegelianism and, 32, 40, 46; pragmatism and, 54–55; significance of, 8, 40; symbolism and language and, 146, 148, 149, 152, 158, 172n58
representationalism, 16, 63, 163; epistemology and, 70; language and, 53; mathematical, 67; metaphysics and, 62; time and, 19; vocabulary and, 61
Riemann, Bernhard, 40, 146
Robb, Alfred A., 172n58
Rorty, Richard, 4, 49, 50; on Brandom, 58; on causal relations, 72n48; on Davidson, 69; on Dewey, 63; on facts, 58–59; on givenness, 62; on James, 63–64; linguistic turn and, 52–53; McDowell on, 54–56, 59, 123; on objectivity, 54–56; on transcendental status, 60
Ross, W. D., 47n24
Rovelli, Carlo, 171n22
Rubenstein, Mary-Jane, 193n64
Russell, Bertrand, 1, 2, 3, 5, 6, 8, 13, 15, 20, 26n8, 28n50, 41, 102, 153; on infinity, 35; Kant and, 22–25, 43; on Leibniz, 34–35; Nunn and, 32; Platonism of, 10; propositions and, 47n22; on 'pure mathematics' usage, 26n17; Redding on, 39, 43–44; Whitehead's criticism of, 22–24

Santayana, George, 173n66
sapience, 44, 104, 128, 156, 157
Scepticism and Animal Faith (Santayana), 173n66
scheme-content dualism, 50, 51, 69, 123, 130

Schiller, Friedrich, 33
Scholium (Newton), 90–91
Science and Metaphysics (Sellars), 115
Science and the Modern World (Whitehead), 159
Scientific Realism, 116
second nature, notion of, 21, 31, 44, 45, 117–19, 133
self-consciousness, 85, 119–22, 132–33, 170; intentionality and, 66, 67; Pittsburgh Neo-Hegelianism and, 31, 39, 42
self-conversation, 168
Sellars, Wilfrid, 4, 10, 43, 49, 50, 119; on belief, 60; on internalist criteria, 120; on intuition, 116; on language, 57; McDowell and, 115–17, 132; on reason, 56; on social practices, 59
"Sellarsian neo-Hegelians", 39
Semitic theory, significance of, 3, 8, 9, 184
sensa, 92, 93, 168; novel, 98–100
sensationalist doctrine, of perception, 82
sensation and reflection dualism, 82
sense-data, 10, 23, 32, 33, 36, 43, 60, 139–41, 157, 159, 164
"Sense-data and Physical Objects" (Nunn), 32, 141
sense perception, 129, 156, 159; aesthetics of experience and, 92, 93, 97, 99, 100, 101, 108
sense reception, 93, 97, 99, 101, 108, 129
sentiency/sentience, 44, 64, 128, 156, 157
shadow Hegel, notion of, 39
Sherburne, Donald, 64, 65
skepticism, 2, 6, 21, 46, 53, 140, 148, 173n66; Cartesian, 16, 49, 60; connivance of world and, 124, 125, 130, 131; epistemological, 51
social practices, 50, 70–71, 72n48, 126, 128; semantic level and, 57–61
"Solidarity or Objectivity?" (Rorty), 54

"Space, Time, and Relativity" (Whitehead), 141
space. *See* extensionality; time
Stengers, Isabelle, 130, 131, 170, 175, 177n1
Stout, G. F., 32, 50, 61–63; on social practices, 70
subjective aim, 181, 185, 186, 188, 189
subjective form, 177n8, 181, 183, 188, 189, 191n7; aesthetics of experience and, 87, 92, 93, 95, 96, 108; symbolism and language and, 158, 163, 165
subjective unity, 181, 186
subjectivity: aesthetics of experience and, 76, 78, 84, 85, 87, 89, 92–96, 102, 103, 108; connivance of world and, 113, 115, 118, 121, 123, 130, 131, 133, 135; givenness and, 123; intentionality and, 62, 70; significance of, 2–3, 17, 21, 42, 177n8, 181–83, 185, 186, 188–90, 191nn7, 15; symbolism and language and, 158, 163, 165, 167
superjection, 96, 97, 181, 183, 185, 191nn7, 15
suppressed principle, of Locke, 125
symbolic reference, 4, 80; error in perception and judgment and, 156–60; significance of, 157; starling murmuration and, 156; symbolism and language and, 140, 141, 149, 150, 152, 155, 163–67, 169
symbolic transference, 163
Symbolism (Whitehead), 149
symbolism and language: absolute time and absolute space and, 145–49; error in perception and judgment and, 155–61; extensionality and, 149–55; meaning and physical explanation of, 141–45; ontological privacy and ontological publicity and, 161–70; significance of, 139–41
synthetic *a posteriori* judgments, 16–17
synthetic *a priori* judgments, 15–18, 25

Tarkian T-sentence, 55–56, 68
Tarski, T., 56, 68
Taylor, A. E., 3, 27n26, 172n50; on absolute space, 13; on bifurcation of nature, 9–10; correct Platonic view of, 8–9
testimony, of senses, 124–25
things-in-themselves, 19, 20, 24, 25, 59, 114, 124, 155
Thinking with Whitehead (Stengers), 130
Timaeus (Plato), 8, 9, 13, 90, 91
time, 6–14, 22–25, 26n10, 37, 41, 65; absolute, 145–49; aesthetics of experience and, 79–81, 83, 85, 86, 88, 93; connivance of world and, 114, 116–18, 132, 133; Kant on, 19–20; Pittsburgh Neo-Hegelianism and, 40, 42, 45; prehension and, 83; symbolism and language and, 140–49, 151–54, 158, 160–61, 167; Whitehead's theology and, 180–81, 183, 185, 186, 189, 190. *See also* duration; extension
"Time, Space, and Material" (Whitehead), 144
timeless space, notion of, 9
"Towards Rehabilitating Objectivity" (McDowell), 123
Tractatus Logico-Philosophicus (Wittgenstein), 39
transcendence, 3, 8, 9, 24, 60, 77, 169, 184, 191n15; absolute, 90; McDowell on, 42; Pittsburgh Neo-Hegelianism and, 42–44, 46
Transcendental Aesthetic, 24, 114–18, 123
Transcendental Deduction, 59, 75, 117
transcendental sociologism, 47n26, 57, 61, 126
transcendental status, significance of, 60
transmutation, of feeling, 94–96, 98, 99
transmuting internalization, 168–69
A Treatise on Universal Algebra (Whitehead), 34, 35

truth, 18, 175, 176, 177n8, 186; aesthetics of experience and, 75, 79, 82, 86–87, 104, 108; belief and, 52; connivance of world and, 120, 122, 124, 126–28, 134; correspondence theory of, 69, 79, 107; definition of, 107; intentionality and, 50–52, 55–58, 60, 62–63; language and, 52, 54, 68, 69, 76; nexus and, 107; objective, 52; as perspicuous, 69; Pittsburgh Neo-Hegelianism and, 36, 37; proposition and, 86–87; symbolism and language and, 140, 160, 173n66
truth claims and truth claimables, 58
truth-makers, idea of, 53
truth-takings, significance of, 51, 68, 126
Tubman, Harriet, 87

ultimate facts, 8, 80, 144–47
undifferentiated endurance, 191n13
unhealthy romanticism, 33

universals, 84, 100, 109
unmoved mover, of Aristotle, 179, 184, 185, 188

vagueness and narrowness, 98
Van Fraassen, Bas, 153, 172n58
Vienna Circle, 41, 153
vocabulary, 55, 58, 60–63, 92, 93; non-conforming, 62, 67; of objectivity, 54
vocabulary of vocabularies, significance of, 60, 61

Watson, Richard, 39
Whitehead, Alfred North, 5, 26n10, 26–27n23, 137n82; conceptual space and, 11–14; on givenness, 10–11; on pure 'mathematics' usage, 26n17. *See also individual entries*
"Whitehead and the Rise of Modern Logic" (Quine), 34
withness, of body, 157
Wittgenstein, Ludwig, 39, 59, 121, 131

About the Author

Lisa Landoe Hedrick is a teaching fellow in the Divinity School and the College at the University of Chicago. She graduated with a BA from Davidson College and completed her MA and PhD at the University of Chicago Divinity School. As a scholar, she focuses on the intersections between analytic philosophy of language, metaphysics, and religious studies. More specifically, she explores the metaphysical assumptions of belief-talk, God-talk, and world-talk, among others, in modern and contemporary philosophy and theology. She has published articles with *Contemporary Pragmatism, The Review of Metaphysics, The Pluralist,* and the *American Journal of Theology and Philosophy,* where she also serves as reviews editor. This is her first book.

www.ingramcontent.com/pod-product-compliance
Lightning Source LLC
Chambersburg PA
CBHW020118010526
44115CB00008B/884